Effective Schooling for English Language Learners:

What Elementary Principals Should Know and Do

Patricia Smiley
Trudy Salsberry

EYE ON EDUCATION
6 DEPOT WAY WEST, SUITE 106
LARCHMONT, NY 10538
(914) 833–0551
(914) 833–0761 fax
www.eyeoneducation.com

For information about permission to reproduce selections from this book, write: Eye On Education, Permissions Dept., Suite 106, 6 Depot Way West, Larchmont, NY 10538.

Library of Congress Cataloging-in-Publication Data

Smiley, Patricia, 1950-
Effective schooling for English language learners : what elementary principals should know and do / Patricia Smiley and Trudy Salsberry.
    p. cm.
    Includes bibliographical references.
ISBN 1-59667-030-4
1. Linguistic minorities—Education (Elementary)—United States. 2. English language—Study and teaching (Elementary)—Foreign speakers. 3. Elementary school administration—United States. I. Salsberry, Trudy. II. Title.

LC3725.S64 2006
372.1829073

2006015828

10 9 8 7 6 5 4 3 2 1

Editorial and production services provided by
Richard H. Adin Freelance Editorial Services
52 Oakwood Blvd., Poughkeepsie, NY 12603-4112
(845-471-3566)

Table of Contents

Preface

In the past 10 years, the number of English language learners (ELLs) enrolled in U.S. schools has dramatically increased. These students, also referred to as limited English proficient (LEP) students, English as a second language (ESL) students, second language learners, or, more recently, English learners (ELs), account for almost 10 percent of the total school population. Currently there are over 5 million English language learners enrolled in U.S. public schools (preK–12), with nearly 70 percent of all ELLs enrolled at the elementary level (Kindler, 2002; National Clearinghouse on English Language Acquisition [NCELA], 2005). In light of the increasing number of second language learners and the requirements of the federal *No Child Left Behind* (NCLB) *Act*, the demands placed upon principals have become increasingly complex. In order to lead their schools in increasing achievement for *all* students, principals must be equipped with additional knowledge and expertise in order to improve the academic achievement of English language learners.

This book is primarily designed as an important first step for elementary principals in need of more knowledge about leadership in implementing effective schooling for these students. Although the book is designed as an introductory framework, it presents a wide range of approaches drawn from theory, research, and practice that will appeal to all levels of knowledge about promoting academic success for English language learners. It could be used as a textbook for administrative leadership courses or training, a resource for personal or building professional development activities, or a book study for principals' professional learning communities. Given the significant demographic changes occurring in our schools, this book will benefit current and potential school administrators, teachers, and educational decision makers.

Each chapter is organized around a series of critical questions related to effective schooling for English language learners. Scattered throughout each chapter are questions for reflection and quotations that have been designed to emphasize important points and provide the principal with reflection about current and future practices. "Building the Vision" questions are provided at the end of Chapters 2 through 5. Each chapter concludes with a "Leadership Challenge" that gives practical guidance and suggestions to increase the principal's understanding of and effectiveness in maximizing instruction for ELLs.

Chapter 1 examines the need for change due to increasing numbers of ELLs, their overall poor academic achievement, and teachers who are ill prepared to serve them. It reviews significant laws and policies that affect services for these students, as well as the attributes of exemplary schools and leadership for ELLs. Chapter 2 focuses on research and theories about second language acquisition and the instructional strategies that promote English, literacy, and content acquisition. Chapter 3 contains information about native language instruction and support, and its impact on student learning, English acquisition, and literacy. Chapter 4 centers on various dimensions of student assessment that are key to improved schooling for ELLs. Chapter 5 addresses the components of a supportive schoolwide climate, various programming and organizational structures, and parent involvement. The concluding chapter reemphasizes the role of the principal in building and sustaining effective change in an ELL-responsive school by highlighting the essential components of professional learning communities and professional development. Because of the complex nature of educating second language learners, additional resources are listed throughout the book and in the Appendix.

We hope that this book will provide knowledge, guidance, and support for principals as they assume a strong role of advocacy and leadership in improving the quality of education for English language learners.

1
The Need for Change

> *That minority and low-income children often perform poorly on tests is well known. But the fact that they do so because we systematically and willfully expect less from them is not. Most Americans assume that the low achievement of poor and minority children is bound up in the children themselves or their families. "The children don't try." "They have no place to study." "Their parents don't care." "Their culture does not value education." These and other excuses are regularly offered up to explain the achievement gap that separates poor and minority students from other young Americans.*
>
> *But these are red herrings. The fact is that we know how to educate poor and minority children of all kinds—racial, ethnic, and language—to high levels.... But the nation as a whole has not yet acted on that knowledge....*
>
> (Commission on Chapter 1, 1992, pp. 3–4)

Chapter Highlights: This chapter examines the need for change—how changing demographics are having an impact on schools and how English language learners (ELLs),[1] also known as limited English proficient (LEP) students, are faring in our schools. It reviews significant laws, court decisions, and policies that affect decisions about services for these students. Research on the attributes of effective schools and effective principals for English language learners is provided. In the Leadership Challenge, you will be able to assess your professional development needs based on what the literature says about effective principals for second language learners.

---

1   The term English language learner is synonymous in this document with the federally defined "limited English proficient" student, which refers to an individual who has sufficient difficulties speaking, reading, writing or understanding the English language and whose difficulties may deny the individual the opportunity to learn successfully in classrooms where the language of instruction is English. A glossary of ELL terminology has been provided at the end of this book.

What Principals Should Know

Critical Questions

1. How are changing demographics having an impact on the nation's schools?

2. How are schools having an impact on English language learners?

3. What are the federal laws, court decisions, and policies that affect the education of English language learners?

4. What are the attributes of effective schools for English language learners?

5. What are the attributes of effective principals for English language learners?

Essential Vocabulary

English language learners (ELLs): Students whose first language is not English and who are in the process of learning English. Unlike terminology such as "limited English proficient," this term highlights what the students are accomplishing, not their temporary deficits (Lacelle-Peterson & Rivera, 1994). Although they are legally referred to as limited English proficient (LEP), the term English language learner (ELL), sometimes shortened to English learner (EL), has become the preferred term. The U.S. Department of Education is currently using the term English language learners.

L1: First or native language.

L2: Second language.

Limited English proficient (LEP): The term used by the federal government and most states to identify students who have insufficient English to succeed in English classrooms (Lessow-Hurley, 1991).

Linguistically and culturally diverse (LCD): Term used to identify individuals from homes and communities where English is not the primary language of communication (García, 1991b).

Native language: First, primary, or home language (L1).

Primary language: First, home, or native language (L1).

Critical Question #1:
How Are Changing Demographics
Having an Impact on Our Schools?

Changing Nation

The first step in being an effective principal for English language learners is being aware of the changing demographics of our nation and our schools. G. N. Garcia (2000) listed three key concerns for school administrators: 1) "the growing number of students who arrive at school ill prepared to learn; 2) the growing number of non-native (foreign) born children and youth who enroll in schools across all grade levels; and 3) the large number of native and foreign-born students who are limited English proficient" (p. 1).

The following statistics support the fact that the United States is becoming more ethnically and linguistically diverse, and the trend is likely to continue.

- The number of U.S. residents not born in the United States passed 34 million in 2004 (almost 12 percent of the total population), tripling the 10 million in 1970 (less than 5 percent of the population). By 2010, it is predicted that the foreign-born population will make up 12 percent of the total U.S. population (Capps et al., 2005).

- In 2000, the number of people over the age of 5 who spoke a language other than English in their home was nearly 47 million, approximately 18 percent of the total U.S. population (U.S. Census Bureau, 2002).

- Between 1980 and 2000, the minority population grew 11 times as rapidly as the white non-Hispanic population, with Asian and Pacific Islanders increasing by 204 percent and the Hispanic population increasing by 142 percent. High levels of immigration and high fertility levels contributed to this growth (Hobbs & Stoops, 2002).

- Between 1990 and 2000, communities saw dramatic increases in their Hispanic populations, with the number of Hispanics increasing from 22.4 million to 35.3 million, a 58 percent increase. The Hispanic population increased nearly fivefold in North Carolina and at least doubled in 21 other states (Hobbs & Stoops, 2002).

- Experts predict that "if immigration and birth rates remain at current levels, the total Hispanic population will grow at least three times faster than the population as a whole for several decades" (Suro, 1998, p. 6).

- By 2050, it is predicted that the concept of a "minority" group will be obsolete, and that no group will form a majority (García, 1994c).

Schools Reflect Changing Population

Administrators must also recognize that the ethnic and linguistic diversity of students enrolling in America's public schools has dramatically increased and is expected to increase even more. In fact, the number of students from non-English speaking backgrounds represents the fastest growing segment of the student population. Furthermore, it is crucial to understand that trends in changing school populations are not confined to specific states or urban schools. Much of the growth has occurred in states that have previously had small numbers of ELLs.

- Nearly one-fifth of all school-age children (ages 5 to 17) are from language minority households in which languages other than English are spoken (U.S. Census Bureau, 2004).

- The number of children (ages 5 to 17) who speak a language other than English at home (19 percent of all children) more than doubled between 1979 and 2003. Of these children, almost one-third speak English with difficulty (National Center for Education Statistics [NCES], 2005).

- From 1979 to 2003, the population of school-age children increased by 19 percent. However, the percentage who spoke a language other than English at home and who spoke English with difficulty increased by 124 percent (NCES, 2005).

- The number of ELLs in the nation's schools more than doubled in the 10-year period from 1990–1991 to 2000–2001, representing a 105 percent growth in the ELL student population as compared to a 12 percent increase in the general K–12 student population (Kindler, 2002).

- The number of students with limited English skills has increased to over 5 million in grades K–12 in U.S. public schools, making up almost 10 percent of the school-age population in 2003–2004 (NCELA, 2005).

- Nearly 70 percent of all ELLs were enrolled at the elementary level in 2000–2001, accounting for almost 12 percent of the PreK–6 total school enrollment (Kindler, 2002).

- By 2000, immigrants represented one-ninth of all U.S. residents, but their children represented one-fifth of all children under age 18. At the elementary level, 25 percent of ELLs were foreign-born, 59 percent of ELLs were second-generation (U.S. born children of immigrants), and 18 percent were third-generation in 2000. Children of immigrants represented one-fourth of all school-age children who were low-income (Capps et al., 2005).

- Although the majority of English learners live in six states, the number of immigrant children in the other states increased by 40 percent between 1990 and 1995 (Ruiz-de-Velasco & Fix, 2000). Between 1990 and 2000, the five states with the greatest percentage growth in the pre-K to grade 5 ELL numbers were Nevada (354 percent increase), Nebraska, South Dakota, Georgia, and Arkansas (243 percent increase) (Capps et al., 2005).

- A widening range of schools across the nation are struggling with rapidly diversifying student populations. In many cases, the capacity of these "new destination" states and schools may be more limited than other traditional gateway communities, which have networks of bilingual and ESL teachers, curricula, and other resources in place (Capps et al., 2005).
- Although ELLs speak almost 400 languages, native Spanish speakers make up approximately 75 percent of the ELL population (Kindler, 2002).

Critical Question #2: How Are Our Schools Having an Impact on English Language Learners?

Poor Performance

English language learners have complex and varied needs. While some ELLs enter U.S. schools with strong academic preparation in their native language that may equal or surpass that of their grade-level peers, others come with limited formal schooling and literacy (LaCelle-Peterson & Rivera, 1994). About half have parents who do not have a high school degree (Center on Education Policy, 2006), and six out of seven elementary age ELLs live in linguistically isolated households (in which everyone over the age of 14 is limited English proficient) (Capps et al., 2005). A disproportionate number also tend to be from disadvantaged socioeconomic backgrounds (McUsic, 1999; Moss & Puma, 1995), which is in itself a risk factor for low achievement (Griffith, 2002; Slavin, 1999). In 2000, half of children of immigrants and two-thirds of ELLs were low income (Capps et al., 2005). Many live in low-income communities and attend schools with student populations that are predominantly minority and low-achieving (Snow, Burns, & Griffin, 1998), and their families tend to be more mobile than average (Center on Education Policy, 2006).

> *Inadequate reading and writing proficiency in English relegates rapidly increasing language-minority populations to the sidelines, limiting the nation's potential for economic competitiveness, innovation, productivity growth, and quality of life.* (August, 2006, p. 6)

Regardless, schools are still faced with the challenge of developing ELLs' English proficiency while maintaining their academic progress in all subjects. However, educational attainment remains low for ELL students.

- A large percentage of ELLs have low levels of academic performance and drop out of school (Bennici & Strang, 1995; Bradby, Owings, & Quinn, 1992). They have four times the dropout rate of their English speaking peers and higher grade repetition rates (U.S. General Accounting Office, 2001).

- By third grade, 25 percent of ELLs (compared to 15 percent of all other students) have been retained at least once (Moss & Puma, 1995), and 76 percent are either below or well below grade level in reading (Zehler et al., 2003). Of the 41 reporting states, only 18.7 percent of ELLS in the 1999–2000 school year scored above the state norms for reading comprehension (Kindler, 2002).

- In general, ELLs receive lower grades, score below their classmates on standardized reading and mathematics tests, are more frequently placed in lower ability groups than native English speakers, and are often judged by their teachers as academic underachievers (Moss & Puma, 1995; Ruiz-de-Velasco & Fix, 2000).

Unprepared Teachers

Many teachers are now experiencing the challenges of educating English learners, a population of students with whom they have little or no familiarity, and with providing effective teaching methodology for which they have little or no training.

> *The reasons for the poor performance of ELLs are complex but are partially caused by educational practices that are not aligned with their needs.*

- During the 1999–2000 school year, 41 percent of all public school teachers taught ELLs, yet only 12.5 percent had had eight or more hours of training in the past three years on how to teach them (NCES, 2002).

- A comprehensive study of teacher quality throughout the United States pointed out that although 54 percent of teachers have bilingual learners in their classrooms, only 20 percent feel well prepared to serve them. Most teachers (83 percent) report that they are unprepared to assess and instruct ELLs (NCES, 1999).

- Enrollment of ELLs is increasing faster than staff can be trained to serve them. The most common challenge reported by districts in working with ELLs was finding and hiring highly qualified staff to teach them (Center on Education Policy, 2006).

- Fewer than a third of the teachers of ELL students are qualified to teach them (Crawford, 1997). The more rural the state, the lower the percentage of staff who have the necessary preparation, down to as low as 2 percent (NCES, 2002).

- According to the Council of Chief State School Officers' report, *Systemic Reform and Limited English Proficient Students* (August & Lara, 1996), the category in which the most needs were cited by states was curriculum and instruction, specifically the need for teachers to become more familiar with the second-language acquisition process and the need to integrate language and content instruction. When states were asked to identify obstacles faced by teachers, the greatest obstacle cited was lack of or inadequate training of teachers.

Despite school reform efforts to increase the achievement of all students, Gandara (1994) warns that "while LEP and other 'at risk' students are frequently cited as justifications for why reforms are needed, they are rarely included in any specific way in the reforms themselves" (p. 46). Adger (1996) states that school reform measures hold just as much potential for ELLs as for other students, but the reform measures must include "continuous and specific attention as to how these students' language skills, cultural backgrounds, and experiences uniquely shape the work of the school" (p. 1).

Questions for Reflection

Has your school responded favorably to the increased numbers of ELLs?

Are all teachers prepared to effectively and appropriately assess and instruct ELLs?

Critical Question #3:
What Are the Federal Laws, Court Decisions, and Policies That Affect the Education of ELLs?

Principal as Advocate

All students, including English learners, are entitled to a quality education that enables them to progress academically while learning English, but some educators have resisted fully serving ELLs and have refused to do what is necessary to provide full access to them. As a result, a large body of law has developed as federal and state legislatures have taken action "to protect the rights of national origin minority students and those who are limited in their English proficiency" (Lyons, 1992, p. 1).

Olsen and Jaramillo (1999) define advocacy as educating staff "about the needs of immigrant students, grappling with what are often low expectations or hostile feelings" toward ELLs, and sometimes "insisting that the school do what is legally required and educationally indicated—whether or not everyone agrees that they want to make that change" (p. 70). Federal and state laws mandate that public education accommodate the needs of ELLs. Administrators must be aware of the laws, legal requirements, and issues related to meeting the educational needs of ELLs in order to be strong advocates for them. Although it is beyond the scope of this book to include state legislation, administrators are also advised to access the information on their state's website.

Federal Law, Significant Court Decisions, Federal Policy

Title VI of the Civil Rights Act of 1964: Title VI prohibits discrimination on the grounds of race, color, or national origin in programs or activities that receive federal financial assistance. The Office for Civil Rights within the U.S. Department of Education is responsible for enforcing Title VI.

No person in the United States shall, on the grounds of race, color, or national origin, be excluded from participation in, be denied the benefits of, or be subjected to discrimination under any program or activity receiving Federal financial assistance. (§ 2000d)

May 25, 1970 OCR (Office for Civil Rights) Memorandum: The director of the Office for Civil Rights issued this memorandum to school districts to clarify their responsibilities to language minority students under Title VI requirements of civil rights law. The memorandum identified four basic school district responsibilities:

1. Where inability to speak and understand the English language excludes national origin minority group children from effective participation in the educational program offered by a school district, the district must take affirmative steps to rectify the language deficiency in order to open its instructional program to these students.

2. School districts must not assign national origin minority group students to classes for the mentally retarded on the basis of criteria which essentially measure or evaluate English language skills; nor may school districts deny national origin minority group children access to college preparatory courses on a basis directly related to the failure of the school system to inculcate English language skills.

3. Any ability grouping or tracking system employed by the school system to deal with the special language skill needs of national origin minority group children must be designed to meet such language skill needs as soon as possible and must not operate as an educational dead end or permanent track.

4. School districts have the responsibility to adequately notify national origin minority group parents of school activities which are called to the attention of other parents. Such notice in order to be adequate may have to be provided in a language other than English. (Pottinger, 1970, pp. 1–2)

OCR issued two updates to this memorandum, one in 1985 and another in 1991. The 1970 memorandum and the 1985 and 1991 updates explain the relevant legal standards for OCR policy concerning discrimination on the basis of national origin.

Section 504 of the Rehabilitation Act of 1973: Section 504 requires that assessments of program recipients be conducted in a way that accurately reflect a student's special education needs rather than English proficiency skills.

Lau v. Nichols **(1974):** This Supreme Court case upheld OCR's 1970 memorandum. The basis for the case was the claim that Chinese-speaking minority students could not understand the language in which they were being taught; therefore, they were not being provided with an equal education. The Supreme Court reaffirmed that all students, regardless of native language, have the right to receive a quality education, stating "there is no equality of treatment merely by providing students with the same facilities, textbooks, teachers, and curriculum; for students who do not understand English are effectively foreclosed from any meaningful education" (*Lau v. Nichols*, 1974, p. 566).

Equal Educational Opportunities Act (EEOA) of 1974: This act, which serves as one of the legal foundations for serving ELL students, requires state and local education agencies to take action in overcoming the language barrier of ELLs (Lyons, 1992). The EEOA states the following:

> No state shall deny equal educational opportunity to an individual on account of his or her race, color, sex, or national origin, by—(f) the failure of an educational agency to take appropriate action to overcome language barriers that impede equal participation by its students in its instructional programs. (§ 1703)

Serna v. Portales Municipal Schools **(1974):** The 10th Circuit Court of Appeals upheld a district court decision that found that Portales Municipal Schools discriminated against Spanish-surnamed students because their achievement levels were below those of their Anglo counterparts and they had higher truancy and dropout rates. The court ordered Portales schools to implement programs of bilingual/bicultural instruction, revise procedures for assessing minority students' achievement, and hire bilingual school personnel.

Cintron v. Brentwood Union Free School District **(1978):** The Federal District Court for the Eastern District of New York rejected the Brentwood School District's proposed alteration of its bilingual program on the grounds that it would violate "Lau guidelines" by unnecessarily segregating Spanish-speaking students from English speaking students in music and art. The court also objected to the program's failure to exit those students who were proficient enough in English to understand mainstream English instruction.

Castañeda v. Pickard **(1981):** This case is said to be the most significant court decision affecting language minority students after *Lau* because it provides important criteria for determining a school's degree of compliance with the EEOA of 1974. The plaintiffs claimed that Raymondville, Texas, Independent School District's language programs violated the EEOA with "ability tracking," hiring practices that discriminated against Mexican Americans, and failure to develop bilingual programs that facilitated learning. In response, the Fifth Circuit Court of Appeals formulated a set of basic standards to determine school district compliance with the EEOA's requirement of "appropriate action." The "Castañeda test" includes three criteria:

1. **Theory:** The school must pursue a program based on an educational theory recognized as sound or, at least, as a legitimate experimental strategy.

2. **Practice:** The school must actually implement the program with instructional practices, resources, and personnel necessary to transfer theory to reality.

3. **Results:** The school must not persist in a program that fails to produce results.

Plyler v. Doe **(1982):** The Supreme Court ruled that undocumented children cannot be denied access to education solely on the basis of their immigration status. Public schools and school personnel cannot adopt policies, take actions, or make inquiries that would deny ELL students access to education based on their immigration status or expose the undocumented status of students or the parents.

Keyes v. School District No. 1 **(1983):** A U.S. District Court found that Denver's public school district had failed to adequately implement the program it had chosen to meet the needs of its national origin minority students, the second element of the "Castañeda test."

Gomez v. Illinois **(1987):** The Seventh Circuit Court of Appeals ruled that a state education agency (as well as a local one) can be sued for failure to take the "appropriate action" required by the EEOA. In both Keyes and Gomez, the courts strongly emphasized the responsibility of education agencies to devote the necessary resources for effective implementation of their planned programs.

September 27, 1991, OCR Memorandum, "Policy Update on Schools' Obligations Toward National Origin Minority Students with Limited-English Proficiency (LEP Students)": OCR issued this policy update to provide additional guidance to schools in applying the May 1970 and December 1985 memoranda within the context of adequacy of program and the need for a formal program. The update notes the following:

> Title VI does not mandate any particular program of instruction for LEP students. In determining whether the recipient is operating a program for LEP students that meets Title VI requirements, OCR will consider whether: (1) the program the recipient chooses is recognized as sound by some experts in the field or is considered a legitimate experimental strategy; (2) the programs and practices used by the school system are reasonably calculated to implement effectively the educational theory adopted by the school; and (3) the program succeeds, after a legitimate trial, in producing results indicating that students' language barriers are actually being overcome. (p. 1)

Other highlights of the update include the following:

Staffing Requirements

A recipient may not in effect relegate LEP students to second-class status by indefinitely allowing teachers without formal qualifications to teach them while requiring teachers of non-LEP students to meet formal qualifications.

If a recipient uses a method other than bilingual education (such as ESL or structured immersion), the recipient should have ascertained that teachers who use those methods have been adequately trained in them.

The recipient should also have the teacher's classroom performance evaluated by someone familiar with the method being used.

Students should not be getting instruction from aides rather than teachers. (pp. 2–3)

Exit Criteria

Some factors to examine in determining whether formerly LEP students are able to participate meaningfully in the regular educational program include: (1) whether they are able to keep up with their non-LEP peers in the regular educational program; (2) whether they are able to participate successfully in essentially all aspects of the school's curriculum without the use of simplified English materials; and (3) whether their retention in-grade and dropout rates are similar to those of their non-LEP peers.

First, exit criteria should be based on objective standards, such as standardized test scores, and the district should be able to explain why it has decided that students meeting those standards will be able to participate meaningfully in the regular classroom.

Second, students should not be exited from the LEP program unless they can read, write, and comprehend English well enough to participate meaningfully in the recipient's program. Exit criteria that simply test a student's oral language skills are inadequate.

...once LEP students become English-proficient, schools retain an obligation to provide assistance necessary to remedy academic deficits that may have occurred in other subjects while the student was focusing on learning English. (p. 3)

Special Education Programs

Special education school systems may not assign students to special education programs on the basis of criteria that essentially measure and evaluate English language skills. (p. 3)

Gifted/Talented Programs and Other Specialized Programs

If a recipient has a process for locating and identifying gifted/talented students, it must also locate and identify gifted/talented LEP students who could benefit from the program. (p. 4)

Need for a Formal Program

If a recipient contends that its LEP students have meaningful access to the district's programs, despite the lack of an alternative program or the presence of a program that is inadequate under Castañeda, some factors to consider in evaluating this claim are: (1) whether LEP students are performing as well as their non-LEP peers in the district, unless some other comparison seems more appropriate; (2) whether LEP students are successfully participating in essentially all aspects of the school's curriculum without the use of simplified English materials; and (3) whether their dropout and retention in-grade rates are comparable to those of their non-LEP peers. Cf. Keyes, 576 F. Supp. at 1519 (high dropout rates and use of "leveled English" materials indicate that district is not providing equal educational opportunity for LEP students). (pp. 4–5)

Segregation of LEP Students

Providing special services to LEP students will usually have the effect of segregating students by national origin during at least part of the school day. Castañeda states that this segregation is permissible because "the benefits which would accrue to [LEP] students by remedying the language barriers which impede their ability to realize their academic potential in an English language educational institution may outweigh the adverse effects of such segregation." (648 F. 2d at 998)

OCR's inquiry in this area should focus on whether the district has carried out its chosen program in the least segregative manner consistent with achieving its stated goals [and] whether the degree of segregation in the program is necessary to achieve the program's educational goals. (p. 5)

"The Provision of an Equal Education Opportunity to Limited-English Proficient Students" (August 2000): This federal policy statement from the Office for Civil Rights outlines the provision of education to ELLs and summarizes relevant requirements of Title VI of the Civil Rights Act of 1964. It addresses two compliance issues: (1) whether there is a need for the district to provide a special language program to meet the educational needs of all language minority students; and (2) whether the district's alternative language program is likely to be effective in meeting the educational needs of its language minority students. The procedures that school districts should use to ensure that their programs are serving this population effectively include the following guidelines:

Districts should:

- identify students who need assistance;
- develop a program which, in the view of experts in the field, has a reasonable chance for success;
- ensure that necessary staff, curricular materials, and facilities are in place and used properly;

- develop appropriate evaluation standards, including program exit criteria, for measuring the progress of students; and
- assess the success of the program and modify it where needed. (p. 3)

The areas that OCR examines to evaluate whether there is a need for a program and whether the program will be effective include the following:

- **Whether a district has identified all LEP students who need special language assistance.** A school district must have a formal system for objectively identifying students whose limited proficiency in speaking, reading, writing, or understanding English denies them the opportunity to meaningfully participate in the regular education environment.

- **Whether a district can ensure the placement of LEP students in appropriate programs.** Once a school district has identified students who need assistance, it must determine what types of assistance are warranted.

- **Whether all LEP students who need a special language assistance program are being provided such a program.** A school district must ensure that all LEP students receive English-language development services.

- **Whether a district has taken steps to modify a program for LEP students when that program is not working.** If the district's alternative language services program is not successful after a reasonable time period, the district must take steps to determine the cause of the program's failure and modify it accordingly.

- **Whether a district ensures that LEP students are not misidentified as students with disabilities because of their inability to speak and understand English.** If national origin minority students are not proficient in speaking, reading, writing, or understanding English, testing them in English may not demonstrate their ability or achievement skills. Steps must be taken so that LEP students are not assigned to special education classes because of their lack of English language proficiency, rather than because they have a disability.

- **Whether a school district ensures that parents who are not proficient in English are provided with appropriate and sufficient information about all school activities.** School districts have a responsibility to adequately notify national origin minority parents of school activities that are called to the attention of other parents. Notification must be sufficient so that parents can make well-informed decisions about the participation of their children in a district's programs and services. Districts may be required to provide notification in the parents' home language. (p. 3)

The Office for Civil Rights' manual, *Programs for English Language Learners: Resource Materials for Planning and Self-Assessment*, provides additional information in addressing a district's legal responsibilities in developing or revising a program for ELLs (see Appendix B).

No Child Left Behind Act (2002): This sweeping educational reform act amends and reauthorizes the Elementary and Secondary Education Act (ESEA) of 1965. NCLB provides for high standards and strong accountability for all schools and all students, including specific provisions for those who are limited English proficient, to be full participants in and beneficiaries of the educational system. This means being held to the same standards, taught the same content, and subject to the same assessments. Under NCLB, and especially under Title I, schools and districts are held accountable for improving the English proficiency and academic achievement of the ELL subgroup (Chapter 4 provides information about the limitations of standardized testing and language proficiency testing for ELLs). The law also emphasizes the use of research-based educational programs and practices, with schools needing to know the research that supports the practices. Title III provides funding to states and districts to ensure that ELLs attain English proficiency, develop high levels of academic competence, and meet the same challenging academic standards as other children. Under Title III, states are required to establish English language proficiency standards, administer English language proficiency assessments to ELLs in speaking, reading, writing, listening, and comprehending English, and define annual measurable achievement objectives (AMAOs) aligned with state standards. Title III also supports a National Professional Development project that makes funds available for "professional development activities that will improve classroom instruction for limited English proficient children and assist educational personnel working with such children to meet high professional standards, including standards for certification and licensure as teachers who work in language instruction educational programs or serve limited English proficient children." (NCLB, Title III, Part A, Subpart 3, Sec. 3131). Under NCLB, parents of ELLs and immigrant parents have the same rights as other parents—to be informed about their child's assessment results and to transfer their child to another school if the school is not making sufficient progress. Additionally, schools must communicate with parents in the languages they speak "to the extent practicable," inform parents of ELLs about the type of language instruction their children are receiving, and grant parents the right to refuse language services for their children. Additional information is available in *No Child Left Behind: A Desktop Reference* (see Appendix B).

Questions for Reflection

How will you use your knowledge of this legislation to advocate for ELLs' rights?

Critical Question #4:
What Are the Attributes
of Effective Schools for ELLs?

Research on Effective Attributes

Clearly then, educating our nation's growing population of ELLs coupled with the demands of NCLB implementation poses many challenges and changes for schools. That means asking pertinent questions. What does research recommend to improve ELLs' achievement? How can we facilitate successful schooling for these students and close the achievement gap between them and native English speakers? How can we accelerate their achievement and sustain their academic growth? Which attributes of effective schooling will transform an ineffective program into an exemplary one for ELLs? What instructional practices work best? What are the implications for resources? In other words, we must seek information far beyond the requirements of the law. We must first educate ourselves about what English learners need (García, 1997b). We must acquire a clear understanding about the essential elements of effective schooling for ELLs.

> *We must first educate ourselves about what English learners need to succeed.* (García, 1997b)

Although no single approach, program, or set of practices fits all students' needs, backgrounds, and experiences, there are many commonalities in effective instruction for ELLs. Empirical studies are limited, but much of the professional literature does provide direction about specific attributes and strategies that make some programs and practices more successful than others and how schools can more effectively serve culturally and linguistically diverse student populations. Since the primary goal of this book is to help principals be effective leaders in meeting the needs of ELLs, it is necessary to take a detailed look at what the research says. In many respects, these best practices are based on similar principles of effective teaching and learning as well as approaches that create highly effective learning environments for all students, such as clear and understandable instructions, modeling, guided practice, checking for understanding, clear learning objectives, challenge that is appropriate to each student's level, a focus on basic and higher-order skills and applications, cooperative learning, and others. While many of these approaches are similar, research does suggest that adjustments are needed in order to maximize benefits with ELLs.

The George Washington University Center for Equity and Excellence in Education [CEEE] (1996) identified the following six research-based principles to assist schools in identifying principles and procedures to facilitate learning for ELLs:

- Limited English proficient students are held to the same high expectations of learning established for all students.

- LEP students develop full receptive and productive proficiencies in English in the domains of listening, speaking, reading, and writing, consistent with expectations for all students.
- LEP students are taught challenging content to enable them to meet performance standards in all content areas…consistent with those for all students.
- LEP students receive instruction that builds on their previous education and cognitive abilities and that reflects their language proficiency levels.
- LEP students are evaluated with appropriate and valid assessments that are aligned with state and local standards and that take into account the language acquisition stages and cultural background of the students.
- The academic success of limited English proficient students is a responsibility shared by all educators, the family, and the community. (p. 4)

Based on a review of 33 different research studies, August & Hakuta (1997) listed the following 13 attributes of effective schooling for ELLs:

- a supportive school-wide climate,
- school leadership,
- a customized learning environment,
- articulation and coordination within and between schools,
- some use of native language and culture in the instruction of language-minority students,
- a balanced curriculum that incorporates both basic and higher-order skills,
- explicit skills instruction,
- opportunities for student-directed activities,
- use of instructional strategies that enhance understanding,
- opportunities for practice,
- systematic student assessment,
- staff development, and
- home and parent involvement. (p. 171)

Based on a recent review of the research, Genesee, Lindholm-Leary, Saunders, and Christian (2005) identified the following program factors and instructional characteristics that promote ELLs' academic success:

- a positive school environment (Battistich, Solomon, Watson, & Schaps, 1997; Berman, Minicucci, McLaughlin, Nelson, & Woodworth, 1995; Montecel & Cortez, 2002);
- a curriculum that is meaningful and academically challenging, incorporates higher order thinking (Berman et al., 1995; Doherty, Hilberg, Pinal, & Tharp, 2003; Montecel & Cortez, 2002; Tikunoff, 1985), is thematically integrated (Montecel & Cortez, 2002), establishes a clear alignment with

standards and assessment (Doherty et al., 2003; Montecel & Cortez, 2002), and is consistent and sustained over time (Ramirez, 1992);

- a program model that is grounded in sound theory and best practices associated with an enriched, not remedial, instructional model (e.g., Montecel & Cortez, 2002);

- teachers in bilingual programs who understand theories about bilingualism and second language development as well as the goals and rationale for the model in which they are teaching (Berman et al., 1995; Montecel & Cortez, 2002); the use of cooperative learning and high-quality exchanges between teachers and pupils (e.g., Berman et al., 1995; Calderón, Hertz-Lazarowitz, & Slavin, 1998; Doherty et al., 2003; Montecel & Cortez, 2002; Tikunoff, 1985). (p.376)

Critical Question #5:
What Are the Attributes
of Effective Principals for ELLs?

Leadership for School Change

In light of the demographic changes and legislative mandates, schools are faced with challenges that may involve changing curricula, changing assessment practices, rethinking professional development, reallocating resources, and examining data differently. It may mean challenging teachers to alter their instructional practices, reorganizing the way students are grouped

> *Research has consistently supported the leadership of the principal as the most important factor in the formula for school change* (Bliss, Firestone, & Richards, 1991; Fullan, 1991; Goldenberg & Sullivan, 1994; Wagner, 1994).

for instruction, and helping others to understand the need for change. As the previous section indicated, research has identified approaches that can help to close the achievement gap for English learners, but where should change begin? Who is responsible? The principal's role is crucial.

Research has consistently supported the leadership of the principal as the most important factor in the formula for school change (Bliss et al., 1991; Fullan, 1991; Goldenberg & Sullivan, 1994; Wagner, 1994). The literature on school reform and educational leadership often notes the importance of visionary and purposeful leaders who can initiate and facilitate school change (Carrow-Moffett, 1993; Goldenberg & Sullivan, 1994; Shachar, 1996) and clearly identifies the role and influence of the school principal on whether or not change will occur (Fullan, 2001). In describing leadership as the "cohesion that makes the other elements and components" of a program work together to create positive change, Goldenberg and

Sullivan (1994) note that without leadership at the school site, the other elements of change will not occur (p. 9). They identify two leadership dimensions that the skillful principal will use to produce a creative tension for change—support and pressure. In his extensive work on educational change, Fullan (1991) also emphasizes the "pivotal role of the principal as the gatekeeper or facilitator of change" (p. 11), stating that "the principal is central, especially to changes in the culture of the school" (p. 145). Miramontes, Nadeau, and Commins (1997) identify the principal as the "keeper of the dream" (p. 87), and Tikunoff (1987) states that the principal is the person most responsible for bringing about an effective school environment.

Critical Role of Principal as Instructional Leader

The principal must not only be a change agent, but must also be an instructional leader. The literature has consistently

> *It's hard to lead if you don't know the way.*

identified the strong instructional leadership of the principal as playing a critical role in providing instruction that responds to the needs of ELLs and in making their achievement a priority (August & Hakuta, 1997; Carter & Chatfield, 1986; Goldenberg & Sullivan, 1994; Gonzáles, 1998; Lucas, Henze, & Donato, 1990; Tikunoff et al., 1991). In their meta-analysis examination of the effects of leadership practices on student achievement, Waters, Marzano, and McNulty (2003) found that there is "a substantial relationship between leadership and student achievement" (p. 3). Carter and Chatfield's research (1986) showed that the priority given to the program for second language learners positively affected student achievement and that the principal played a key role in guiding this process.

As such, today's instructional leaders need additional skills and knowledge. Batsis (1987) found that principals in language minority settings "need to be equipped with additional knowledge and skills in order to be most effective" (p. 3). Miramontes and colleagues (1997) note that effective principals of ELLs must have a "firm grasp of curricular issues" that are crucial to successful programs for linguistically and culturally diverse students (p. 87). School leadership and expertise were found to be the most important factors in Goldenberg's (2004b) studies about creating settings that improve teaching and learning for language minority students. Research by Waters and colleagues (2003) also confirms the importance of the principal's instructional leadership:

> [J]ust as leaders can have a positive impact on achievement, they also can have a marginal, or worse, a negative impact on student achievement. When leaders concentrate on the wrong school and/or classroom practices, or miscalculate the magnitude…of the change they are attempting to implement, they can negatively impact student achievement. (p. 5)

In addition to being knowledgeable about effective practices, leaders must also create the settings and conditions for successful school change and provide a "school-wide intensive focus on increasing student achievement" (Goldenberg,

2004b, p. 177). Principals must create and maintain this commitment through distributed leadership, practice-oriented professional development, and high levels of collaboration found in professional learning communities. Olsen and Jaramillo (1999) specify the following tasks that leaders must be able to execute:

- build the capacity to deliver programs that address the needs of this new population,
- build understanding about the needs of newcomers and about the impacts of language and culture on education,
- provide the leadership, build the will, and create the attitudes so that educators welcome and embrace English language learners,
- create the structures that support learning for English language learners,
- build accountability and ownership for serving English language learners into the life of the school and district. (p. 24)

Interstate School Leaders Licensure Consortium Standards

In redefining the portfolio of skills that school leaders should possess, the Interstate School Leaders Licensure Consortium (ISLLC), a program of the Council of Chief State School Officers, and member states created a set of model standards that have become the basis for administrator licensure tests (see Appendix A). These standards represent a common core of knowledge, dispositions, and performances that link educational leadership to productive schools and enhanced educational outcomes, and that tie "significant trends in society and education" to "emerging views of leadership" (Council of Chief State School Officers [CCSSO], 1996, p. 5). While the following standards do not specifically address the issues of English learners, those issues are certainly implied:

A school administrator is an educational leader who promotes the success of all students by:

- **Standard 1:** Facilitating the development, articulation, implementation, and stewardship of a vision of learning that is shared and supported by the school community.
- **Standard 2:** Advocating, nurturing, and sustaining a school culture and instructional program conducive to student learning and staff professional growth.
- **Standard 3:** Ensuring management of the organization, operations, and resources for a safe, efficient, and effective learning environment.
- **Standard 4:** Collaborating with families and community members, responding to community interests and needs, and mobilizing community resources.
- **Standard 5:** Acting with integrity, fairness, and in an ethical manner.

- **Standard 6:** Understanding, responding to, and influencing the larger political, social, economic, legal, and cultural context. (CCSSO, 1996, pp. 10–24)

The literature on educational leadership, change, and English language acquisition clearly emphasizes the importance of a principal's knowledge and skills in leading effective schools for English learners, but "a principal is not going to improve academic achievement for all students unless she engages in her work differently" (National Association of Elementary School Principals [NAESP], 2001, p. v). In order to close the achievement gap for ELLs, it is imperative that principals possess the knowledge and skills to create a framework for success. The principal's leadership role in increasing school effectiveness for these students will be discussed throughout this book. A first step in helping you to determine your own professional development needs is to assess your knowledge and performance by taking the survey on the following pages. The descriptors, aligned to the ISLLC standards, have been developed from what the literature reveals about the attributes of effective principals for ELLs.

Leadership Challenge:
What Principals Should Do

Survey of Attributes of Effective Principals for ELLs

The value of this book can be measured in part by how it increases your knowledge about the components of effective schooling practices for ELLs. The following self-assessment, based on what the literature says about the attributes of effective principals for ELLs and aligned to the ISLLC standards, will help you to assess your own knowledge and performance.

Directions: For each question, circle the number that best represents the answer as it relates to your present knowledge and performance based on the following scale:

4	=	fully achieved	3	=	partially achieved
2	=	beginning to achieve	1	=	not achieved

Self-Assessment: Attributes of Effective Principals for ELLs

Vision and Leadership				
Standard 1: Facilitate "the development, articulation, implementation, and stewardship of a vision of learning that is shared and supported by the school community" (CCSSO, 1996, p. 10). **Standard 5:** Act "with integrity, fairness, and in an ethical manner" (CCSSO, 1996, p. 18).				
1.	I have a clear understanding of the elements that are necessary for an effective program for ELLs with a focused vision of what outcomes are to be expected from the program (Valverde & Armendáriz, 1999).	4	3	2	1
2.	I facilitate and communicate the school's vision to the staff, faculty, and the community in order to form a partnership in which all are motivated to achieve these outcomes (Valverde & Armendáriz, 1999).	4	3	2	1
3.	I have extensive training and certification in bilingual/ESL education (Texas Education Agency, 2000), spend time staying current on the recent research and practice in bilingual/ESL education (Lucas et al., 1990), and confidently share this information with others (Carter & Chatfield, 1986).	4	3	2	1
4.	Because I have a thorough understanding of the research findings and pedagogical principles underlying programs for ELLs, I am prepared to advocate for the programs that are best for our students (Genesee, 1999).	4	3	2	1
5.	I facilitate discussions with my staff that examine existing organizational practices and key ideas for reform that center on critical questions such as "Who benefits from what goes on here?" (Sirotnik & Oakes, 1986), and what these mean in terms of specific school improvement plans (Rollow & Bryk, 1993).	4	3	2	1
6.	I emphasize and create norms of "staff-wide concern for continual school improvement" (García, 1987, p. 6), assist in helping to establish the goals, obtain the resources, stimulate the understandings, change the structures, and promote and maintain the practices that improve learning experiences and outcomes for ELLs (García, 1987; Leithwood, 1994; Meyer, 1984; Murphy & Louis, 1994).	4	3	2	1
7.	I take an advocacy approach regarding various forms of discrimination or inequity (Bishop, Foster, & Jubala, 1993; Korinek, Walther-Thomas, & Laycock, 1992; Lipsky & Gartner, 1997).	4	3	2	1

Positive School Culture and Instructional Program				
Standard 2: Advocate, nurture, and sustain "a school culture and instructional program conducive to student learning and staff professional growth" (CCSSO, 1996, p. 12).				
8.	My school has researched effective programs and/or practices that have been effective in similar settings and made recommendations for implementation on a specified timeline (Hispanic Dropout Project, 1998).	4	3	2	1
9.	I continually advocate for the inclusion of ELLs (Berman et al., 1995; Goldenberg & Sullivan, 1994; Minicucci & Olsen, 1992) and "ensure sustained attention to these students by explicitly keeping language and culture on the reform agenda and insisting that every teacher participate in the school's continuous improvement process" (Adger, 1996, p. 1).	4	3	2	1
10.	I practice shared leadership (Texas Education Agency, 2000).	4	3	2	1
11.	I support educational equity and excellence for all students (Carter & Chatfield, 1986; Lucas et al., 1990), hold high expectations for all students (Baptiste, 1999; Genesee et al., 2005; Lein, Johnson, & Ragland, 1997, Purkey & Smith, 1983; Rosenholtz, 1985), and make the achievement of ELLs a priority (August & Hakuta, 1997; Carter & Chatfield, 1986; Lucas, 1993).	4	3	2	1
12.	I promote instructional approaches that foster biliteracy development and content acquisition (Villareal, 2001) and advocate for the use and development of students' native languages (Genesee et al., 2005; Lucas & Katz, 1994; Thomas & Collier, 1997).	4	3	2	1
13.	I help to create a school climate that values cultural and linguistic diversity (Berman et al., 1995; Collier, 1995).	4	3	2	1
14.	I have current and substantial knowledge about curricular issues and effective instructional strategies crucial to successful programs for ELLs (García, 1987), and I play a critical role in promoting and monitoring effective teaching and learning for them (August & Hakuta, 1997; Tikunoff et al., 1991).	4	3	2	1
15.	I have restructured the school to be a professional learning community that helps to improve teaching quality and raise student achievement (Adger, 1996).	4	3	2	1
16.	I place high priority on professional development for all school staff with training that is designed to serve ELLs more effectively (August & Hakuta, 1997; Lucas et al., 1990; Villareal, 2001).	4	3	2	1
17.	I help to create a climate of professional growth and accountability to support teachers in their efforts to become proficient teachers of ELLs, and I develop structures to strengthen curriculum and instruction (Lucas, 1992; Lucas et al., 1990).	4	3	2	1
18.	I have current and substantial knowledge about trends in effective professional development (Clair & Adger, 1999), and I am engaged in ongoing professional development activities for myself and my teachers (Gonzáles, 1998).	4	3	2	1
19.	I provide procedures for early data collection on students, particularly ELLs, that enable my staff to make informed and appropriate decisions regarding students' instructional needs (Texas Education Agency, 2000).	4	3	2	1
20.	I monitor ELLs' language and academic development (Texas Education Agency, 2000).	4	3	2	1

21.	I assist teachers in increasing their certainty about the goals for student achievement and their ability to meet the goals, and provide feedback when they have met the goals (Berman et al., 1995; Rosenholtz, 1985).	4	3	2	1
22.	I am highly visible in my school, I make frequent visits to classes to assure that quality instruction is provided (Edmonds, 1979; Purkey & Smith, 1983; Rosenholtz, 1985), and I provide substantial feedback to teachers on their teaching (Rosenholtz, 1985).	4	3	2	1

School Management				
Standard 3: Ensure "management of the organization, operations, and resources for a safe, efficient, and effective learning environment" (CCSSO, 1996, p. 14).				
23. I play a key role in the improvement of teaching and learning by influencing the organization of instruction (Bossert, Dwyer, Rowan, & Lee, 1982), examining the impact of various organizational alternatives on access to instruction and on student achievement, and making appropriate changes that promote both equity and excellence for all students (Baptiste, 1999).	4	3	2	1
24. I recruit and keep talented and dedicated staff (August & Hakuta, 1997; Lucas, 1993).	4	3	2	1
25. I hire bilingual staff who have cultural backgrounds similar to those of the students (Lucas et al., 1990) and who are role models (Lucas, 1993).	4	3	2	1
26. I provide and facilitate ample opportunities for collaborative planning and design of curriculum and lessons (Villareal, 2001).	4	3	2	1
27. I allocate funding for appropriate materials, translation of materials, professional development, and innovation within the classroom (Milk, Mercado, & Sapiens, 1992).	4	3	2	1

School and Community				
Standard 4: Collaborate "with families and community members, responding to community interests and needs, and mobilizing community resources" (CCSSO, 1996, p. 16). **Standard 6:** Understand, respond to, and influence "the larger political, social, economic, legal, and cultural context" (CCSSO, 1996, p. 20).				
28. I take strong steps to work with ELLs' parents, meeting parents in their homes and work sites, establishing linguistic equity by providing translators whenever needed, and developing parent competencies in leadership and other areas (Miron, 1997; Parker & Shapiro, 1993).	4	3	2	1
29. I ensure that all communication to parents is provided in their native languages as much as possible (Lucas et al., 1990; Sosa, 1990).	4	3	2	1
30. I encourage ELL parents to participate in literacy-rich activities with their children (Valverde & Armendáriz, 1999).	4	3	2	1
31. I send a strong message to parents that they should use and extend the family's primary language at home (Crawford, 1997; Wong Fillmore, 1991b).	4	3	2	1

32.	I actively solicit bilingual parents, extended family members, and community volunteers to help in the school (Bermúdez & Márquez, 1996; Tse, 1996) and become involved in their children's schooling (Lucas et al., 1990).	4	3	2	1
33.	I involve language minority parents in the decision-making process (Valverde & Armendáriz, 1999).	4	3	2	1
34.	I learn about the communities our students represent, and I attend activities sponsored by language minority groups in the school and community (Lucas, 1993).	4	3	2	1
35.	I advocate for language minorities in the school and community, and I speak up in favor of programs and services for ELLs and their families in various forums (Lucas, 1993).	4	3	2	1

Tally of Self-Assessment Answers

	Number of Questions	Number Answered with 3 (Partially Achieved)	Number Answered with 2 or 1 (Beginning to Achieve or Not Achieved)
☐ Vision and Leadership	7		
☐ Positive School Culture & Instructional Program	15		
☐ School Management	5		
☐ School and Community	8		

Check the areas that indicate a need for growth in your knowledge and performance as an effective principal of ELLs. These areas will serve as guideposts as you seek new ideas, strategies, and actions in each chapter's Leadership Challenge.

Questions for Reflection

How do your answers on the Survey of Attributes of Effective Principals for ELLs inform you of your own professional development needs?

2

Second Language Acquisition and Instructional Strategies

> *Immigrant children in our schools enter an educational system that is foreign, where the language is incomprehensible, where the faces of classmates are of many colors, and where parents feel unconnected and frustrated. It is alarming but not surprising that so many fail and drop out of school. While we talk democracy and equal opportunity, in reality many of our students are barely given a chance to get out of the gate. The basic question is not how can we teach these students, but whether we really want to.*
>
> (Olsen, 1988, p. 40)

Chapter Highlights: This chapter examines how students acquire a second language, factors that affect second language acquisition, and the research on effective instructional strategies for ELLs. In the Leadership Challenge, you will be able to identify specific ways that you and your staff can promote second language and content acquisition.

What Principals Should Know

Critical Questions

1. How do students acquire proficiency in a second language?
2. What are the dimensions of language proficiency?
3. What variables affect second language acquisition?
4. What instructional practices promote second language acquisition and content development?

Essential Vocabulary

Affective filter: A metaphor that describes a learner's attitudes that affect the relative success of second language acquisition. Negative feelings such as lack of motivation, lack of self-confidence, and learning anxiety act as filters that hinder and obstruct language learning (Baker & Prys Jones, 1998; NCELA, 2002).

BICS (Basic Interpersonal Communicative Skills): Also known as conversational fluency or social language (Cummins, 1984), everyday communication skills that are helped by contextual support (Baker & Prys Jones, 1998).

CALP (Cognitive Academic Language Proficiency): Also known as academic language proficiency (Cummins, 1984), the level of second language proficiency needed by students to perform the more abstract and cognitively demanding tasks of a classroom. Academic language is often abstract and has few contextual supports such as gestures and the viewing of objects (Baker & Prys Jones, 1998).

Cognates: Two words that have a common origin; most often, words in two languages that have a common etymology and thus are similar or identical in meaning (azure [English], *azul* [Spanish]).

Comprehensible input: A construct developed to describe understandable and meaningful language directed at second language learners under optimal conditions (Cloud, Genesee, & Hamayan, 2000, p. 203).

Context-embedded/context-reduced instruction: Context-embedded instruction provides a wide range of cues to meaning to support verbal input (facial expressions, gestures, visual clues). However, context-reduced instruction lacks such contextual support and provides few clues to meaning other than the words themselves (Cummins, 1984).

Conversational fluency: Also known as BICS or social language, the ability to carry on a conversation in familiar face-to-face situations (Cummins, 2002).

Discrete language skills: Aspect of language proficiency referring to the specific phonological, literacy, and grammatical skills that students acquire (Cummins, 2002).

False cognates: Words that are thought to be related (have a common origin) but are not (embarrassed [English], *embarazado* ["pregnant" in Spanish]).

Scaffolding: Adult support for learning and student performance through instruction, modeling, questioning, feedback, and so on. These supports are gradually withdrawn as students are able to demonstrate strategic behaviors in their own learning activities (Harris & Hodges, 1995).

Second language acquisition: The process of acquiring a second language. Some linguists distinguish between *acquisition* and *learning* of a second language, with acquisition used to describe the informal development of a second language, and learning used to describe the process of formal study of a second language. Other linguists maintain that there is no clear distinction between the two (NCELA, 2002).

Sheltered instruction (SI): An approach to teaching that extends the time students have for receiving English language support while they learn content subjects. SI classrooms, which may include a mix of native English speakers and English language learners or only ELLs, integrate language and content with sociocultural awareness. Teachers scaffold instruction to aid student comprehension of content topics and objectives by adjusting their speech and instructional tasks and by providing appropriate background information and experiences. The ultimate goal is accessibility for ELLs to grade-level content standards and concepts while they continue to improve their English language proficiency (Echevarria, Vogt, & Short, 2000, p. 200).

Critical Question #1:
How Do Students Acquire Proficiency in a Second Language?

Theoretical Models of Language Acquisition

Acquiring proficiency in a second language is a complex process. Although similar processes are used in acquiring a first language, such as progression through developmental stages of language development and reliance on others' modified speech to comprehend meaning, other factors play a stronger role in influencing second language acquisition than they do in influencing first language development. Furthermore, when the context of second language use is school, a deeper level of language proficiency is necessary. Theoretical models of second language acquisition that are prevalent in the literature include Krashen's hypotheses, Cummins' aspects of language proficiency, and Thomas and Collier's Prism Model.

Krashen's Hypotheses

Many of the current classroom practices for second language learning are based on Krashen's (1981, 1985) five hypotheses:

"People acquire second languages only if they obtain comprehensible input and if their affective filters are low enough to allow the input 'in'" (Krashen, 1985, p. 2).

1. **The Acquisition-Learning Hypothesis** Krashen (1985) distinguishes between two ways of acquiring a second language, acquisition and learning. Acquisition is a subconscious process in which students acquire language in a natural environment, out of the need to communicate and without formal instruction, "when the learner hears the language spoken in meaningful contexts and…[is] able to understand the message conveyed by the language he hears" (Krashen & Terrell, 1983, p. 27). On the other hand, language learning is a conscious process that results in conscious "knowing about a language" (Krashen, 1985, p. 1), such as knowl-

edge of grammar rules. According to Krashen, "learning" is less important than "acquisition."

2. **The Natural Order Hypothesis** Language learners acquire the rules of a language in a predictable sequence, a natural order. Certain grammatical features tend to be acquired early, while others tend to be acquired late. The order of language acquisition is developmental, and errors, inevitable and temporary, will gradually disappear.

3. **The Monitor Hypothesis** The consciously learned rules about language play just a small part in the development of students' language proficiency, but these rules can be used to monitor or check their spoken or written language. However, students must first be concerned about speaking or writing correctly and must know the rule.

4. **The Input Hypothesis** A key element of this hypothesis is that students acquire, not learn, language by receiving understandable messages, thus the term "comprehensible input." Input can be made comprehensible as a result of context, which includes extralinguistic information such as gestures, pictures, background knowledge, and previous linguistic knowledge. Students acquire language best in natural communication situations when they receive second language input slightly beyond their current levels of language proficiency (i = actual level; $i + 1$ = potential language development level).

5. **The Affective Filter Hypothesis** Affective or socioemotional variables influence students' ability to acquire language. Negative feelings act as filters that hinder and obstruct language learning, thus the term "affective filter" (Baker & Prys Jones, 1998) describing the wall of anxiety that ELLs may put up to protect themselves from embarrassment, failure, or taking risks with the language. However, when students have low affective filters (which includes a lower anxiety level), they will interact more with native speakers, receive more natural language input, and be more open to learning the difficult aspects of the language. The most important affective variables are motivation to learn the language, self-confidence, a low-anxiety learning environment, and self-esteem.

Krashen (1985) summarizes his five hypotheses with the statement that "people acquire second languages only if they obtain comprehensible input and if their affective filters are low enough to allow the input 'in'" (p. 2). He urges teachers not to force language production, but rather to allow students a "silent period" during which they can initially acquire some language knowledge by listening and understanding. During the silent period, comprehension precedes production; the learner listens to the sounds of the language and attempts to make sense of the sounds, but often doesn't produce any linguistic output.

Krashen's theories have influenced language teaching practices that focus on meaningful communication rather than rote learning; promote the use of comprehensible input; and produce low-anxiety, learner-centered classrooms. However, one should not overgeneralize "natural language acquisition" to mean that language skills should not be taught. Aspects of language proficiency can and should be developed and accelerated through focused and explicit instruction (Wong Fillmore & Snow, 2000). This includes explicit instruction in skills and subskills for reading and writing (de la Luz Reyes, 1991; Kucer & Silva, 1999)—skills that are needed to understand text, such as vocabulary building in context, comprehension strategies, and academic oral language (American Educational Research Association, 2004)—as well as how to use language learning strategies (O'Malley, Chamot, Stewner-Manzanares, Russo, & Kupper, 1985).

Stages of Language Acquisition

Theorists believe that second language learners progress through a continuum of predictable and sequential stages of language development as they acquire a new language, from very little knowledge about the new language (preproduction) to competency resembling that of a native English speaker (advanced fluency). Krashen and Terrell (1983) identified five stages of language development (see page 30): (1) preproduction (listening and gestures); (2) early production (short phrases); (3) speech emergence (long phrases and sentences); (4) intermediate fluency (conversation); and (5) advanced fluency (effective communication, both oral and written). Students go through these stages naturally and cannot be forced from one stage of linguistic development to the next before they are ready. As they progress through the stages, their receptive language abilities will exceed their productive abilities, and they will understand more than they can say or write. According to a recent research synthesis (Genesee et al., 2005), ELLs need three to five years to reach advanced proficiency in oral English, and while progress from the beginning to the middle stages of proficiency occurs rapidly, progress from the middle to the upper levels of proficiency takes much longer. Also, the strategies that ELLs use to learn language vary with their stage of language development. Students in the early stages use receptive strategies, such as repetition and memorization, to learn words and phrases; students in the middle stages use more interactive strategies, such as verbal attention-getters and elaboration in order to interact with others; and those in the advanced stages use language and communication monitoring strategies to clarify, ask for assistance, and maintain and repair communication with others (Genesee et al., 2005). Therefore, it is very important for educators to understand ELLs' stages of language development, use a wide variety of strategies to modify instruction and make content comprehensible, and appropriately assess students' progress. In addition, instruction and programs must accommodate the changing needs of students to facilitate progression to the next stages. More information on the stages of language development may be found on the pages that follow.

Stages of Language Development

Language Development Stage	Teacher Strategies
Stage I: Preproduction/Preconversational • Student is totally new to English, but experiences rapid oral language growth and has 500 "receptive" words (words they understand but may not be comfortable using) • Minimal comprehension, minimal verbal production • Student spends much time listening and observing surroundings, understanding more than he or she can produce • Usually involves a "silent period" during which student may be reluctant to speak • Student uses physical responses to understand and communicate, such as facial expressions, pointing, acting out, gesturing, nodding, drawing • Student is dependent on visual clues for understanding • Student experiences mental fatigue from unfamiliar surroundings • Stage can last from two weeks to six months	• Honor silent period; avoid forcing student to speak prematurely • Build on/expand background knowledge • Pair students with more advanced learners; use cooperative learning • Provide total physical response and extensive visual support; use pictures, physical movement, gestures, real objects, manipulatives, repetition, and verbal cues to support and expand language acquisition • Use physical response to check comprehension (show/point/draw answers); ask yes/no questions • Read aloud to students; use books with lots of visuals and repetitive patterns • Provide native language reading materials • Encourage parents to read to the child in the first language • Preview/review key vocabulary and phrases (in both languages if possible); show/write key words • Use alternative assessment and modified grading
Stage II: Early Production • "Low beginner"; 1,000 receptive/active words (words they can understand and use) • Limited comprehension and disconnected speech; student speaks in one- to two-word short phrases; omits words or parts of words; mispronounces words • Student is dependent on context for understanding • Student can demonstrate comprehension physically and by giving short answers to simple questions • Uses mostly present-tense words • Can last up to an additional six months after preproduction stage	• Provide extensive modeling and support • Provide extensive visual cues (gestures, objects, pictures) and repetition to convey meaning • Use shared reading, echo reading, choral reading, rhymes, songs, and word banks • Continue total physical response techniques • Ask questions that require one- to two-word responses: who, what, when, where, which one • Have students label or manipulate pictures and/or objects • Use authentic and rich literature with read-alouds and story/picture books on tape • Explicitly teach reading strategies • Preteach/teach key vocabulary and concepts (in native language if possible) • Provide native language reading materials • Encourage parents to read to the child in the first language • Provide lots of easy reading materials, visually supported content area texts, trade books • Use pictorial-based graphic organizers with key phrases • Pair students with more advanced learners; use cooperative learning • Use alternative assessment and modified grading

Language Development Stage	Teacher Strategies
Stage III: Speech Emergence ■ "Beginner"; 3,000 active words, noticeable increase in listening comprehension ■ Student functions on a social level; uses language more freely; begins to use dialogue; uses short phrases and simple sentences; can ask and answer simple questions; makes basic grammatical errors ■ Student is developing reading comprehension and writing skills in English; understands more, but is still dependent on context ■ Student is able to participate in many mainstream academic subjects and small-group activities; makes some errors in speech ■ Student can demonstrate comprehension and academic knowledge in a variety of ways with assistance ■ Stage can last up to an additional year or more	■ Preteach/teach key vocabulary and concepts ■ Introduce concepts through K-W-L charts, webs, and story maps ■ Build on/expand background knowledge ■ Provide lots of visually supported content area texts, trade books ■ Use teacher modeling and support student comprehension of main ideas ■ Rely less on cues from pictures and context ■ Engage students in producing language: describing, retelling, comparing, contrasting, defining, summarizing, reporting ■ Ask application questions; require more writing ■ Explicitly teach reading comprehension strategies ■ Transition students to word-based graphic organizers ■ Use cooperative learning ■ Use alternative assessment and modified grading as needed
Stage IV: Intermediate Fluency ■ Students are "high beginners, intermediate or advanced"; 6,000 active words with continued vocabulary expansion ■ Student uses more complex sentence patterns and extended speech; makes complex grammatical errors ■ Student is expected to participate in all classroom reading and writing activities, can understand most of what is said in the classroom, and is able to read most grade-level materials (may need some modifications) ■ Student can express ideas in both oral and written communication; uses simple/complex sentence responses, states opinions, shares thoughts, and asks for clarification ■ Student still needs help with vocabulary development in content areas, may experience difficulties in abstract, cognitively demanding subjects, especially when a high degree of literacy is required ■ Stage may require three to five years to achieve peer-appropriate fluency in academic settings	■ Continue to shelter instruction and check for understanding ■ Use teacher modeling and support to help students begin making inferences and understand meanings of text ■ Use context to support meaning; gradually decrease visual supports for reading and writing ■ Teach students to systematically apply reading comprehension strategies ■ Engage students in higher-order thinking activities; ask why questions ■ Expect more advanced reading and writing in English; develop academic language, figurative language ■ Preteach/reteach key vocabulary for content areas ■ Use cooperative learning ■ Use alternative assessment and modified grading as needed

Language Development Stage	Teacher Strategies
Stage V: Advanced Fluency ■ Student is on the verge of exiting the program, can easily express thoughts and feelings using grammar and vocabulary comparable to that of native speakers ■ Student comprehends what is taught in the mainstream classroom, can participate fully in grade-level classroom activities with some modifications and occasional extra support in understanding specialized academic language in content areas, may be unfamiliar with some of the nuances of the language ■ Academic language increases in development; student has some specialized content-area vocabulary ■ Stage may last three to seven years as growth continues in cultural and background knowledge of the language and content area vocabulary	■ Provide minimal support for students to be successful with grade-level material ■ Continue to focus on all reading strategies ■ Be aware of possible gaps in content due to lack of prior experience with specific topics ■ Expect reading and writing skills to approach that of a native speaker ■ Model strategies for comprehension of texts ■ Continue ongoing development through integrated language arts and content area activities

Characteristics of English Language Proficiency Levels

Adapted and modified from New Mexico State Department of Education, 2003.

English Proficiency Level	Preproduction	Early Production	Speech Emergence	Intermediate Fluency	Advanced Fluency
Listening	■ Understands very little or no spoken English ■ Progresses to understanding simple questions and statements	■ Understands simple and familiar conversations (limited academic conversations), at normal speeds	■ Understands most social and academic conversations on familiar topics at normal speeds; occasionally misunderstands	■ Understands most social and academic conversations; rarely misunderstands	■ Understands social and academic language without difficulty
Speaking	■ Produces little or no spoken English ■ Communicates basic and routine needs primarily through gestures or single words ■ Uses objects or things to communicate	■ Uses basic words, simple phrases, and routine expressions for needs and preferences ■ Lacks vocabulary to fully convey ideas. ■ Needs assistance in handling some academic language tasks	■ Develops social and academic language, but participation is hesitant. ■ Speaks in longer phrases and sentences ■ Speech contains errors (idioms, vocabulary, structure) that may prevent communication	■ Speaks the language in most situations with more complex sentences and phrases ■ Occasional errors in idioms, vocabulary, structure, but errors do not hinder communication	■ Uses both social and academic language with a high degree of fluency, approximating that of a native speaker

Reading	<ul><li>Listens to read alouds.</li><li>Participates in chanting, singing</li><li>Relies heavily on pictures in shared reading</li><li>Can participate in shared-to-guided reading</li><li>Demonstrates awareness of print and some knowledge of like phonemes</li></ul>	<ul><li>Starts to understand and participate in read alouds, shared reading, chanting, singing</li><li>Memorizes rhymes, songs, and chants</li><li>Relies on pictures in shared reading</li><li>Participates in shared-to-guided reading</li></ul>	<ul><li>Reads aloud familiar, predictable text with minimal self-correction and appropriate pacing and phrasing</li><li>Actively participates in shared and guided reading</li><li>Relies on high-frequency words and patterns in shared reading</li></ul>	<ul><li>Develops more fluency in oral reading with minimal self-correction</li><li>Participates in reading materials near to scope and difficulty of grade-level peers</li><li>Begins to use multiple strategies to construct meaning</li></ul>	<ul><li>Reads aloud predictable or grade-level text with fluency and accuracy</li><li>Reads or demonstrates progress toward reading at independent and instructional level appropriate to grade level</li><li>Uses multiple strategies to construct meaning</li></ul>
Writing	<ul><li>Communicates through pictures</li><li>May be able to write in native language</li><li>Copies print, labels drawings, may be able to dictate or write a simple message</li><li>Begins to use spacing and sound-symbol relationships to spell</li></ul>	<ul><li>Writes labels or a few words</li><li>Can dictate or write a simple message</li><li>Produces phrases or sentences on one topic</li><li>Uses sound-symbol relationships to spell</li><li>Uses upper and lower case letters</li><li>Participates in language-experience activities</li></ul>	<ul><li>Actively participates in shared writing</li><li>Writes longer phrases or simple sentences</li><li>May have to dictate message</li><li>Writing has inconsistent accuracy, will resemble spoken language</li><li>Produces past tenses</li><li>Participates in scaffolded guided writing</li></ul>	<ul><li>Writes complete sentences with errors but still has some difficulty with complex sentences</li><li>Uses common conventions, but has errors in spelling and punctuation</li><li>Organizes paragraphs</li><li>Participates in shared and guided writing</li></ul>	<ul><li>Writes effectively in most situations</li><li>Demonstrates knowledge of spelling, punctuation, and vocabulary appropriate to grade level</li><li>Writes varied sentence structures and/or paragraphs to express ideas clearly</li></ul>

Building Staff Knowledge: Stages of Language Development

Materials: Stages of language development sheets (pages 30–32).

Time: 20–30 minutes

Explanation: As ELLs acquire English, they progress through a series of language proficiency stages. It is important to remember that students will pass through each stage at different rates and that the length of time in each stage may also differ. Usually, students reach proficiency in this order: listening, speaking, reading, writing. It is also important to think about English language proficiency levels when designing lessons, as learning needs vary and levels provide access points to content.

Activity: Number teachers by five for a jigsaw activity. Give each group a language development stage on which to become experts. Teachers in the same groups meet to discuss their language development stage and the impact on their students. They then plan how to teach the information to their peers. Have each group create a t-chart poster summarizing the information on their specific stage by characteristics and strategies. Teachers will then return to their original groups where one member of each expert group will teach what they have learned to their group members. Have each teacher think of a particular ELL student and circle the listening, speaking, reading, and writing level (page 32) exhibited by that child. Emphasize that children can be at different stages for the four language areas, and that levels help teachers differentiate instruction.

Discuss in groups:
- Why should we be aware of the stages of language development for English language learners? What are the implications for instruction?
- What is good about using a jigsaw activity with ELLs? What would you want to consider before using a jigsaw activity? How would you use it in your classroom?

Have each group briefly report to the rest of the staff.

Follow-up: Post the t-chart posters in the teachers' lounge for a period of time to promote further conversations about the stages of language development. Provide time for teachers to design differentiated lesson plans in their study groups that consider the various stages of language acquisition of the ELL children in their classrooms. When an ELL is referred to the student improvement team, revisit and identify the child's stage of language development for each domain.

Questions for Reflection

Are all staff aware of how children acquire a second language?

Are all staff aware of the stages of language proficiency?

Critical Question #2:
What Are the Dimensions
of Language Proficiency?

Cummins' Dimensions of Language Proficiency

Underlying many issues about second language acquisition is the question of what is meant by "language proficiency" and how it relates to academic achievement. Cummins (2002) makes important distinctions between three aspects of "language proficiency" to consider when implementing programs for sustained academic development of ELLs: conversational fluency, discrete language skills, and academic language proficiency. Each dimension of language proficiency develops and responds differently to various types of instructional practices.

Conversational fluency is characterized by the "ability to carry on a conversation in familiar face-to-face situations" (Cummins, 2002, p. 19). Sometimes called BICS (Basic Interpersonal Communicative Skills) or social language, conversational fluency is context-embedded and low in cognitive demand. It is easily acquired through daily living activities (Cummins, 1979, 1981b, 1984, 1991b) with the use of high-frequency words and simple grammatical structures. Most native speakers already have conversational fluency when they enter school, but it takes ELLs at least one to two years of intense second language exposure to develop it (Collier, 1989; Cummins, 1981a, 1981b, 1996, 2000).

Discrete language skills refers to the specific phonological, literacy, and grammatical skills that students acquire. Cummins (2002) states that students acquire discrete language skills through direct instruction or through immersion in a language- and literacy-rich environment. Students acquire some discrete skills early, such as knowledge of the letters of the alphabet, sound-symbol relationships, and decoding. Students acquire other discrete language skills (e.g., spelling, punctuation, capitalization, grammar) throughout their schooling. Discrete skills such as phonemic awareness and knowledge of the letters of the alphabet show consistently moderate relationships with the acquisition of decoding skills (National Reading Panel, 2000; Snow et al., 1998). ELLs can acquire these skills while they are developing basic vocabulary and conversational fluency, but there is little transfer to other aspects of academic oral language proficiency such as linguistic concepts, vocabulary, sentence memory, and word memory (Geva, 2000; Kwan & Willows, 1998).

Academic language proficiency, sometimes called CALP (Cognitive Academic Language Proficiency) (Cummins, 1979, 1981b, 1984, 1991b), requires students to know and understand less frequently used vocabulary and to produce increasingly complex oral and written language (Cummins, 2002). As students progress through grades, they are faced with increasingly complex language demands, encountering more low-frequency words, complex syntax, and abstract concepts and expressions that occur in environments without much context reduced and are not used in every-day conversations. Generally not related to conversational fluency or discrete language skills, academic language proficiency is needed for linguistically and cognitively demanding tasks such as reading and understanding content-specific texts and understanding and using spoken and written academic language. Learning academic language is a complex endeavor for all students, and is even more so for ELLs, who need a minimum of three to five years to reach advanced oral proficiency (Genesee et al., 2005) and a minimum of five years of academic language exposure to catch up to their English speaking peers (Cummins, 1981a; Klesmer, 1994).

Implications of the Three Dimensions

While it is important for ELLs to develop all three dimensions of language proficiency, teachers often incorrectly assume that once children can comfortably converse in English, they are in full control of the language.

> *"Just learning English will not guarantee a student's success"* (Samway & McKeon, 1999, p. 24).

However, children who have conversational fluency have not necessarily achieved proficiency in the more abstract academic language needed for many classroom activities, especially in the later grades (McLaughlin, 1992). In fact, they may still have great difficulty reading and writing proficiently in English, and the direct instruction approaches that are effective in developing decoding skills (discrete language skills) have little value in promoting reading comprehension and academic language proficiency (Cummins, 2002). Failure to take account of these different dimensions of language proficiency may result in the following:

- Many ELLs who have acquired conversational fluency and discrete language skills, such as decoding in English, are often misinterpreted as having on-grade-level academic language proficiency (Cummins, 2001; Krashen, 2001).

- Students who can read English fluently because they have the decoding skills may have limited comprehension of what they have read (Cummins, 2002).

- If phonics instruction is all that these students get, and they are not offered any special language assistance because they have oral fluency and some discrete language skills, they tend to fall behind in later elementary grades due to their lack of academic language proficiency, also referred to as the "fourth grade slump" (Chall, Jacobs, & Baldwin, 1990; Cummins, 2002; Rand Reading Study Group, 2002). From fourth grade on, "reading materials become more complex, technical and abstract and are beyond the everyday experiences of most children" (Chall et al., 1990, p. 45).

- When making assumptions that are solely based on conversational and discrete language skill proficiencies, educators might assume that ELLs no longer need language development support and exit them too soon from second language programs (Cummins, 1984).

- Educators may label some ELLs as unmotivated or resistant to learning when their academic performance is below grade level (Meyer, 2000).

Academic Language Development and Reading Comprehension

ELLs do not need to be proficient speakers before they start to read and write. Practice in one language process (reading, writing, listening, speaking) promotes development in the others. For example, the importance of oral language development in English is supported by several studies which have found a positive relation between oral proficiency in English and English reading achievement (Carlisle, Beeman, Davis, & Spharim, 1999; Garcia-Vásquez, Vásquez, Lopez, & Ward, 1997; Goldstein, Harris, & Klein, 1993; Saville-Troike, 1984). In order to promote academic language proficiency and the development of reading comprehension for ELLs, Fielding and Pearson (1994) state that students need the following: "large amounts of time for actual text reading, teacher-directed instruction in comprehension strategies, opportunities for peer and collaborative learning, and occasions to talk to a teacher and one another about their responses to reading" (p. 62). According to Cummins (2002), ELLs must have "immersion in a rich literacy environment where students have ample encouragement and opportunity to read (and write) extensively....This is true for all students but it is particularly significant for ESL students who are attempting to catch up to native-speakers in academic language proficiency" (p. 21).

Although much vocabulary and syntax are incidentally acquired through interactions and opportunities in language-rich classrooms, mere exposure to English is not enough to assure full academic proficiency (Doughty & Williams, 1998). Academic language proficiency must be systematically developed and explicitly taught across all language areas. Academic language development includes linguistic structures used to summarize; analyze; evaluate; combine sentences; compose and write text; interpret graphs, charts, and word problems; and extract information from texts (Scarcella, 1996; Wong Fillmore & Snow, 2000).

Critical Question #3:
What Variables Affect
Second Language Acquisition?

Thomas and Collier's Prism Model

Educators often assume that the first thing ELLs need to do is to learn English, but Thomas and Collier's (1997) Prism Model, reproduced here, explains that this one-dimensional perspective does not apply to a school-aged child because second language acquisition is only one of many processes that are occurring. Instead, Thomas and Collier (1997) propose a multidimensional perspective of English language acquisition involving four interdependent components—sociocultural, language, academic, and cognitive processes—all of which must be developed in order for a child to reach full cognitive maturity and achieve overall growth and academic success.

The Prism Model

Language Acquisition for School
L1 + L2 Academic Development
L1 + L2 Cognitive Development
L1 + L2 Language Development
Social & Cultural Processes

L1 +L2 Academic Development

L1 + L2 Language Development

Social & Cultural Processes

L1 + L2 Cognitive Development

Copyright 1997, Wayne P. Thomas & Virginia Collier, National Clearinghouse for Bilingual Education, The George Washington University, reproduced by permission of the authors.

The sociocultural dimension of the model, the core of the student's acquisition, includes the social and cultural processes occurring in all contexts of the student's life—home, school, community, and society. Sociocultural processes that affect second language acquisition include affective student variables (self-esteem, embarrassment, anxiety) and sociocultural factors such as the instructional environment in a classroom, peer acceptance, discrimination, the subordinate status of a minority group, or acculturation versus assimilation forces (Collier, 1995; Thomas & Collier, 1997).

The linguistic dimension of the model encompasses all aspects of language development: the subconscious aspects of language development; acquisition and proficiency in the first and second languages; the conscious, formal teaching of language in school; and acquisition of the oral and written systems in both languages across the reading, writing, speaking, and listening domains. The cognitive component involves the subconscious process of cognitive development, challenging ELLs continually in both languages through grade-level classroom experiences, teaching students how to use learning strategies, and providing students with the "tools" of higher-level thinking.

The academic development component includes all school work in all subjects. Academic development cannot be addressed separately from language development; content should drive language development. Thomas and Collier (1997) note that "with each succeeding grade, academic work dramatically expands the vocabulary, sociolinguistic, and discourse dimensions of language to higher cognitive levels" (p. 43). However, if instruction is "remedial" and only focuses on simple tasks, it does not support language development to the same degree as on-grade-level instruction. Also, postponing or interrupting academic development "to learn English first" will likely promote academic failure in the long run (Collier, 1995).

Thomas and Collier (1997) assert that all four components of the model must be supported simultaneously for ELLs to develop deep levels of academic English proficiency. They cite three key predictors of long-term school success:

- On-grade-level academic instruction using students' first language for as long as possible and on-grade-level academic instruction using students' second language for part of the school day
- Interactive, discovery learning and other approaches that foster active learning
- A sociocultural context of schooling in which ELLs are integrated with non-ELLs in a safe and supportive learning environment, bilingualism is considered an asset, and the bilingual program is perceived as the gifted and talented program.

Other Variables Affecting Language Acquisition

Like their native English speaking peers, ELLs vary in abilities, motivation, and readiness to learn (August & Hakuta, 1997). Verbal intelligence plays only a small part in second language acquisition. Factors that are more important include students' attitudes toward acquiring the language, the motivation that a child has to learn the language, and the level of relaxation that the student feels in the second language environment (Cloud et al., 2000). The degree of acculturation—the way that newcomers adapt and socialize to the new culture—can also delay or accelerate learning (García, 1994c) and depends on factors such as the desire to leave home, psychological trauma or warfare, age, educational background, urban versus rural orientation, and similarities and differences between the new and previous cultures.

> *The most significant student background variable regarding the "how long" question is the amount of formal schooling students have received in their first language.*

Other factors that impact the rate of acquisition include age (the older student learns the language more efficiently); language distance (the ease or difficulty of learning English based on the similarities and differences of English as compared to the native language); first language development; language status (the prestige of the target language); home support (parents who value both languages and show support for their children's progress); personality (the more gregarious child will take more risks in learning the language); learning style; cultural background; classroom interaction; and quality of instruction in the second language (McLaughlin, 1992; Walqui, 2000). Access to effective teaching and educational services also strongly influences the length of time it takes for students to learn English. The most significant student background variable regarding "how long" is the amount of formal schooling that students have received in their first language, whether it's been received only in the home country or in both the home country and the United States (Cummins, 1991a, 1996; García, 1994c; Genesee, 1994; Lessow-Hurley, 1990; McLaughlin, 1992; Pérez & Torres-Guzmán, 1996; Snow, 1990). The Thomas and Collier studies (Collier, 1989, 1992; Collier & Thomas, 1989; Thomas & Collier, 1997, 2002) have found that the following pattern exists across student groups, regardless of native language, country of origin, socioeconomic status, and other student background variables:

- Where all instruction is given in English, non-native speakers of English with no schooling in their first language take 7 to 10 years or more to reach age and grade level norms of their native English speaking peers.
- Immigrant students who have had two to three years of first language schooling in their home country before they come to the United States take at least five to seven years to reach typical native-speaker performance.

- Students who are schooled bilingually take four to seven years to reach parity with native English speakers.

Because of the many variables that influence and affect language acquisition, time frames for learning language and subject matter are difficult to determine. On average, English learners require about 2 years to acquire conversational proficiency, whereas at least 5 years (within a range of 4 to 10 years) of exposure to academic English is needed in order to acquire grade level native-speaker proficiency (Collier, 1992; Cummins, 1981a, 1981b, 1996; Klesmer, 1994; Ramirez, 1992). Initially, this may seem to be a very long period of time, but when one considers that English speaking students spend 12 years or more studying and acquiring academic language, it is quite plausible. In addition, ELLs are competing with a moving target; while they are learning academic English, their native-speaking peers are also learning academic English. So in order to catch up to English speaking students in 6 years, an ELL must make more than 1 year of academic gain (typically 15 months for every 10-month school year) in each of several consecutive years, while the typical English student is expected to make 10 months of achievement gain every school year (Thomas & Collier, 1997).

Questions for Reflection

What are the implications for curriculum and instruction when considering the dimensions of language proficiency? For programming?

When considering the variables that affect second language acquisition, what are the implications for gaining comprehensive information about new ELL students? For parent interviews? For program placement?

What are the educational considerations for social and cultural support?

What are the implications for instruction when considering this information? For special education referrals? For exit criteria from ELL programs, knowing that students are often exited too quickly?

Critical Question #4:
What Instructional Practices Promote Second Language Acquisition and Content Development?

Integrated Content and Language Instruction

Because ELLs may need 4 to 10 years to become proficient in academic English, they can not afford to "learn English first." Schools must integrate the teaching of language into the existing academic program, not teach it separately. Integrated content and language instruction can combine academic learning with language and literacy opportunities for ELLs (Brinton, Snow, & Wesche, 1993), but the instruction must be modified in ways that make it comprehensible and meaningful.

Second language development and academic learning are fostered by using a variety of strategies that make the second language comprehensible. This type of instruction, based on Krashen's concepts about comprehensible input, is known as sheltered instruction, sheltered English, or Specially Designed Academic Instruction in English (SDAIE) (California State Department of Education, 1994). In addition to techniques that make language comprehensible, sheltered instruction also includes cognitive strategies; promotion of student participation and communication through all four language domains; and cooperative grouping strategies, enabling ELLs to access additional support from their peers.

Sheltered instruction can be used for English language development, literacy development, and content development; it can be used in English-only classrooms, content ESL programs, bilingual programs, or newcomer programs (Echevarria et al., 2000). Genesee (1999) states that sheltered instruction "is an instructional strategy that can and should be used in conjunction with all of the program types....It can also be implemented as the sole approach for educating English language learners" (p. 7). For example, some schools offer sheltered classes for language-sensitive content instruction, such as sheltered science or sheltered social studies. Whatever the mode of delivery, all teachers should be trained in sheltered instruction techniques so that they can adjust their instruction to meet the needs of ELLs. When considering the implementation of sheltered instruction, it is essential that several issues be addressed: academic discourse and literacy; standards-based instruction; differentiation and scaffolding; and quality teacher training to provide ELLs with rigorous, on-grade-level work. Structured collaboration time facilitates the planning and coordination of instruction that supports grade-level standards and provides opportunities for demonstration of sheltered instruction combined with peer coaching.

Teaching to grade-level standards while meeting the needs of ELLs requires knowledgeable use of differentiation and scaffolding. Several resources guide instruction in this approach. The Sheltered Instruction Observation Protocol (SIOP) model (see page 44) consists of 30 descriptors organized into eight sections covering lesson preparation, building background, comprehensible input, strategies, interaction, practice and application, lesson delivery, and review and assessment (Echevarria et al., 2000). The authors have also developed an observation instrument that teachers and administrators can use as a tool for instructional planning, delivery, and observation. Findings from a study of the SIOP observation instrument indicate that it is a highly reliable and valid measure of sheltered instruction (Guarino et al., 2001), and ELLs in classes whose teachers had been trained in implementing SIOP to a high degree outperformed control students in narrative and expository writing (Echevarria, Vogt, & Short, 2004). The Cognitive Academic Language Learning Approach (CALLA) is another content-based instructional model. The CALLA approach, which integrates grade-appropriate content, language development, and explicit instruction in learning strategies, can also be used in ESL, bilingual, and mainstream classrooms (Chamot & O'Malley, 1994).

Sheltered Instruction
Observation Protocol (SIOP) Components
Echevarria et al., 2000, pp. 191–194

I. **Lesson Preparation**
   1. Clearly defined *content objectives* for students
   2. Clearly defined *language objectives* for students
   3. *Content concepts* appropriate for age and educational background level of students
   4. *Supplementary materials* used to a high degree, making the lesson clear and meaningful (e.g., graphs, models, visuals)
   5. *Adaptation of content* (e.g., text, assignment) to all levels of student proficiency
   6. *Meaningful activities* that integrate lesson concepts (e.g., surveys, letter writing, simulations, constructing models) with language practice opportunities for reading, writing, listening, speaking

II. **Building Background**
   7. *Concepts explicitly linked* to students' background experiences
   8. *Links explicitly* made between past learning and new concepts
   9. *Key vocabulary* emphasized (e.g., introduced, written, repeated, and highlighted for students to see)

III. **Comprehensible Input**
   10. *Speech* appropriate for students' proficiency level (e.g., slower rate, enunciation, and simple sentence structure for beginners)
   11. *Explanation of academic tasks* clear
   12. Uses a variety of *techniques* to make content concepts clear (e.g., modeling, visuals, hands-on activities, demonstrations, gestures, body language)

IV. **Strategies**
   13. Provides ample opportunities for students to use *strategies*
   14. Consistent use of *scaffolding* techniques throughout lesson, assisting and supporting student understanding, such as think-alouds
   15. Teacher uses a variety of *question types, including those that promote higher-order thinking skills* throughout the lessons (e.g., knowledge, comprehension, application, analysis, synthesis, evaluation)

V. **Interaction**
   16. Frequent opportunities for *interactions* and discussion between teacher and student and among students, which encourage elaborated responses about lesson concepts
   17. *Grouping configurations* support language and content objectives of the lesson
   18. Consistently provides sufficient *wait time for student responses*
   19. Ample opportunities for students to *clarify key concepts in L1* as needed with aide, peer, or L1 text

VI. **Practice/Application**
   20. Provides *hands-on* materials and/or manipulatives for students to practice using new content knowledge

21. Provides activities for students to *apply content and language knowledge* in the classroom
22. Uses activities that integrate all *language skills* (e.g., reading, writing, listening, and speaking)

VII. **Lesson Delivery**

23. *Content objectives* clearly supported by lesson delivery
24. *Language objectives* clearly supported by lesson delivery
25. *Students engaged* approximately 90 to 100 percent of the period
26. *Pacing* of the lesson appropriate to the students' ability level

VIII. **Review/Assessment**

27. Comprehensive *review of key vocabulary*
28. Comprehensive *review of key content concepts*
29. Regularly provides *feedback* to students on their output (e.g., language, content, work)
30. Conducts *assessment* of student comprehension and learning of all lesson objectives (e.g., spot checking, group response) throughout the lesson

Regardless of the model, effective teachers of ELLs use a vast repertoire of instructional practices to shelter instruction and to enhance student understanding. Besides use of the native language (see Chapter 3), effective instructional practices for ELLs draw from the professional literature on reading, second language acquisition, and effective teaching (Echevarria et al., 2000). In their examination of effective practices, August and Hakuta (1997) specifically noted the use of routines and specific strategies to provide comprehensible input, collaborative/cooperative interaction, thematic curriculum, a balanced literacy program, explicit skills instruction, metacognitive strategies, and comprehension strategies. Gersten and Jiménez (1994) identified instruction that challenged the students, encouraged their involvement, provided them with opportunities for success, included scaffolding with a variety of graphic organizers to draw on their background knowledge, and gave them access to content.

Even though sheltered instruction models share some of the same strategies found in high-quality teaching for native English speaking students, it is important to note that they are characterized by careful attention to ELLs' language development needs. Sheltered instruction models (Echevarria & Graves, 1998; Echevarria et al., 2000, 2004; Short, 1999) recommend that teachers specifically plan for language objectives with activities and techniques that support and promote students' language development as they are learning content.

Strategies for Making Language and Content Comprehensible

The literature is replete with strategies that help make instruction comprehensible to ELLs (Chamot, 1992; Echevarria & Graves, 1998; Echevarria et al., 2000, 2004; Gersten & Jiménez, 1994; Gersten & Woodward, 1992; Peregoy & Boyle, 2005; Saunders, O'Brien, Lennon, & McLean, 1996). These include the following:

- Modified speech and language
  - Adjusting the rate and pace of speech
  - Speaking clearly with repetition if needed
  - Simplifying language by using shorter sentences, active voice, and paraphrasing
  - Using explicit discourse markers such as "first" and "next"
  - Limiting the use of idioms and slang
  - Defining new words in context
- Increased use of visuals, multiple modalities, and nonverbal cues
  - Pictures, charts, graphs, maps, diagrams, props, and realia (real objects)
  - Gestures, facial expressions, and actions to demonstrate meaning
  - Multimedia and objects related to the subject matter
  - Modeling and demonstration
  - Reinforcement of oral language with written cues, written material on the board or overhead, and visual representations of academic concepts (e.g., graphic organizers)
- Multiple opportunities to practice with hands-on materials, manipulatives, and activities
- Theme-based content
- Activating students' prior knowledge and building background knowledge (through the first language when necessary)
- Flexible grouping formats (skill groups, pair work, heterogeneous groups)

Active Learning

Researchers agree that active learning produces the greatest success for ELLs. Active learning implies the development of a community of learners that promotes and provides authentic communication among all students in a variety of self-directed activities emphasizing student production rather than reproduction of knowledge and language (Rossi & Stringfield, 1997). Active learning environments include the following:

- Students actively involved in peer instruction (Anstrom, 1998)

- Students regularly engaged in instructional conversation (Goldenberg, 1992; Tharp & Gallimore, 1991) and functional communication (García, 1991b)
- Teachers understanding that learning is a social act involving personal invention or construction of knowledge (Prawatt, 1992)
- Prior knowledge, skills, and abilities of students incorporated into the curriculum (Anstrom, 1998; Peregoy & Boyle, 2005)
- Students' home, community, and culture integrated into the curriculum (Anstrom, 1998; Echevarria & Graves, 1998)
- Learning activities that draw on students' multiple intelligences (Gardner, 1993), focus on complex meaningful problems, and embed basic skills instruction into global contexts (Anstrom, 1998; Echevarria & Graves, 1998)

Cooperative/Collaborative Interaction

Research on second language acquisition finds that for students to reach high levels of proficiency, they must engage in high levels of oral interaction, negotiating meaning and solving problems (Chamot & O'Malley, 1987; Krashen, 1985; Wong Fillmore, 1991a). In fact, children learn a language best when frequently trying to communicate with others in meaningful and interactive contexts in which language and knowledge are socially constructed, language acquisition is fostered naturally, and highly interactive opportunities for both linguistic and academic input and output are present (McLeod, 1996; Slavin, 1995). Saunders and Goldenberg's study (1999) found that students who were encouraged to use language to elaborate and develop ideas performed better academically than those who did not engage in forms of extended language use.

> "One of the more jarring paradoxes in education is th e gap between the rich research on cooperative learning and its unfortunate underuse in the classroom" (Schmoker, 1999, p. 73).

Successful classrooms for ELLs use cooperative and collaborative approaches to learning (Calderón, Hertz-Lazarowitz, Ivory, & Slavin, 1997; McLeod, 1996; Pease-Álvarez, García, & Espinoza, 1991). Cooperative learning provides opportunities for students to work together to construct meaning and share understandings (Durán & Szymanski, 1993), increases the amount and quality of practice in English than would otherwise be available (Long & Porter, 1985), and helps to provide more comprehensible input and output (Kagan, 1995). Cooperative learning also creates a positive affective climate, increases student motivation (McLeod, 1996), and promotes problem-solving (Arreaga-Mayer, 1998; Slavin, 1995). The research findings of García (1994b); Kagan (1989); McLeod (1996); and Tinajero, Calderón, and Hertz-Lazarowitz (1993) noted the importance of cooperative learning practices, especially for Latinos, because these learning strategies are more compatible with the social and family structures in which Latino language minority students are most productive (Huerta-Macías, 1998). A study of Cambodian-American students acquiring English also showed positive effects utilizing cooperative learning techniques (Slavin, 1995; Slavin & Yampolsky, 1992).

However, ELLs cannot simply be paired with native English speakers to produce positive oral language benefits—tasks have to be carefully designed, English peers need interaction training, and the language proficiency of ELLs must be considered (Genesee et al., 2005). Teachers must also provide opportunities for interaction through the kind of extended dialogue that occurs in instructional conversations (Patthey-Chavez & Goldenberg, 1995; Saunders & Goldenberg, 1999).

Balanced Curriculum

Effective schools in August and Hakuta's report (1997) focused on a balanced curriculum of basic skills and higher-order skills. Cummins (2000) defines a balanced curriculum as one that includes "balance between, on the one hand, extensive meaning-focused oral and written language input and use designed to promote problem-solving and higher-order thinking, and, on the other hand, explicit formal instruction designed to develop linguistic and metacognitive awareness" (p. 267). Schools that reported an increase in ELL student achievement used explicit skills instruction to help students acquire basic skills (Rosenshine & Stevens, 1986; Sternberg, 1986) and devoted substantial amounts of time to explicit skills instruction (Carter & Chatfield, 1986; Escamilla, 1994; Goldenberg & Gallimore, 1991b; Goldenberg & Sullivan, 1994; Slavin & Yampolsky, 1992; Tikunoff, 1983). Teachers in effective classrooms for ELLs supplement explicit skills instruction by providing many opportunities to produce oral and written English and to exchange ideas in intellectual opportunities and collaborative inquiry (August & Hakuta, 1997). The research on effective schools and effective teachers for second language learners includes the following approaches to achieving a balanced curriculum:

- "Meaning-centered thematic curriculum," allowing students to be exposed to the repetition of concepts and vocabulary across a variety of settings and contexts (Berman et al., 1995)
- A wide range of meaningful activities or experiences focused on a particular concept (Pease-Álvarez et al., 1991)
- A combination of basic and higher-order skills that focuses on comprehension, thinking skills, fluency, pleasure reading, and an increasing use of complex material (Dianda & Flaherty, 1995; Slavin & Yampolsky, 1992)
- A balanced literacy program in which key skills and subjects such as phonics, word recognition, specific comprehension skills, and writing conventions are taught (Goldenberg & Gallimore, 1991b; Goldenberg & Sullivan, 1994)
- Enhanced learning and language development using integrated holistic approaches that involve prereading and prewriting activities instead of rote drill and practice (Saravia-Shore & García, 1995)

Literacy and Five Components

The National Reading Panel (2000) identified five major elements that contribute to the early reading success of English-proficient children: phonemic awareness, phonics, vocabulary, comprehension, and fluency. Researchers have identified these same elements as contributing to the reading success of ELLs (August, 2002, 2004, 2006; Fitzgerald, 1995b; G. E. Garcia, 2000; Genesee et al., 2005; Gersten & Geva, 2003), along with the three-tier model of delivering literacy instruction (August, 2004). Genesee and colleagues (2005) found that ELLs with solid phonological awareness skills in English acquire beginning reading skills more easily than those with poorly developed skills. Slavin and Cheung (2003) state:

> This does not mean that no accommodations are necessary for English language learners, but it does suggest that with allowances for the language issues themselves, effective reading instruction for non-English-proficient children may be similar to effective instruction for English-proficient children, whether the ELLs are taught in their native language or in English. (p. 22)

August (2004) notes that ELLs need the following considerations regarding the five components:

Phonemic awareness and phonics issues

- Specific sounds and sound placement in words differ for different languages.
- Phonological tasks with unknown words are more difficult.
- Unfamiliar phonemes and graphemes make decoding and spelling difficult.
- For literate ELLs, English graphemes have different sounds in L1.
- Limited English proficiency prevents children from using word meaning to figure out how to read a word. (p. 6)

Fluency issues

- Fluency embraces both word recognition and comprehension.
- ELLs often have less opportunity to read aloud in English with feedback. (p. 10)

Vocabulary issues

- ELLs arrive at school with a much more limited English vocabulary than English speaking students. There are many basic words that English speaking students know that ELLs do not.
- ELLs may lack labels in English for concepts they know and have labels for in their first language.
- ELLs and English speakers may have different concepts for the same label.

- There is some English vocabulary that may be especially important in comprehending connected text—cohesion markers, for example—that necessitates explicit instruction.
- ELLs literate in a first language that has many cognates with English have an important resource.
- Words with multiple meanings can be a source of confusion. (pp. 14–15)

Comprehension issues

- Limited word recognition skills and fluency impede comprehension.
- Limited vocabulary impedes comprehension.
- Structural differences between languages can mislead ELLs.
- Text structures vary across cultures, and this may influence comprehension.
- Culture influences, but does not completely determine, background knowledge. (p. 21)

Although instruction in the five key components is necessary, it is not sufficient. Early, ongoing, and intensive efforts to develop extensive oral proficiency in English are also critical to the success of ELLs, but are often neglected (August, 2006; Genesee et al., 2005). Well-developed oral proficiency in English is associated with English reading comprehension (vocabulary knowledge, listening comprehension, syntactic skills, and metalinguistic aspects of language), and ELLs who have well-developed English oral skills achieve greater success in English reading than those who have less well-developed skills (August, 2006; Genesee et al., 2005).

Goldenberg (2004a) agrees that "teaching/learning in L1 literacy and L2 literacy (in alphabetic languages) is more alike than different, but adjustments are probably needed to account for language differences and possible cross-language confusions." Phonemic awareness and phonics instruction in English does not need to be delayed until a particular threshold of oral language is reached (August, 2004), but further instructional adjustments for maximum benefit include explicit teaching and guidance in the aspects of oral language development and written English—word identification skills, vocabulary, idioms, syntax, English sounds, and spelling patterns. Examples of adjustments include the following:

- Explicit instruction about the similarities and differences between the first and second languages (e.g., sound-letter correspondences, particular phonemes, and combinations of phonemes that do not exist in their native languages) (August, 2006; Jiménez, 2000)
- Helping students hear and reproduce particular sounds (e.g., /ch/, /sh/) that don't exist or are not salient in their home language
- Teaching syntax differences (order and relationship of parts of a sentence)
- Teaching of cognates and false cognates (e.g., embarrassed, *embarazado* ["pregnant" in Spanish]), especially for ELLs who are native Spanish speakers

- Preteaching vocabulary
- Explicit instruction in vocabulary that is especially important in comprehending connected text (e.g., cohesion markers)
- Explaining cultural concepts or background knowledge that influences comprehension

(August, 2004, 2006; Goldenberg, 2004a; Jiménez, 2000)

Chapter 3 includes a further discussion of reading strategies that relate to native language instruction and support. The following chart also includes more information on literacy and ELLs.

Building Staff Knowledge:
Literacy and ELLs

A strong and positive correlation exists between literacy in the native language and learning English (Baker, 1993). ELLs need rich literacy environments with ample opportunities to read and write extensively (Cummins, 2002). The same five elements that contribute to the reading success of English-proficient children contribute to the reading success of ELLs: phonemic awareness, phonics, vocabulary, comprehension, and fluency (Genesee et al., 2005). However, extensive oral language development must be incorporated as well (August, 2006).

Phonemic Awareness Considerations

- Not all English phonemes are present in ELLs' first languages, making it difficult for ELLs to pronounce them, distinguish them auditorily, and place them into meaningful context (August, 2003).
- ELLs can be taught to hear the sounds that are not in their first languages (August, 2003).

Implications/Tips

- Learn the linguistic characteristics of students' native languages, including the phonemes that exist and do not exist in those languages (Antunez, 2003).
- Teach students the different sounds (e.g., /ch/, /sh/; /b/, /v/) (Goldenberg, 2004a).
- Teach phonemic awareness while explicitly teaching vocabulary (Antunez, 2003).
- Use meaningful activities such as language games and word walls to focus on particular sounds and letters (Antunez, 2003).
- Use rhythm and repetition (songs, poetry) to teach phonemic awareness and print concepts (Antunez, 2003).

Phonics Considerations

- Students not literate in their native languages or who speak languages that do not have a written form may have trouble understanding certain concepts and will need to be taught concepts of print (Peregoy & Boyle, 2000).
- Students who already read might have difficulty because certain graphemes represent different sounds in the second language than they do in the first (e.g., /b/ in English can be pronounced either /v/ or /b/ in Spanish; short /i/ in English as in "it" has a long /e/ sound in Spanish as in "eat") (August, 2003).
- Some languages have a different orthography than English (e.g., Russian, Arabic) (August, 2003).
- ELLs are often not aware if they are reading correctly (whether it sounds right or makes sense) and have difficulty using meaning to support decoding because they lack knowledge about the language (August, 2003).

Implications/Tips (Phonics Considerations)

- Teach students the similarities and differences between their first and second languages (August, 2006; Goldenberg, 2004a). The letters b, c, d, f, l, m, n, p, q, s, and t in Spanish are similar enough to English to transfer readily, resulting in the need for minimal phonics instruction for these consonants. However, vowel letters in both languages represent very different sounds and will need explicit instruction (Peregoy & Boyle, 2000).
- Group children by word reading level; provide structured phonics work and decoding with language development (Slavin & Madden, 2001).
- Provide one-to-one or small group assistance to students who need further intervention (Slavin & Madden, 2001).

Vocabulary Considerations

- Some vocabulary development is acquired through reading, but is not the most effective method (August, 2003).
- Students are likely to acquire and retain more words when they use the words in various tasks (Laufer, 2001).

Implications/Tips

- Explicitly teach vocabulary before students read a text (Antunez, 2003).
- Preview the key vocabulary in students' native language before introducing it in English.
- Use cognates in English and in the students' native language to create meaningful connections (McLaughlin et al., 2000).
- Use visuals, objects, and printed contexts with explicit and redundant information for learning vocabulary (Neuman & Koskinen, 1992).
- Provide more opportunities for vocabulary acquisition than just reading or hearing new words. Have the students use the new vocabulary words in various tasks (Laufer, 2001).
- Provide direct intervention for ELLs who are below a threshold of linguistic competence in English (August, 2003).
- Provide vocabulary instruction that builds vocabulary breadth and depth and teaches strategies for acquiring word knowledge (McLaughlin et al., 2000).
- Provide multiple opportunities for peer and collaborative learning (Fielding & Pearson, 1994).
- Explicitly teach text markers (August, 2004).

Comprehension Considerations

- ELLs are less likely to comprehend what they're reading because of their limited English proficiency (August, 2003).
- Comprehension is disrupted due to a high proportion of unknown words and a lack of knowledge about English grammar and structure (August, 2003).
- Comprehension is enhanced when students read culturally familiar content (August, 2003).

Implications/Tips (Comprehension Considerations)

- To the extent possible, develop literacy skills in the first language (Snow et al., 1998).
- Explicitly teach structural features of English that are not present in students' first languages (order and relationship of parts of a sentence—e.g., in English, an adjective precedes the noun that it's modifying; in Spanish, the adjective follows the noun that it's modifying) (August, 2003; Goldenberg, 2004a).
- Scaffold instruction through discourse (August, 2003). Use literature logs and provide opportunities for instructional conversations about the content and concepts of stories (Fielding & Pearson, 1994; Saunders & Goldenberg, 1999).
- Provide large amounts of time for actual text reading (Fielding & Pearson, 1994).
- Provide teacher-directed instruction in multiple comprehension strategies, such as asking questions, making inferences, and looking for cognate vocabulary (Fielding & Pearson, 1994).
- Provide multiple opportunities for students to read authentic and culturally familiar literature, and challenge students with tasks that require higher-order thinking skills (graphic organizers, think-alouds, questioning, summarizing) (Antunez, 2003).
- Translate key concepts into the students' native language to ensure that ELLs make connections to background knowledge.
- Furnish bilingual texts or translations ahead of time whenever possible so students can listen or read on their own or with a bilingual paraprofessional, community member, parent, or bilingual peer before the text is read in English.

Fluency Considerations

- ELLs have less opportunity to read aloud with feedback because many of their parents are not literate in English (August, 2003).
- ELLs do not read as fluently due to their limited comprehension (August, 2003).
- Fluency should not be confused with accent (Antunez, 2003).

Implications/Tips

- Provide opportunities for ELLs to participate in read-alouds of big books, read-alongs with proficient readers, and repeated listening to books read aloud (Hiebert, Pearson, Taylor, Richardson, & Paris, 1998).
- Provide assisted reading opportunities to increase ELLs' reading rates, word accuracy, and comprehension (Van Wagenen, Williams, & McLaughlin, 1994):
  - Have the student read silently while listening to a recording of the passage.
  - Have the student read the passage aloud.
  - Have the student read the passage three times silently with the tape.
  - Have the student read the passage aloud again.

Vocabulary Instruction

Vocabulary instruction has consistently emerged as a key area in second language learning, bilingual education and literacy instruction (Nagy & Scott, 2000; Saville-Troike, 1984; Tikunoff, 1983). Research shows a strong relationship between vocabulary knowledge in English and academic achievement (Saville-Troike, 1984) and a direct correlation between vocabulary knowledge and reading proficiency and comprehension (Chall et al., 1990; Cunningham & Stanovich, 1997; Nagy & Scott, 2000). In addition, there are strong relationships between opportunities to read and the development of vocabulary and reading comprehension abilities (Elley, 1991; Krashen, 1993; Postlethwaite & Ross, 1992).

Because daily oral language experiences such as conversations and watching television do not bring about significant vocabulary growth (Anderson, 1996; Cunningham & Stanovich, 1998), vocabulary development for ELLs must be intensively targeted from the earliest grades, and the time spent on learning vocabulary must be expanded (August, 2004, 2006). Graves (2005) states that comprehensive vocabulary programs include four parts: rich and varied language experiences, teaching individual words, teaching word learning strategies, and fostering word consciousness. Intentional, explicit teaching of specific words and word-learning strategies can increase students' vocabularies (Tomeson & Aarnoutse, 1998; White, Graves, & Slater, 1990) and improve reading comprehension (McKeown, Beck, Omanson, & Pople, 1985; Stahl & Fairbanks, 1986). Pearson and Fielding (1991) note that effective teachers design activities to emphasize vocabulary development, providing explicit discussion and teaching of vocabulary and structure. Nagy, Garcia, Durgunoglu, and Hancin-Bhatt (1993) found that instruction in how to use cognate knowledge was highly beneficial to native Spanish-speaking ELLs.

Beck, McKeown, and Kucan (2002) recommend teaching about 400 "tier two" words per year, words that are characteristic of mature language users, appear frequently across a variety of domains, have instructional potential, and for which students already have conceptual understanding. The Vocabulary Improvement Project for upper elementary ELLs, an adaptation of Beck and McKeown's (2001) Text Talk method, involved explicit instruction in developing word-learning strategies, such as analyzing morphological aspects of words. This program led to improved performance in ELLs' word knowledge and reading comprehension (Carlo et al., 2004). McLaughlin and colleagues (2000) found that an enriched vocabulary development program substantially closed the gap between native and non-native speakers in vocabulary development and reading comprehension. The structure of each unit consisted of the following 20- to 30-minute lessons:

- Day 1: Teacher introduced the story, defined the words, and developed vocabulary inferencing strategies.
- Day 2: Students worked in groups to learn words in context.

- Day 3: Students engaged in activities to deepen their knowledge of different uses and meanings of the words.
- Day 4: Students participated in activities to develop their appreciation of English/Spanish cognates and took assessments to determine their progress in learning the week's identified words.
- Day 5: Students learned other strategies for developing word knowledge, such as using roots, affixes, and comprehension monitoring (McLaughlin et al., 2000).

Cummins (2002) advocates for large amounts of time for actual text reading, stating that "extensive reading is crucial for academic language development because less frequent vocabulary, most of which derives from Greek and Latin sources, is found primarily in written text" (p. 21).

Elley (1998) reported that ELLs made significant gains in vocabulary acquisition simply by having someone read to them. The key point was that teachers used interesting books and techniques for comprehensible input such as gesturing, paraphrasing, and pointing to the pictures to ensure that students understood the story. Additional vocabulary information follows.

Building Staff Knowledge:
Vocabulary and ELLs

- Explicitly and directly teach key vocabulary (Rousseau, Tam, & Ramnarain, 1993). This might include saying the word, writing it on the board, asking students to say it and write it, and defining the terms with pictures, visuals, realia, multisensory experiences, examples, demonstrations (Echevarria, 1998). Instruction should include student involvement and student-generated word meanings. When students use their experiences and background knowledge to define words, they understand and remember the words better.
- Use both direct instruction and cooperative learning to teach vocabulary (August, 2004).
- Select vocabulary words for direct instruction. Focus on a relatively small number (7–12 each week) of critical words that are usable and that students are likely to encounter repeatedly across texts in different domains. Restricting the number of words will help students develop a deeper understanding of meanings (Gersten & Baker, 2000; McLaughlin et al., 2000).

- Develop activities that help make semantic links to other words and concepts for a deeper and richer understanding of a word's meaning and to learn other words and concepts related to the target words (McLaughlin et al., 2000). Children learn vocabulary better when the words are related to concepts they already know. Existing concepts should be used as a basis for acquiring new concepts. Use vocabulary related to a theme or instruction in "word webs."

- Use stories and writing projects as contexts for vocabulary learning (Gersten & Baker, 2000).

- Choose reading selections containing only a limited number of new words. Readings should be considered comprehensible input, that is, just slightly above the student's true reading level (Gersten & Baker, 2000).

- Preteach critical vocabulary prior to student reading (Rousseau et al., 1993).

- Emphasize words over time. Provide multiple exposures of words to build depth of knowledge (Gersten & Baker, 2000).

- Teach students to infer meanings from context (McLaughlin et al., 2000). The contextual setting gives student clues to word meanings.

- Teach students to use roots, affixes, cognates, morphological relationships, and comprehension monitoring (McLaughlin et al., 2000). Specifically teach students how to look at morphological cues within a word that might indicate its meaning or part of speech (Osburne & Mulling, 2001).

- Explicitly teach the use of cognates to improve reading and vocabulary (McLaughlin et al., 2000). Since many words in English share common roots in Greek and Latin with other languages, there are many cognates or words that have the same meaning. Knowledge of Spanish cognates transfers to ESL reading (Garcia & Nagy, 1993; Jiménez, Garcia, & Pearson, 1995, 1996; Nagy et al., 1993). Have students raise their hands and identify cognates when they hear them, create a cognate word chart, and have students do cognate word sorts.

- Provide ELLs with frequent opportunities to use oral language in the classroom. Active, daily language use should be structured to include both conversational and academic discourse (Gersten & Baker, 2000).

- Teach students to learn to distinguish and look up words that seem most essential to the meaning of the text, such as those that are repeated four or five times (Birch, 2002). They need to learn to use the dictionary, thesaurus, and glossary to develop understanding of word meanings when they cannot figure out the meanings from experience, context, or structural analysis.

- Teach students different word learning and recognition strategies to apply on their own while they are reading (Rousseau et al., 1993)

- When reading to students, use interesting books and a variety of techniques for comprehensible input (gesturing, paraphrasing, pointing to the pictures) to ensure that students understand the story and acquire new vocabulary (Elley, 1998).

- Use research-based practices such as those in Beck's *Bringing Words to Life* (August, 2003).

I. Explicitly teach tier two words.
   A. Choose for importance and utility.
      1. Characteristic of mature language users.
      2. Useful across a variety of domains—words that students will encounter often, functionally important words.
   B. Choose for conceptual understanding—students understand the general concept (e.g., forlorn—students understand the concept of sad).
   C. Select three to six vocabulary words per week to teach from books you are reading aloud.
   D. Explain definitions in everyday connected language, rather than dictionary definitions.
II. Explain tier one words when needed for meaning.
   A. Tier one consists of basic words that rarely require instructional attention in school and are highly frequent in life for English speakers.
   B. ELLs know many of these words in first language and just need English labels. Add pictures to word cards and use pantomime, gesture, real objects, quick draws, first language equivalent.
   C. Spanish cognates (family/*familia*) rarely require instruction, but should be pointed out. False cognates should also be pointed out.
   D. Multiple-meaning words need to be deliberately taught to ELLs.
   E. ELLs need instruction in idioms, metaphors, or everyday expressions (make up your mind, let's hit the books, once upon a time).

Building Background

ELLs may have difficulty understanding a text or concept because their schemata or background knowledge does not match the topic of the text (Anderson, 1994; Jiménez et al., 1996). Research indicates that students learn better and have increased comprehension when teachers activate students' prior knowledge and refer to relevant student experiences during instruction (Lim & Watson, 1993; Moll, 1988; Muniz-Swicegood, 1994; Saunders, O'Brien, Lennon, & McLean, 1999), taking students from where they are and leading them to higher levels of understanding (Krashen, 1985; Vygotsky, 1978). August (2006) states that background knowledge, acquired through oral language, should be targeted intensively throughout high-quality literacy instruction. When building background, effective teachers link new concepts and information to students' background experiences, both personal (including cultural) and academic, and build upon and make explicit connections to new learning and previously covered material, vocabulary, skills, and concepts (Echevarria et al., 2000; Saunders et al., 1999; Tierney & Pearson, 1994). Strategies for developing background knowledge prior to reading include using prereading activities that focus on previewing content and activating existing schemata, or knowledge already stored in the memory. This may include verbal explanations and discussions, structured overviews of the topic, preview guides, anticipation guides, indirect experiences to provide background (pictures, video clips, demonstrations, role plays, simulations), or direct and concrete experiences (field trips, experiments).

Learning Strategies

O'Malley and Chamot (1990) define learning strategies as "the special thoughts or behaviors that individuals use to help them comprehend, learn, or retain new information" (p. 1). According to the authors, "learning a language has more in common with learning complex cognitive skills than it does with learning facts, isolated pieces of information, or even meaningful texts" (Chamot & O'Malley, 1989, p. 112). Providing ELLs with the metacognitive skills they can use to "think about and prepare for a task, monitor themselves as they complete the task, and evaluate the outcomes helps language-minority students deal with context-reduced tasks" (Dianda & Flaherty, 1995, p. 8). Cognitive development includes teaching students how to explicitly use learning strategies, providing students with the "tools" of higher-level thinking.

Effective teachers of ELLs explicitly model and teach learning strategies and metacognitive strategies that facilitate the learning process and enhance understanding (August & Hakuta, 1997; Echevarria & Graves, 1998; Garcia & Pearson, 1990; Palincsar & Brown, 1984; Palincsar & Klenk, 1992; Pearson & Fielding, 1991). According to Pressley and Woloshyn (1995), students are likely to become more effective strategy users when teachers model strategies and then provide scaffolded opportunities for students to practice the strategies. Direct explanation of strategies involves the following components:

- An explicit description of the strategy and when and how it should be used
- Teacher and/or student modeling of the strategy in action
- Collaborative use of the strategy in action
- Guided practice using the strategy with gradual release of responsibility
- Independent use of the strategy (Duke & Pearson, 2002, pp. 208–210).

Research supports the importance of explicit instruction in comprehension strategies and explanation of word meanings (Biemiller, 1999; Rand Reading Study Group, 2002). Dole, Duffy, Roehler, and Pearson (1991) recommend that teachers incorporate strategy instruction that includes prediction, self-questioning, monitoring, determining importance, and summarizing. Chamot and O'Malley (1987, 1994) specifically speak to the explicit teaching and application of metacognitive, cognitive, and social/affective strategies in their CALLA approach. Echevarria and colleagues (2000) and Chamot and O'Malley (1994) add that teachers can promote strategy use by asking higher-level thinking questions that are accompanied by appropriate wait time.

Effective schools in the literature incorporated the following approaches to specifically teach learning strategies:

- Explicit teaching of why, when, and how to use metacognitive strategies (Calderón et al., 1997; Dianda & Flaherty, 1995; Slavin & Yampolsky, 1992)
- Instruction in self-generated questioning strategies in metacognitive reading strategy training (Muniz-Swicegood, 1994)
- Teaching and modeling of comprehension strategies, such as question generating, summarizing, and predicting in which the reciprocal teaching

form of assisted performance was modified to include discussion (Hernandez, 1991)

- Explicit instruction in problem-solving procedures and learning strategies including metacognitive strategies such as planning and self-evaluation, cognitive strategies such as elaboration of prior knowledge, and social/affective strategies such as cooperation (Chamot, Dale, O'Malley, & Spanos, 1992).

Questions for Reflection

Does your literacy program balance explicit basic skills instruction with multiple opportunities to produce oral and written English?

Does your literacy program adjust for language differences and possible cross-language confusions for ELLs?

Do all teachers explicitly teach vocabulary?

Do all teachers explicitly build background?

Do all teachers explicitly teach strategies?

Do all teachers use a variety of instructional strategies to promote language and content acquisition for ELLs?

Building Staff Knowledge: A Checklist
for Adapting Curriculum and Instruction for ELLs

The purpose of adapting curriculum and instruction is to decrease the language demands on students and to make the English used in lessons as comprehensible as possible. Therefore, lessons should be designed to build upon the students' background knowledge and to rely on contextualized or nonlinguistic cues so that ELLs can comprehend the material and the teacher's message.

Adapting Instruction

☐ Simplify the language of instruction, not the concept being taught.
  ✓ Use simple sentence structure (subject-verb-object). Avoid complex sentence structure.
  ✓ Use high-frequency words.
  ✓ Use active voice; avoid passive voice (e.g., active voice: "The boy hit the ball."; passive voice: "The ball was hit by the boy.").
  ✓ Avoid negative phrasing, such as "all but," "except," "everything is _____ except," or "which answer is NOT the reason/cause?"
☐ Consistently use gestures and animated delivery. Provide clues to meaning through drawings, acting out, and emotions.
☐ Emphasize key words and phrases using intonation and repetition.
☐ Modify your speech.
  ✓ Speak slowly.
  ✓ Enunciate.
  ✓ Avoid idioms and slang.
☐ Teach students the phrases "I don't understand," "Slowly, please," and "Please repeat" so they can provide feedback to you when they need clarification.
☐ Go for depth of information, not breadth. Present materials in a clear, concise, comprehensible manner. Eliminate nonessential information.
☐ Present information through a multisensory approach. Provide concrete examples through hands-on activities that make abstract concepts comprehensible and meaningful.
  ✓ Tape recordings.
  ✓ Role playing and drama.
  ✓ Simulations.
  ✓ Songs, chants, kinesthetic activities.
☐ Consistently use visuals.
  ✓ Use pictures, drawings, illustrations, videos, picture books, demonstration lessons, maps, charts, graphs, posters, and realia.
  ✓ Use samples of finished products as models.
☐ Use graphic organizers to make information more comprehensible—webs, Venn diagrams, timelines, K-W-Ls.
☐ Provide written as well as aural (listening) messages.

   ✓ Write key points or outline what you are saying on the board or overhead, reading aloud what you've written as you present the lesson.

   ✓ Summarize key points on the board or an overhead as you review them at the end of the lesson.

☐ Write clearly, legibly, and in print—many ELLs have difficulty reading cursive.

☐ Present content area vocabulary and concepts using realia, visuals, hands-on activities, and native language support.

   ✓ Preview and review key vocabulary and phrases (in both languages if possible) before and after the lesson.

   ✓ Provide practice and application of vocabulary words with concrete examples— visuals, interactive computer programs, and activities.

☐ Explicitly teach learning strategies.

☐ Build background knowledge before teaching a lesson. Because ELLs have such varied educational and life experiences, they may need more comprehensive background information than other students. Do not take for granted that ELLs will understand or have experiences with some of the concepts being taught.

☐ Model "think-alouds"—saying out loud the various thought processes that students must use to apply information and solve problems.

☐ Structure opportunities for interaction by having students work in pairs or small groups. Rotate members of the group to provide varied language and learning-style experiences.

   ✓ Flexible grouping (mixed-ability groups, similar-ability groups, cooperative groups, same-language groups).

   ✓ Paired learning (peer buddies, more proficient ELLs with less proficient ELLs).

   ✓ Cross-age tutoring.

☐ Provide advance organizers.

   ✓ Concise organized listings of important points in lesson presentation, reading selection, video.

   ✓ Summaries of the most important concepts.

   ✓ Vocabulary preview lists defined in simple, easily understood terms.

   ✓ Preview questions that focus on significant ideas and concepts.

   ✓ Mnemonic devices—strategies that are helpful for organizing and learning information.

☐ Allow longer wait time (10–20 seconds) for ELLs' responses. They must translate the questions into their native language, formulate a response, and translate the response into English.

☐ Provide additional resources for students to use:

   ✓ Bilingual dictionaries, picture dictionaries, speaking dictionaries, electronic translators.

   ✓ Video clips.

   ✓ Interactive computer programs.

   ✓ Books/text on audio tapes.

   ✓ Native language reference materials.

   ✓ Native language content texts.

✓ High-interest/leveled reading books for content materials

☐ Provide frequent positive feedback. Model error correction.

Adapting Assignments

☐ Highlight texts/reading material.

☐ Provide native language materials.

☐ Consider student's level of language proficiency when grading for errors in spelling, punctuation, and grammar.

☐ Use a multitude of leveled books—both fiction and nonfiction—that supplement science and social studies themes.

☐ Use cooperative learning strategies.

☐ Explicitly teach reading strategies. Use before, during, and after reading strategies such as THIEVES, SQP2RS, textbook tours, K-W-L charts.

☐ Provide lots of visually supported content area texts, trade books, and narratives.

☐ Allow student to dictate answers on tape recorders or to others.

☐ Allow extra time in class or outside of class for work completion.

☐ Simplify written directions by limiting words and numbering steps.

Assessment

☐ Remember to ask yourself, "Am I testing reading comprehension or content concepts?"

☐ Design alternative assessment activities—demonstrations, oral interviews, portfolios, projects, exhibitions, story or text retelling, writing samples, teacher observations. Consider other approaches for finding out what students know or can do. Manipulatives and other hands-on items or activities lend themselves to being effective assessment tools.

☐ Allow students to retell or restate orally and in writing.

☐ Preteach "test language."

☐ Instruct students to write or tell what they have learned in the native language (for students with adequate native language literacy).

☐ Underline or use a highlighter to point out important words in test directions or test items.

☐ Increase time for test completion.

☐ Simplify the language on test items:

✓ Eliminate unfamiliar or infrequent words.

✓ Shorten long nominals.

✓ Change complex phrases to simple phrases.

✓ Change passive verbs to active.

✓ Reduce conditional clauses with separate sentences.

✓ Remove or rephrase relative clauses.

☐ Provide study guides with key concepts and vocabulary.

☐ Provide extra review time (emphasizing key points to study).

☐ Provide students with examples of test content and format.

Leadership Challenge:
What Principals Should Do

Critical Question

How will you promote and encourage second language acquisition and the use of effective instructional strategies?

Directions: As you read the following list of suggestions, check items that best align to the school's vision, program goals, resources, and needs of your students. Items from the Principal's Survey in Chapter 1 are designated in bold font and ◆.

Vision and Leadership: Standards 1, 5

◆ **Have knowledge and understanding about the elements of effective programs.**

◆ **Communicate the vision.**

◆ **Examine current practices.**

◆ **Promote and maintain best practices.**

    ☐ When developing the schoolwide vision and school goals, consider the school's instructional practices.

        ✓ What instructional practices should be added to increase ELL achievement? What should be eliminated?

        ✓ Do all students have adequate and appropriate opportunities to meet state standards?

        ✓ To what extent do your school's instructional practices and curriculum promote second language acquisition and content development?

        ✓ Do teachers use a variety of instructional strategies?

        ✓ Do teachers provide for flexible grouping based on students' needs? Do the groupings consider the language and academic needs of ELLs?

        ✓ Does the current programming model consider the differences in ELLs' language proficiency and the various stages of language development?

        ✓ Is instruction active and student-centered?

        ✓ Are ELLs provided with a full core curriculum? Have the same academic goals been set for ELLs as for mainstream students?

        ✓ Is instruction provided in a comprehensible manner through sheltered instruction?

        ✓ Is the school culture collaborative and supportive of efforts to improve instructional practices and achievement for all students?

        ✓ Are staff members appropriately trained in effective instructional strategies for ELLs? Do they consistently and effectively implement best practices?

☐ Examine the long-term data on ELLs' achievement levels in your school. Consider your staff's instructional practices. Create a detailed vision of how changes in instructional strategies will benefit students, and engage the staff in a continuous process of restructuring and rethinking about how the school's instructional practices support and enhance the education of ELLs and all students.

☐ Actively promote instructional strategies such as active learning, cooperative learning, and sheltered instruction.

◆ **Foster knowledge and understanding about the research.**

☐ Set aside time to stay current on the recent research and practices in second language acquisition and instructional strategies. The following newsletters are free:

✓ *ERIC/CLL Language Link,* a quarterly online newsletter from the ERIC Clearinghouse on Languages and Linguistics. Issues are available at http://www.cal.org/resources/news

✓ OELA's (Office of English Language Acquisition) electronic weekly *Newsline Bulletin* at http://www.ncela.gwu.edu/newsline

✓ WETA's *Reading Rockets* at http://www.readingrockets.org/newsletters/

✓ Additional websites are listed in Appendix B.

☐ Use staff meetings and other avenues to build staff awareness about second language acquisition and effective instructional strategies.

☐ Inform all staff, including classified staff, about how students acquire a second language, the dimensions of language proficiency, and the stages of language development.

✓ Model some of the strategies during the meetings.

✓ Use Building Staff Knowledge lists and activities (pages 32, 34, 52, 56, 61) as springboards for in-depth reading and discussion for study groups.

☐ Make sure that staff members are familiar with the research and professional literature on second language acquisition, the conditions that foster second language development, and effective strategies for teaching ELLs. Assist teachers in understanding that the traditional way of teaching might not be effective in a classroom of mixed language proficiencies and that the majority of strategies cited to be effective in the research are good for all students. Determine how you will assess staff's knowledge base.

Positive School Culture and Instructional Program: Standard 2

◆ Recommend implementation of effective programs/practices.

◆ Promote instructional approaches that foster content acquisition.

◆ Restructure the school to be a professional learning community.

◆ Place high priority on training for all school staff to help them serve ELLs more effectively.

   ☐ Have staff complete training on sheltered instruction.

     ✓ Access http://www.siopinstitute.net/index.html for training information.

     ✓ Establish your own key trainers within the school.

   ☐ Organize study groups on sheltered instruction and effective teaching and learning strategies. Suggestions for book studies might include the following:

     ✓ Chamot, A. U. (2003). *The Elementary Immersion Learning Strategies Guide.* Georgetown, VA: National Capitol Language Resource Center, The George Washington University Center for Applied Linguistics

     ✓ Chamot, A. U., & O'Malley, J. M. (1994). *The CALLA Handbook: Implementing the Cognitive Academic Language Learning Approach.* Reading, MA: Addison-Wesley

     ✓ Echevarria, J., & Graves, A. (1998). *Sheltered Content Instruction: Teaching English Language Learners with Diverse Abilities.* Boston: Allyn and Bacon

     ✓ Echevarria, J., Vogt, M., & Short, D. J. (2004). *Making content comprehensible for English learners: The SIOP model* (2nd ed.). Boston: Allyn and Bacon

   ☐ Consider purchasing supplemental materials that will assist in staff development (http://www.cal.org/resources):

     ✓ *Helping English Learners Succeed: An Overview of the SIOP Model* (video).

     ✓ *The SIOP Model: Sheltered Instruction for Academic Achievement* (video).

     ✓ *Using the SIOP Model: Professional Development Manual for Sheltered Instruction.*

     ✓ *Teaching Alive for the 21st Century: The Five Standards for Effective Pedagogy in Elementary Settings* (CD-ROM).

   ☐ Provide pressure, support, and leadership to classroom teachers and other staff in using effective instructional practices that promote second language and content development.

     ✓ Together with staff, study the research on effective instruction for ELLs. Explicitly define what effective instruction consists of and create a professional development plan to facilitate the practices.

     ✓ Set goals and benchmarks regarding the implementation of effective instructional practices and tie them to teacher observation and assessment of students' academic performance. Focus on a few key elements initially and set goals as to which key strategies will be learned and practiced during the identified timeline.

✓ Provide opportunities for teachers to observe each other, videotape their lessons, and reflect upon their own use of effective instructional strategies. Peer videotaping and reflection are powerful tools in sharing good practices.

✓ Provide support through peer coaching or mentoring. Structure specific times when teachers will meet to discuss how the identified strategies worked and how to improve upon them.

☐ Organize grade-level meetings to coordinate effective lesson planning for ELLs. Pool resources, time, and effort to plan lessons that incorporate all components of sheltered and effective instruction.

✓ Have teachers identify content and language objectives (long-range and unit-specific).

✓ Have teachers identify tier two words as key vocabulary for each unit. Make sure they include academic vocabulary ("school language").

✓ Provide time for teachers to modify and adapt materials.

✓ Have teachers decide which learning strategies will be emphasized at each grade level and which ones will be reinforced and extended through all grade levels.

✓ Have teachers decide which graphic organizers will be emphasized at each grade level and which ones will be reinforced and extended through all grade levels.

✓ Ensure that all teachers, not just bilingual or ESL teachers, interact with each other to coordinate instruction and to discuss plans for meeting the needs of ELLs.

☐ Have staff identify similarities and differences between English phonology and ELLs' phonologies. Decide who, when, and how the similarities and differences will be taught. The following resources will provide information on phonics instruction for many languages.

✓ Au, K., Garcia, G. G., Goldenberg, C., & Vogt, M. E. (2002). *Handbook for English Language Learners.* Boston: Houghton Mifflin.

✓ Calderón, M., August, D., Durán, D., Madden, N., Slavin, R., & Gil, M. (2003). *Spanish to English Transitional Reading: Teacher's Manual.* Baltimore: The Success for All Foundation.

✓ Freeman, D. E., Freeman, Y. S., Stack, L., García, A. C., McCloskey, M. L., Silva, C., & Gottlieb, M. (2004). *On Our Way to English: Teacher's Guide.* Barrington, IL: Rigby.

✓ Schifini, A., Short, D., Tinajero, J. V., García, E., García, E. E., Hamayan, E., & Kratky, L. (2004). *Avenues: Teacher's Edition.* Carmel, CA: Hampton-Brown.

☐ Visit another school site that has successfully implemented effective instructional strategies for ELLs.

☐ Assess professional development needs. Topics for workshops/professional development could include the following:

✓ Adapting mainstream lessons and learning materials to meet the needs of ELLs

✓ Providing comprehensible input to ELLs

✓ Literacy instruction for ELLs

✓ Vocabulary instruction for ELLs

✓ Learning strategies instruction

✓ Identifying appropriate learning materials and matching them to the instructional needs of ELLs

✓ Promoting English language development with cooperative classroom activities

✓ Designing classroom environments that provide differentiated instruction and promote English language development

✓ Managing multiple language levels in a classroom environment.

◆ **Develop structures to strengthen curriculum and instruction.**

◆ **Assist teachers in increasing their certainty about the goals for student achievement.**

☐ Establish "concrete goals for all curriculum, instruction, and assessment" (Waters et al., 2003, p. 10) with clear expectations that all students will meet the high goals. Continually focus attention on the established goals.

✓ Ensure that the curriculum for all students, especially ELLs, focuses on a common set of grade-level standards that aligns with state standards, school goals, instruction, and assessments.

✓ Provide structures and opportunities for teachers to collaboratively create a year-long, standards-based curriculum map, with horizontal and vertical articulation. Coordinate work across languages, settings, programs, and grade levels.

✓ Determine multiple measures of assessment that will be used to assess academic achievement and language proficiency (see Chapter 4).

☐ Facilitate the development of integrated thematic units. Plan opportunities and time for teachers to develop schoolwide themes that incorporate grade-level content standards into their thematic units. Have them create concept maps for each theme and align them with the content to be taught in each grade.

◆ **Promote and monitor effective teaching and learning for ELLs.**

◆ **Provide substantial feedback to teachers on their teaching.**

☐ Make "systematic and frequent visits to classrooms" to assure that quality instruction is provided (Waters et al., 2003, p. 10).

    ✓ Observe classroom practices to assure that all teachers consistently use effective instructional practices that promote active learning and content and language acquisition.

    ✓ Provide specific feedback to teachers on effective instructional practices (See Echevarria et al., 2000, 2004; National Reading Panel, 2000).

☐ Observe classroom practices and provide feedback on indicators that promote cooperative and collaborative interaction.

    ✓ How often are cooperative learning methods used?

    ✓ Are students engaged in cooperative learning or just group work?

    ✓ Are ELLs participating in classroom activities?

School Management: Standard 3

◆ **Influence and examine the organization of instruction.**

◆ **Facilitate ample opportunities for collaborative planning and design of curriculum and lessons.**

☐ Reorganize teachers' schedules and responsibilities to provide smaller groupings for integrated content and language instruction, especially during math and literacy blocks.

    ✓ Consider the use of staggered schedules, with ESL teachers arriving earlier or staying late.

    ✓ Create larger groups of students for nonacademic subjects to provide more flexibility for collaboration time, observation time, and smaller groupings for academic skills.

    ✓ Some schools provide low student-to-teacher ratio instruction through a "pod concept"— ESL classes at the K, 1, 2–3, and 4–5 levels, with each class taught collaboratively by two teachers: an ESL or bilingual education teacher and a grade-level teacher. ELLs spend part of the day in the ESL class, and part of their day in a grade-level "buddy class" with students who are proficient in English. The buddy concept allows the ELLs to gain appropriate content-based instruction and provides contact with other students in the school (Seaman, 2000).

    ✓ A modified pod concept can be accomplished during literacy blocks, with the ESL teacher providing two to three hours of literacy instruction to multiage groups, such as first and second graders in the morning and third and fourth graders in the afternoon.

◆ **Recruit and keep talented and dedicated staff.**

☐ Hire and retain high-quality teachers who understand the long-term process of second language acquisition, use sheltered instruction strategies, provide differentiated instruction, promote active learning for all students, and conscientiously provide caring and supportive classrooms.

☐ Recruit and assign the "best and brightest" to teach ELLs.

☐ Provide additional stipends to recruit and retain exemplary ESL teachers.

◆ **Allocate appropriate funding for materials, translation, and professional development.**

☐ Purchase appropriate support materials for teaching English language development, second language reading, and "sheltered" academic content. See Illinois Resource Center website at http://www.thecenterlibrary.org/ cwis/index.php for an extensive list of recommended materials. When purchasing materials, look for the following:

✓ Standards-based instruction in English reading and language arts designed to accelerate ELLs' growth in language, literacy, and content.

✓ Literature selections in both fiction and nonfiction that build vocabulary and language and facilitate the fundamentals of reading (phonemic awareness, phonics and decoding), development of comprehension skills, writing, and applications in content-area studies through a balanced literacy approach.

✓ Literature selections that are organized thematically.

✓ Levelized books for guided reading groups that connect oral proficiency to print.

✓ Resources that provide multisensory modalities through visual, auditory, and kinesthetic activities: poetry, songs, chants, pictures, manipulatives, audio CDs.

✓ Literature that is authentic and multicultural.

✓ Assessments that are systemic, comprehensive, and authentic.

✓ Resources for home activities.

☐ Purchase software programs, laser discs, and other interactive software that will support students in acquiring English, content, and literacy (e.g., Leap Pads, Zip Zoom English, Soliloquy Learning).

☐ Have the school librarian and technology specialist acquire and organize an extensive collection of visuals and objects that teachers may check out or access through a shared network to aid them in building background and providing comprehensible input.

☐ Ensure that the school library has a good collection of multicultural and authentic literature, as well as videotapes and audiotapes that support the curriculum and assist in providing comprehensible input to ELLs.

School and Community: Standards 4, 6

- ◆ **Take strong steps to work with ELLs' parents.**
- ◆ **Ensure that all communication to parents is provided in their native languages.**
    - ☐ Ensure that parents and the school community are well informed about the goals and standards of the school. Prepare brochures that outline grade-level expectations for each core subject area. Have brochures translated and explained to parents in all needed languages.
    - ☐ Require ESL teachers and mainstream teachers to regularly discuss ELL students' progress and hold joint parent conferences.
    - ☐ If needed, explore commercial translation and interpretation services. One example is Language Line Services (http://www.languageline. com/).
- ◆ **Encourage ELL parents to participate in literacy-rich activities with their children.**
- ◆ **Actively solicit bilingual parents, family members, and community volunteers to be involved.**
    - ☐ Link instruction with the home and community.
        - ✓ Extend learning opportunities beyond the classroom by encouraging teachers and their classrooms to visit museums, libraries, galleries, nature preserves, historical sites, and planetariums.
        - ✓ Make materials available for home study. Provide materials for use at home such as take-home activities, books, videos, monthly newsletters. ReadingA-Z.com (http://www.readinga-z.com) offers downloadable and printable books that would be ideal take-home books. Their selections include books in different languages.
        - ✓ Purchase and send home Reading Rainbow Family Literacy Kits that are available in English and Spanish (http://gpn.unl.edu/rainbow/).
        - ✓ Send notes home about television programs or rental videos that correspond to current units of study.
        - ✓ Survey parents to identify interests or expertise in particular units of instruction. Use parents as classroom resources, especially when they have expertise related to units of study that they can share with their child or the entire class.
- ◆ **Advocate for language minorities in the school and community.**
    - ☐ Ensure that teachers, parents, and community members are informed about the federal and state legal requirements, policies, and research that affect instruction for ELLs. Keep all stakeholders informed about language acquisition and instructional practices that support language and content acquisition.

☐ Advocate for increased funding at local and state levels, and identify sources of additional funding. Check with state department coordinators of federal funding, especially Titles I and III. Let policymakers and the public know about the school's efforts to increase the achievement of ELLs and the additional resources that are needed.

Building the Vision

As you answer each of the following questions, think about what might be done to facilitate change. Seek staff, parent, and community input in identifying goals that will promote second language acquisition and instructional strategies based on the school's vision, resources, and population.

1. How will you effectively share the research on second language acquisition and instructional strategies with all staff?
2. Which strategies and suggestions in the Leadership Challenge will be implemented? How will you share the strategies and suggestions with all staff?
3. How will you empower staff to support each other and reflect on practice?
4. How are English language learners viewed in the school? What is the school's vision about integrating language and content instruction?
5. What instructional strategies need to be changed, added, or upgraded? How will teachers be trained in these strategies? How will exemplary instruction be fostered in every classroom?
6. How can the school actively involve parents and the community in linking instruction to the home and community?
7. How will you fund materials that support second language acquisition and sheltered instruction?
8. What goals will the school implement that will promote second language acquisition and content instruction for English language learners based on the school's vision, resources, and population?

3

Native Language Instruction and Support

Native language instruction is critical. Anyone that is familiar with the research will tell you that the fastest way to get children into a second language is if they know their first language well. You only learn to read and write once—after that, everything else is a transfer. If that is the case you have to make sure you do an excellent job of teaching them to read and write well first, because if that is not in place, then they will not have anything solid to transfer into the second language. Much of bilingual education is based on the premise of transfer. That's not to say that once you move into English you drop the Spanish—on the contrary. Children need to continue in their native language because that is where higher-level thinking skills are developed. Once children know how to sequence, how to infer, how to predict, and how to summarize, it will be easy to do it in English. But they have to know it well in their native language first.

So, when I became principal and they were teaching math in English to Spanish monolingual students, I said, "That's ridiculous! We're wasting precious time!" You see, I believe that we should be learning while learning English, not learning English at the expense of learning!

Guadalupe Escamilla (Guadarrama, 1993, p. 20)

Chapter Highlights: This chapter explores the research on native language instruction and its impact on student learning, English acquisition, and literacy. In the Leadership Challenge, you will be able to identify specific ways that you and your staff can encourage and support native language instruction and support.

What Principals Should Know

Critical Questions

1. How does native language instruction affect student learning and second language acquisition?
2. What is the relationship between first and second language literacy?
3. What program models are most effective in providing native language instruction and support?

Essential Vocabulary

Additive bilingualism: The learning of a majority language in an environment in which the addition of a second language and culture does not replace the first language and culture; rather, the first language and culture are promoted and developed (Lambert, 1982; NCELA, 2002).

Bilingual education: Generally understood to be an instructional program for language minority students that makes use of the students' native language(s), bilingual education in practice takes many different forms. An important distinction is between those programs that use and promote two languages and those where bilingual children are present, but bilingualism is not fostered in the curriculum (Baker, 1993; NCELA, 2002).

Bilingualism: Simply defined, the ability to use two languages. However, individuals with varying bilingual characteristics may be classified as bilingual. Categories of bilingualism include ability and use of a language; proficiency across the language dimensions of listening, speaking, reading, and writing; differences in proficiency of both languages; and variation in proficiency over time (Baker, 1993; NCELA, 2002).

Common underlying proficiency: Two or more languages contributing to the central, unified thinking system in an individual. The indications of linguistic interdependence in language learning are the understandings common across languages that make possible the transfer of such skills. Thus, ideas, concepts, attitudes, knowledge, and skills can transfer into either language (Baker & Prys Jones, 1998; Cummins, 1989).

Language transfer: The effect of one language on the learning of another. There can be two types of transfer: negative transfer, sometimes called interference, and more often positive transfer, particularly in understandings and meanings of concepts (Baker & Prys Jones, 1998).

Native language instruction: Use of a child's home language (generally by a classroom teacher) to provide lessons in academic subjects or to teach reading and other language arts (Crawford, 1997; NCELA, 2002).

Native language support: Use of a child's home language (generally by a teacher aide) to translate unfamiliar terms or otherwise clarify lessons taught in English (Crawford, 1997; NCELA, 2002).

Preview-view-review method: An instructional approach in which content areas are previewed in the first language, presented in the second, and reviewed in the first (Lessow-Hurley, 1990).

Subtractive bilingualism: The learning of a majority language in an environment in which the second language and culture is intended to replace the first language and culture (Lambert, 1982).

Threshold hypothesis: Hypothesis that suggests that first language literacy transfers to a second language only when a person has reached a critical level of language competence in the first language in order to gain cognitive benefits from owning two languages (Baker & Prys Jones, 1998).

Universal aspects of literacy: Those characteristics of literacy that are similar for all languages and once learned in the first language can be transferred to learning a second language (Harris & Hodges, 1995).

Critical Question #1:
How Does Native Language Instruction Affect Student Learning and Second Language Acquisition?

Native Language and Effective Schools Research

Past and ongoing research shows that the most effective way for ELLs to develop both academic concepts and English language proficiency is through the development of their first language and the use of native language instruction (August & Hakuta, 1997; Collier, 1995; Cummins, 1996; Krashen, Tse, & McQuillan, 1998). Study after study emphasizes the importance of supporting and valuing the native language of ELLs. August and Hakuta (1997) identified the use of native language and culture as one of the primary factors related to effective schooling for ELLs, stating that "the degree of children's native-language proficiency is a strong predictor of their English language development" (p. 28).

Many research studies explicitly cite the advantages of native-language use (August, 2006; Berman et al., 1995; Calderón et al., 1997; Hernandez, 1991; Lucas et al., 1990; Muniz-Swicegood, 1994; Pease-Álvarez et al., 1991; Rosebery, Warren, & Conant, 1992), whereas others implicitly support the native language and culture (Carter & Chatfield, 1986; Goldenberg & Sullivan, 1994). Even in schools designed to provide instruction primarily in English, findings from a study of nine sheltered instruction programs indicated that the classrooms were "multilingual environments in which students' native languages served a multitude of purposes and functions. Across sites, native language use emerged as a persistent and key instructional strategy realized in very site-specific ways" (Lucas & Katz, 1994, p. 545).

The Role of Native Language in English Language Acquisition

Research indicates that use of the native language does not adversely affect students' mastery of English (Cummins, 1996), nor is English development delayed (Ramirez, 1992). Instead, the first language facilitates and helps develop second language proficiency and academic skills (August, 2006; Goldenberg, 2001; Thomas & Collier, 1997). Cummins (1981b, 1989) explains that even though the surface aspects of different languages (e.g., pronunciation and fluency) are clearly separate, there is an underlying cognitive/academic proficiency that is common across languages. This common underlying proficiency (CUP), in which skills, knowledge, and concepts learned in any language can be accessed through different languages, is what makes the transfer of cognitive, academic, and literacy-related skills across languages possible. In fact, many studies have found that the most effective way to develop academic concepts and English proficiency is through cognitive and academic development in the first language (Collier, 1989, 1992; García, 1994c; Genesee, 1994; Thomas & Collier, 1997, 2002). Instruction in the primary language has a number of benefits for students:

- Academic skills, literacy development, concept formation, subject knowledge, and learning strategies developed in the first language will all transfer to the second language (Collier, 1995). As students expand their vocabulary, oral skills, and written skills in the second language, they will be able to demonstrate the knowledge gained in their first language.

- The primary language can be used to develop literacy that transfers to the second language, which is highly effective in promoting academic English language development (Collier, 1995; Krashen & Biber, 1988). Students are able to take advantage of cognate relationships between L1 and L2 to understand English words, which facilitates comprehension, and of higher-order vocabulary skills in their first language when speaking a second language (August, 2006).

- Sustained use of a child's native language for longer periods of time allows the student to experience normal linguistic development, strengthening the foundation for the acquisition of the second language (Ramirez, 1992; Spangenberg-Urbschat & Pritchard, 1994; Wong Fillmore & Meyer, 1992).

- First language instruction provides the comprehensible input that students need to develop academic concepts. When students receive substantial primary language support, they progress in learning content. However, they fall behind when they are too quickly switched to all English instruction (Ramirez, 1992).

- The more academic support students receive in their native language, in combination with high-quality second language development, the higher the academic achievement in English with each succeeding year, in comparison with ELLs instructed only in the second language (Collier, 1992; Krashen & Biber, 1988; Ramirez, 1992).

- Bilingual proficiency and biliteracy are positively related to academic achievement in both languages (Genesee et al., 2005).

- When primary language instruction is part of a program, minority language parents are more involved in their children's schooling (Ramirez, 1992).

Questions for Reflection

To what extent are students' first languages developed in your school?

To what extent are students' first languages used to facilitate second language development?

Building Staff Knowledge:
Common Underlying Proficiency Activity

Materials: Separate Underlying Proficiency (SUP)/Common Underlying Proficiency (CUP) Handout (page 79).

Time: 15 minutes

Activity Information: Go over the information on the SUP/CUP handout. Point out that the left head in Figure 3.1 illustrates the myth that there's only enough room in the head for one language, and if the balloon of the first language (L1) gets too big, there won't be enough room for the second language (L2). This is based on the Separate Underlying Proficiency (SUP) hypothesis about language learning—that the skills of one language are learned separately and independently from the skills of another language. Cummins (1981b) proposed the Common Underlying Proficiency (CUP) hypothesis for explaining how literacy development in the first language relates to success in second language literacy. Because there is a common underlying proficiency, academic language proficiency that is developed in any language supports all languages, and a concept learned in one language transfers to the second (Cummins, 1981b, 1989). According to Cummins, once children become competent in their first language, their literacy skills can transfer readily to English.

Examples to use: When you were learning how to read, write, and speak a foreign language in high school, you didn't have to relearn those things you already knew. You didn't have to relearn how to read, how to write a paragraph, how to use punctuation, how to make a prediction, and how to do algebraic equations. You just needed to learn those elements that were unique to the new language you were studying (new vocabulary or different verb forms, for example).

If you were to move to Madrid today, you wouldn't lose your current knowledge as you acquire Spanish. It would all transfer as you learn Spanish, and once you became competent in Spanish, you would have the language skills to demonstrate that knowledge.

Just as you only needed to learn to read once, second language learners only learn to read once. They will need to learn a new set of sound-letter correspondences, but if they know how to read in their first language, they do not have to start at the beginning and relearn the entire process of reading. Those skills and strategies will transfer.

Highlight and discuss the following information: Following the principles of the Common Underlying Proficiency theory, primary language instruction strengthens ELLs' ability to speak, read, and write English, and it will not hinder the rate at which the students learn English. Academic language proficiency that is developed in the first language transfers to the second language, and the primary language is helpful, not harmful, in attaining English proficiency.

Discuss: What are the implications of this theory for instructional strategies, programming, materials, and staff development?

Figure 3.1. Handout:
Separate and Common Underlying Proficiency

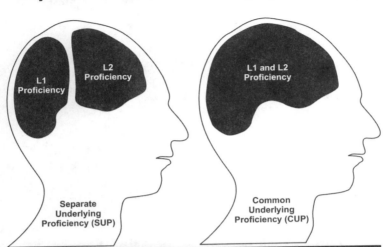

The Common Underlying Proficiency (CUP) and the Separate Underlying Proficiency (SUP) theories are sometimes compared to balloons. The Separate Underlying Proficiency (SUP) model views the mind as housing two languages separately within it like two balloons (Baker & Prys Jones, 1998), with the two languages working against one another. In the CUP theory, the one balloon theory, Cummins (1981b, 1989) explains that even though the surface aspects of different languages such as pronunciation and fluency are separate, an underlying cognitive/academic proficiency is common across languages. Therefore, bilingualism is possible because people have the capacity to easily store and function in two or more languages. This common underlying proficiency allows the skills, knowledge, and concepts learned in one language to be accessed through different languages, making the transfer of cognitive/academic and literacy-related skills across languages possible.

The rationale for using the primary language in instruction is based on Cummins' theory of the Common Underlying Proficiency. Following the principles of this theory, speaking, listening, reading, or writing in either language helps to develop the whole cognitive system. Because academic language proficiency that is developed in the first language transfers to the second language, native language instruction strengthens ELLs' literacy in both languages, and the primary language is helpful, not harmful, in attaining English proficiency.

Since knowledge developed in the first language (L1) transfers to the second language (L2) and will not have to be relearned when acquiring a second language, elements of literacy common to most languages (such as concepts of print, phonological awareness, word reading, vocabulary knowledge, and comprehension) also transfer.

Critical Question #2:
What Is the Relationship Between
First and Second Language Literacy?

The Role of Native Language in Literacy

A consistent body of research correlates the importance of native language literacy to the development of second language literacy. Specifically, strong oral and literacy skills developed in the first language provide a solid basis for the acquisition of literacy and other academic language skills in English (Baker,

Instruction in students' first language can help them develop literacy and academic skills in a second language. (Goldenberg, 2001, p. B1)

1993; Lanauze & Snow, 1989; Saunders & Goldenberg, 1999). Reviews of research by Fitzgerald (1995a, 1995b) and Garcia (2000) cite substantial evidence that students use their native language knowledge as they read in a second language. For example, knowledge of Spanish cognates transfers to reading in English (Garcia & Nagy, 1993; Nagy et al., 1993), and knowledge that is used to guide native-language comprehension is also used in reading in English (Langer, Bartolome, Vasquez, & Luca, 1990; Jiménez et al., 1996). In addition, good writing in the first language by native Spanish-speaking students is related to good writing in English as a second language (Lanauze & Snow, 1989).

This transfer of literacy skills from one language to another is due to the universal aspects of literacy; reading and writing processes function in similar ways for native and second language learners (Grabe, 1991). Moreover, the transfer is a reciprocal process—ELLs use their native language literacy skills to become literate in English, and what they learn in English enhances their native language literacy and cognitive abilities (Escamilla, 1993; Fitzgerald, 1999). Some studies indicate that if students do not reach a certain threshold in their first language, including literacy, they may have cognitive difficulties in English (Collier & Thomas, 1989; Cummins, 1981b, 1991a; Thomas & Collier, 1997). Von Vacano (1994) notes that if a child is forced into English too early or without proper support, there is a strong likelihood that the child will develop what is known as semilingualism or subtractive bilingualism. Collier (1995) explains

> The key to understanding the role of the first language in the academic development of the second language is understanding the function of uninterrupted cognitive development. When students switch to second language use at school and teachers encourage parents to speak in the second language at home, both students and parents are functioning at a level cognitively far below their age. Whereas, when parents and children speak the language that they know best, they are working at their actual level of cognitive maturity. (p. 4)

When the parents of ELLs have limited literacy in English, they serve as poor models for children acquiring English. Wong Fillmore (1991b) explains that when parents use their weaker language (English, for example) to communicate, parents are not as able to elaborate and extend the language of their children or to communicate complex ideas. Their relatively weaker ability to speak in English may then result in causing them to speak less to their children, or even avoid interaction altogether. Consequently, the children's language may be inadequately developed in both languages, and the home language loss can result in negative consequences for parent-child relationships (Wong Fillmore, 1991b).

Native Language in Reading Instruction

The question about the most effective reading programs for ELLs has primarily centered on the language of instruction, as to whether students should be taught to read in their primary language or in English. Native language advocates assert that children should learn to read in their native language first and should be transitioned to English instruction after they have developed substantial oral proficiency in English, whereas others advocate paired bilingual instruction, in which students are taught to read in both languages (their native language and English) at different times of the day. Opponents of bilingual education state that English-only instruction with support in teaching vocabulary is more effective. In a review of the research on beginning reading instruction for ELLs, Slavin and Cheung (2004) stated

> First, the literature supports the use of native language in early reading instruction, especially for paired bilingual strategies that teach reading both in the native language and in English from 1st grade onward. Although not every study found benefits from bilingual instruction, most studies supported this strategy and the remainder found no differences. None found English-only strategies to be superior. Second, research indicates that paired bilingual strategies—part of most two-way bilingual programs—tend to be effective. (p. 56)

In their best-evidence synthesis, Slavin and Cheung (2003) stated

> English language learners may learn to read best if taught both in their native language and in English, from the beginning of formal instruction. Rather than confusing children, as some have feared, reading instruction in a familiar language may serve as a bridge to success in English, as decoding, sound blending, and generic comprehension strategies clearly transfer among languages that use phonetic orthographies, such as Spanish, French, and English (see August, 2002; August & Hakuta, 1997; Fitzgerald, 1995b; Garcia, 2000). (p. 20)

> Language of instruction must be seen as only one aspect, however, of instructional programming for English language learners…quality of instruction is at least as important as language of instruction. (p. 40)

Other information that supports developing literacy in the child's first language includes the following:

- Developing literacy skills in children's first language not only facilitates learning to read in the second language but, more importantly, accelerates it (Snow et al., 1998; Thomas & Collier, 1997). A recent synthesis of research (Genesee et al., 2005) found that "ELLs with emergent L1 (first language) literacy skills, prior experiences with L1 literacy in the home, knowledge of cognate vocabulary, and well-developed L1 phonological awareness acquire reading skills in English more readily than ELLs who lack these L1 skills" (p. 371). Reese, Garnier, Gallimore, and Goldenberg (2000) found that the ELLs who were the best first language readers were able to transition to English reading much earlier than other ELLs. August (2006) states that "language minority students instructed in their native language as well as in English perform better, on average, on measures of English reading proficiency than language minority students instructed only in English" (p. 6).

- Literacy instruction in the native language is the most pedagogically sound way to teach English learners about the relationship between meaning and print in both the first and second languages (Cummins, 1989; Krashen & Biber, 1988; Ramirez, 1992; Snow et al., 1998).

Questions for Reflection

What do staff members know about the research supporting the teaching of reading to ELLs?

What are ELL parents told about using the primary language at home?

What components of the school's literacy program help to develop literacy in ELLs' first languages?

Building Staff Knowledge:
Exploring Native Language Use

Adapted from Murphy & Lick, 2001.

Materials: Article for discussion (regarding language use at home and school)
Examples of articles:

- Brown, Z. A., Hammond, O. W., & Onikama, D. L. (1997, September). *Language use at home and school: A synthesis of research for Pacific educators.* Honolulu, HI: Pacific Resources for Education and Learning. Available: http://www.prel.org/products/products/Language-use.pdf (use pages 5–9).

- Soto, L., Smrekar, J., Nekcovei, D. (1999, Spring). *Preserving home languages and cultures in the classroom: Challenges and opportunities* (Directions in Language and Education, No. 13). Washington, DC: National Clearinghouse for Bilingual Education (ERIC Document Reproduction Service No. ED436085). Available: http://www.ncela.gwu.edu/pubs/directions/13.htm

Time: 30–40 minutes

Activity: The Final Word, Text Exploration Protocol
The Final Word is a protocol designed to explore a piece of text, clarify thoughts, expand perspectives, and build on each other's thinking.

Key to Facilitation: Timing, avoid dialogue

Guidelines:

- Prior to the meeting, read the article, highlighting significant quotes or sections that you agree with, disagree with, or have questions about.
- Sit in circles containing four people each.
- Have the facilitator keep the conversation moving, keep it clear and directed to the article, make connections, and keep time so that everyone gets an opportunity to speak and listen.

Directions for Activity:

1. Round 1 (6–10 minutes for a four-person circle).
   - The first person starts by sharing a line or two from the article that he or she agreed with, disagreed with, or had a question about, and why (2–3 minutes).
   - Proceeding around the circle, each person comments on the same section shared by the first person, responding to what the first person has said or speaking to the section in ways that extend understanding of the text (1–2 minutes each).
   - The first person who started has the Final Word. He of she can share what was learned from colleagues or summarize what was said (1 minute).
2. Rounds 2 and Following.
   - The next person in the circle shares a different section, and the round follows the same format as Round 1.

Final Point: "How could you use The Final Word in the classroom? Why would it be good for ELLs?"

Critical Question #3: What Program Models Are Most Effective in Providing Native Language Instruction and Support?

Program Models for Bilingualism and Biliteracy

Lambert (1982) identified two possible outcomes of program models—additive bilingualism and subtractive bilingualism. The concepts of additive and subtractive bilingualism are often used when considering the theory, program implementation, and assessment of bilingual programs. Additive bilingualism maintains the first language while students are acquiring the second, valuing and enhancing

> *Your language minority students...do need to acquire English, but don't let them fall behind the constantly advancing native-English speakers...while they are learning English.*
> (Thomas & Collier, 1997, p. 72)

both cultures. In subtractive bilingualism, students lose their first language and culture in the process of acquiring their second language.

According to Thomas and Collier (1997, 2002), the following three program models provide strong native language support for academic and cognitive development (ranging from the most to the least instructional support using the minority language) and are additive programs because biliteracy and bilingualism are expected outcomes of each model. In bilingual immersion (also known as dual language or two-way immersion) and in two-way bilingual education, both English speaking and non-English speaking students are schooled bilingually in the same classroom. In one-way bilingual education, most or all of the students are language minority.

1. Bilingual Immersion Education (also referred to as Dual Language Education): Academic instruction through both L1 and L2 for Grades K–12.

   • The 90-10 Model:

     Grades K–1: All or 90% of academic instruction through minority language (literacy begins in minority language)

     Grade 2: One hour of academic instruction through majority language added (literacy instruction in majority language typically introduced in Grade 2 or 3)

     Grade 3: Two hours of academic instruction through majority language added

     Grades 4–5 or 6: Academic instruction half a day through each language

     Grades 6 or 7–12: 60% of academic instruction through majority language and 40% through minority language

   • The 50-50 Model:

     Grades K–5 or 6: Academic instruction half a day through each language

Grades 6 or 7–12: 60% of academic instruction through majority language and 40% through minority language

2. Two-Way Bilingual Education: Language majority and language minority students are schooled together in the same bilingual class, and they work together at all times, serving as peer teachers. Both the 90-10 and the 50-50 are two-way BE [bilingual education] models.

3. Developmental Bilingual Education (also referred to as Maintenance Bilingual Education or Late-Exit Bilingual Education): Academic instruction occurs half a day through each language for Grades K–5 or 6. (Thomas & Collier, 1997, p. 58).

In comparing all program types in their retrospective study, Thomas and Collier (2002) stated

Enrichment 90-10 and 50-50 one-way and two-way developmental bilingual education…are the only programs we have found to date that assist students to fully reach the 50th percentile in both L1 and L2 in all subjects and to maintain that level of high achievement, or reach even higher levels through the end of schooling. Bilingual immersion (two-way) programs were the most effective, with students reaching the 50th NCE before middle school, and eventually reaching approximately the 60th NCE [normal curve equivalent] (nearly 70th percentile); late exit bilingual programs brought ELL achievement up to the 50th NCE/percentile by middle school, and slightly rose in high school. In addition, bilingually schooled students were found to outperform their peers who were educated monolingually in English in all subjects after 4–7 years.

In a recent synthesis of research, Genesee and colleagues (2005) also found strong evidence that educational success for ELLs is positively related to sustained instruction in the first language with the "educational outcomes of bilingually educated students, especially in late-exit and two-way programs, at least comparable to, and usually higher than their comparison peers" and "the longer they stayed in the program, the more positive the outcomes" in "reading or mathematics achievement, GPA [grade point average], attendance, high school completion, or attitudes toward school and self (e.g., Cazabon, Nicoladis, & Lambert, 1998; Curiel, Rosenthal, & Richek, 1986; Lambert & Cazabon, 1994; Lindholm-Leary, 2001; Lindholm-Leary & Borsato, 2001; Thomas & Collier, 2002)" (Genesee et al., 2005, pp. 374–375).

Native Language Support

Of course, bilingual education is not possible in many schools due to a lack of bilingual teachers or a wide variety of primary languages (see Chapter 5 for programming information). However, even without bilingual programs, there are many ways that schools

> *There are always ways to nurture the primary language regardless of school resources.* (Miramontes et al., 1997, p. 40)

can develop and support students' native languages (see the Leadership Challenge section in this chapter and Figure 3.2, p. 83).

When using native language support, rather than native language instruction models, an important consideration is the prevention of concurrent translation. Concurrent translation occurs when a teacher speaks in one language and then immediately translates (or has a bilingual aide translate) what was said in the second language. Concurrent translation in instruction fails to facilitate second language acquisition because children are not compelled to attend to what is being said in English when the translation occurs immediately thereafter (Wong Fillmore, 1985). They simply tune out the language they do not understand and wait for the information in the language they do understand. When children alternate between both languages (known as code switching), that's normal and perfectly acceptable. However, bilingual aides and teachers should be discouraged from doing this. Instead, bilingual personnel should use the native language to assist the students when previewing the lesson, explaining or clarifying concepts, preteaching vocabulary, pointing out similarities in cognates, reading to the students, and reviewing the lesson's concepts and vocabulary with the students.

Questions for Reflection

What components of your current ELL program help to build additive bilingualism?

How could your school or community resources be used to provide native language instruction and/or support to your ELL students? To what extent?

Figure 3.2. Resource Questionnaire

In small groups, identify and brainstorm resources for native language instruction and support. Create an action plan based on your input.

What resources does our school or community have to provide native language instruction and support to our ELL students and families?

	English only	Some native languages spoken by our students	All native languages spoken by our students	What do we need?
Core Subject Area Materials				
Reading/language arts				
Math				
Social studies				
Science				
Other				
Library Resources				
Books				
Multimedia				
Other				
Technology Resources				
Computer-assisted learning				
Taped books				
Other				
Parent Information				
Enrollment/orientation information				
Home language survey				
Parent notification letter				
Newsletters				
Notes home				
Student handbook				
Other				
Personnel				
Certified staff				
Classified staff				
Parent/community volunteers				
Other				

Leadership Challenge:
What Principals Should Do

Critical Question

How will you promote and encourage native language instruction and support?

Directions: As you read the following list of suggestions, check items that best align to your school's vision, program goals, resources, and student needs. Items from the Principal's Survey in Chapter 1 are designated in bold font.

Vision and Leadership: Standards 1, 5

- **Have knowledge and understanding about the elements of effective programs.**
- **Communicate the vision.**
- **Have knowledge and understanding about the research.**
- **Advocate for programs.**
- **Examine current practices.**
- **Advocate for equity.**
  - ☐ When developing a schoolwide vision and school goals, consider the role and impact of native language instruction and support.
    - ✓ What are the school's beliefs about bilingualism and about programs that foster bilingualism?
    - ✓ What are the beliefs about use of the primary language for instruction? To what extent?
    - ✓ What are the beliefs about language loss?
    - ✓ Are the beliefs, values, and commitments about student learning evident in the school's use of native language instruction and/or support?
    - ✓ Are the beliefs reflected in daily learning opportunities for ELLs?
    - ✓ To what extent do the school's instructional practices and curriculum support use of the native language?
    - ✓ What should be added to the school's program and culture regarding use of the native language to increase ELL achievement? What level of primary language instruction or support is possible? Who would this affect? What practices should be eliminated?
    - ✓ Is there a plan in place for informing and involving parents in supporting the native language?
    - ✓ Is the school culture supportive of efforts to encourage use of the native language?
    - ✓ What community support can be expected?

✓ How do these decisions affect curriculum, resources, organizational structures, and assessment?

☐ When examining the long-term data on the achievement levels of your ELLs to see if they are closing the achievement gap, consider the native language components of your current program.

☐ Implement inquiry groups, where teachers raise questions about ELLs' success in your school, gather and analyze data, and make a plan regarding the data (Joyce & Calhoun, 1995). Ask questions such as, "What language needs of these students are not being addressed by the current academic program? What does the program need in order to serve these students better?"

☐ Make sure that *all* staff members are familiar with the research and professional literature so they are confident about the level of native language instruction and support your school has selected and why native language instruction and/or support are used. Ensure that staff understand that knowledge and skills developed in a child's first language support literacy and language acquisition in the second language. Classified employees such as school secretaries, teacher aides, and cafeteria employees play important roles in promoting or deterring the success of a program that uses native language instruction.

☐ Actively pursue and defend programs and services that promote native language instruction and support. Use your vision of native language instruction and support as a guidepost when making decisions about professional development, hiring, and budget.

☐ Actively seek external partners and research information to advance your understanding of how to realize your school's vision. National and state bilingual associations (see Appendix B) are excellent resources.

☐ With staff input, establish a schoolwide native language use policy that provides teachers and staff consistent guidance as to when it's appropriate for students to use their native languages and that eliminates individual policies within each classroom and setting.

Positive School Culture and Instructional Program: Standard 2

◆ **Recommend implementation of effective programs/practices.**

◆ **Ensure sustained attention to ELLs.**

◆ **Hold high expectations for all students and make the achievement of ELLs a priority.**

◆ **Promote instructional approaches that foster biliteracy development and content acquisition.**

◆ **Advocate for equity.**

☐ Examine the various programming options that promote native language instruction and literacy. Establish a dual language/bilingual education program development team or study group. You may want to link up with other local elementary schools to consider neighborhood versus magnet site options, financial obligations, curricular issues, and personnel issues.

✓ If resources and personnel are available, implement a bilingual program.

✓ If a bilingual program is not possible, explore other options such as providing literacy instruction or support in students' native languages.

✓ Once your school has decided upon a program option, demonstrate commitment to the program in terms of curriculum, materials, professional development, staffing, space, and allocation of resources.

☐ Provide professional materials on bilingual programming.

✓ Calderon, M., & Minaya-Rowe, L. (2003). *Designing and Implementing Two-Way Bilingual Programs: A Step-by-Step Guide for Administrators, Teachers, and Parents.* Thousand Oaks, CA: Corwin Press.

✓ Cloud, N., Genesee, F., & Hamayan, E. (2000). *Dual Language Instruction: A Handbook for Enriched Education.* Boston: Heinle & Heinle.

✓ Howard, E. R., & Christian, D. (2002). *Two-Way Immersion 101: Designing and Implementing a Two-Way Immersion Education Program at the Elementary School Level* (Educational Practice Report 9). Santa Cruz, CA: Center for Research on Education, Diversity & Excellence.

✓ Howard, E. R., Christian, D., & Genesee, F. (2003). *The Development of bilingualism and biliteracy From Grades 3 to 5: A Summary of Findings From the CAL/CREDE Study of Two-Way Immersion Education.* Santa Cruz, CA: Center for Research on Education, Diversity & Excellence.

✓ Howard, E. R., Olague, N., & Rogers, D. (2003). *The Dual Language Program Planner: A Guide for Designing and Implementing Dual Language Programs.* Santa Cruz, CA: Center for Research on Education, Diversity & Excellence.

✓ Howard, E. R., Sugarman, J., & Christian, D. (2003). *Trends in Two-Way Immersion Education: A Review of the Research* (Report No. 63). Baltimore: Center for Research on the Education of Students Placed at Risk. Available: http://www.csos.jhu.edu/crespar/techReports/Report63.pdf

✓ Lindholm-Leary, K. J. (2001). *Dual Language Education.* Clevedon, England: Multilingual Matters.

✓ Sugarman, J., & Howard, E. R. (2001). *Development and Maintenance of Two-Way Immersion Programs: Advice From Practitioners* (Practitioner Brief 2). Santa Cruz, CA: Center for Research on Education, Diversity & Excellence. Available: http://www.cal.org/crede/pubs/PracBrief2.htm

- ✓ Sugarman, J., & Howard, L. (2001). Two-Way Immersion Shows Promising Results: Findings From a New Study. *ERIC/CLL Language Link.* Available: http://www.cal.org/resources/langlink/current2.html
- ☐ Contact and visit other districts with established bilingual programs. A directory of two-way bilingual immersion programs in the United States can be found at http://www.cal.org/twi/directory/. If you are looking for a program that is a total or partial immersion program for native English speakers, check the Directory of Total and Partial Immersion Programs at http://www.cal.org/ericcll/immersion
- ☐ Examine the New Mexico dual language program standards for ideas about programming at http://www.duallanguagenm.org/standardspdf.html

- ◆ **Foster a school climate that values cultural and linguistic diversity.**
- ◆ **Promote and monitor effective teaching and learning for ELLs.**
  - ☐ Encourage students to develop their primary language skills and allow them to speak their native languages (Lucas et al., 1990). Make sure that all staff understand the reasons and are supportive of allowing students to speak their native languages.
  - ☐ Ensure that bilingual students are allowed to orally respond and write in their primary languages to demonstrate comprehension of content taught in English. If the students are not literate in their native languages, teachers should encourage them to draw to demonstrate what they have understood (Freeman & Freeman, 1998, 2001).
  - ☐ Encourage teachers to pair less fluent students with more fluent students of the same language background during classroom activities so that the more fluent students can provide language assistance in understanding instructions and classroom routines. The buddy system also provides social support for the students.
  - ☐ Urge teachers and aides to provide instructions and key concepts in students' native languages to facilitate student understanding to ensure that students have access to academic content and to check students' comprehension (Lucas et al., 1990).
  - ☐ Encourage teachers to set up situations or activities specifically calling for students to use their native languages with each other (Lucas & Katz, 1994). Examples include the following:
    - ✓ A group writing assignment using the native language, such as having students write journals in their primary languages or English (allow students to choose which language they will use). Bilingual aides, peers, or parent volunteers can read and respond to the journal entries.
    - ✓ Students read or tell stories from their own countries to each other in their native languages and then translate them into English to tell other students.

      ✓ Form literature circles of second language learners to read and study books in their native languages, meet weekly to discuss the books' themes and characters, and keep a log in which they write chapter summaries, opinions, and critiques.

      ✓ Print or publish stories, newsletters, newspapers, or books that students write in their primary languages, which also increases the number of primary language resources in the classrooms and student self-esteem. Students could share their stories with other students and families (Freeman & Freeman, 2001).

    ☐ Facilitate the forming of small groups of students to provide additional instruction in the native language by bilingual teachers or teacher aides.

      ✓ Implement the preview-view-review method. During the preview, a bilingual teacher, teacher aide, tutor, peer, or volunteer gives a preview or overview of the lesson, activity, or key concepts in the students' native language prior to the upcoming lesson. During the view, the regular teacher conducts the lesson or activity in English. During the review, a bilingual person summarizes the lesson, clarifies key concepts, and answers and/or asks questions in the student's native language about the lesson. This could also be accomplished by allowing students who speak the same language to meet in groups to review the lesson and report back in English (Lessow-Hurley, 1990).

      ✓ Have bilingual teacher aides read to and with students in their primary languages.

    ☐ Explore how students' native languages could be incorporated not only into the structure of the curriculum, but also into other programs that serve them, such as extracurricular activities and events supporting instruction (Lucas et al., 1990; Lucas & Katz, 1994). See all school activities as opportunities to teach and enrich language.

◆ **Place high priority on training for all school staff to help them serve ELLs more effectively.**

◆ **Develop structures to strengthen curriculum and instruction.**

    ☐ Provide or arrange for ongoing staff development on native language instruction and support, increasing staff awareness of the key role that native language literacy plays in students' literacy and English language development.

    ☐ Offer courses in a language other than English to all staff. Encourage all staff to learn a second language and use it with the students, even if it's just a few words or greetings.

School Management: Standard 3

◆ **Influence and examine the organization of instruction.**

☐ Assign teachers and instructional aides who are fluent in other languages to roles that will use their bilingual abilities to help the students whose language they share (Lucas et al., 1990; Lucas & Katz, 1994).

☐ Form cross-age reading groups where older students read to younger students in their primary languages. Older students can also write stories and books for the younger students (Freeman & Freeman, 1998, 2001).

☐ If your ESL teachers have the students for a two- to three-hour literacy block, assign bilingual aides to that time so they can do the following to support L1:

✓ Preview (and review) materials orally with ELL students in L1—read the actual text in the native language prior to the student reading the material in English, do a picture walk, preview/review the vocabulary, and point out similarities/differences of languages in phonological activities.

✓ Prepare adapted materials to support more limited ELLs.

✓ Review written assignments in L1.

✓ Translate key concepts and content (orally or written) in the native language, avoiding concurrent translation.

◆ **Recruit and keep talented and dedicated staff.**

◆ **Hire bilingual staff with cultural backgrounds similar to those of the students.**

☐ With district personnel, work with colleges and universities to ensure that they are aware of the need for bilingual teachers and aides in your school.

☐ Reserve classified teacher aide positions for prospective bilingual teachers so they can work for the district while preparing to become teachers. Work with universities to offer courses at times that are more compatible with family and job responsibilities, provide credit for district work experience to fulfill certain observation requirements, and assist with loans, scholarships, and grants.

☐ Assist in forming partnerships with universities to form career ladders for bilingual teacher aides.

☐ Work with your chamber of commerce and local high schools to sponsor scholarships for "grow your own" programs.

☐ Urge your school district to formulate comprehensive packages of recruitment activities and stipends for bilingual teachers, and invest in recruitment booths at state and national bilingual education conferences and recruitment fairs.

☐ Consider sharing teachers between other districts or using interactive television.

☐ Contact your state department of education for more information on programs involving visiting teachers from Spain or Mexico.

◆ **Facilitate ample opportunities for collaborative planning and design of curriculum and lessons.**

☐ Provide opportunities and structures for bilingual and monolingual teachers to jointly develop and sequence curriculum and instruction so that the bilingual instruction is aligned with the mainstream curriculum and state standards.

◆ **Allocate appropriate funding for materials, translation, and professional development.**

☐ Require your school librarian to purchase library books, magazines, and other resources in students' native languages and encourage students to read them. The school library should have a substantial section of authentic children's literature at different literacy levels in students' native languages.

☐ Purchase materials in students' primary languages. The combined use of thematic teaching, content-based learning, and authentic literature is necessary to create optimal learning environments for bilingual students. Materials can include the following:

✓ Bilingual dictionaries for each classroom.

✓ Reference books.

✓ Software.

✓ Children's literature at different literacy levels.

✓ Audiotaped or recorded books.

✓ Corresponding textbooks in students' native languages.

✓ Electronic translators or reading pens.

☐ Purchase or produce videos that support primary language development, academic learning, and student self-esteem.

✓ Students could produce native language videos on big books with pictures, discussion, and a reading of each story.

✓ Students could produce videos of dramatizations of stories in their native languages (Freeman & Freeman, 2001).

School and Community: Standards 4, 6

◆ **Take strong steps to work with ELLs' parents.**

◆ **Encourage ELL parents to participate in literacy-rich activities with their children.**

◆ **Send a strong message to parents to use and extend the family's primary language at home.**

☐ Ensure that bilingual and monolingual teachers regularly discuss ELL students' progress and hold joint parent conferences.

☐ Encourage families to continue to use their native language in the home.

✓ Help families understand that children do not need to stop using their first language in order to learn English and that children who have a strong basis in their native language will learn English more easily.

✓ Point out the benefits for children who continue to use their native languages in being able to communicate with family members who do not speak English and to maintain close ties to their cultural heritages.

✓ Help parents access information about the benefits of being bilingual and provide reasons to their children about the benefits. Helpful websites include the following:

- http://www.pbs.org/teachersource/prek2/issues/1103issue.shtm
- http://www.yearoflanguages.org/i4a/pages/index.cfm?pageid=3651
- http://www.cal.org/sns/sns-fieldrpt.html#BENEFITS
- http://www.prel.org/products/Products/Samoan-Conversation.pdf

☐ Help parents to understand that they can promote literacy in English by developing early literacy in their children's native language (Genesee, 1993). Encourage parents to read to their children, assist children in reading in their first language, and tell stories to their children in their home language. Parents who are not literate should be encouraged to read wordless books, tell stories to their children, encourage their children to read to them, and discuss current events and news in the home language.

☐ Send home writing folders and fun writing pens and pencils to encourage children to write at home. Provide parents with ideas they can use to encourage their children to write. Consult the Reading Is Fundamental website at http://www.rif.org or the Colorín Colorado website at http://www.colorin colorado.org/ for brochures and ideas (also in Spanish).

☐ Talk to parents about the importance of stimulating cognitive development using the primary language (Thomas & Collier, 1997) and providing learning activities in the primary language (Crawford, 1997). Encourage parents to do the following:

✓ Provide time when they and their child can talk in the first language. This can occur during any family activities—at the dinner table, playing games, telling stories, driving in the car, discussing a television program, or celebrating.

✓ Share stories about the family's history in the first language.

✓ Engage their children in daily interactive problem solving—discussing daily activities, making decisions, and sharing values.

☐ Have teachers talk to the parents about ensuring that the home offers an environment that is rich in first language materials. Encourage parents to supply children with books and magazines written in the first language.

      ✓ Provide take-home books and media-based materials to encourage literacy outside of school.

      ✓ Video storybooks, CD-ROM "living storybooks," or books on tape are useful resources for parents who are unable to read to their children.

☐ Encourage students to seek help at home in their native language from family members (Lucas & Katz, 1994).

☐ Survey families to find out what forms of literacy occur in the home (see Figure 3.3).

☐ For parents who are not fully literate, provide meaningful opportunities to enhance their literacy skills, such as the following:

      ✓ Literacy programs in the home language to help parents develop and/or strengthen their native language literacy skills. The best literacy development training programs for parents are those that build on the strengths and skills of the parents and what they have to offer to their child in their native language (Lee & Patel, 1994).

      ✓ A family literacy program in which the whole family is involved in reading by creating a take-home library with a variety of books and magazines in the parents' native language.

      ✓ ESL classes for parents, GED classes in English or the native language if available, and workshops on writing skills.

      ✓ Parent-child learning activities in reading and writing.

☐ Help parents get connected to the public library to find resources in their native language. Make sure that they understand that a library card is free in this country, which is not true in all countries.

◆ **Actively solicit bilingual parents, family members, and community volunteers to be involved.**

☐ Ask bilingual parents, family members, college students, and community volunteers to use their native language skills for oral and written translations, concept explanations, and concept previews and reviews (Cary, 2000).

☐ Organize a pen pal system for writing letters in the primary languages between students of different classes or in different schools. For example, high school or college students studying another language might write to elementary ELLs.

☐ Organize a "Teachers of Tomorrow" program where bilingual middle school and high school students read and write with elementary ELLs (Freeman & Freeman, 2001).

☐ Organize a monthly "community teaching time," when parents or bilingual adults or high school students use their native languages to teach a poem or song, tell a story, or do a presentation about a hobby or their occupation. All presenters should be encouraged to use visuals, gestures, movement, dramatic techniques, and objects (comprehensible input) to make their presentations understandable. Bilingual storytellers are particularly effective, because many well-known children's stories are common to many cultures and are available in other languages (Cary, 2000).

- ◆ **Involve language minority parents in decision making.**
- ◆ **Advocate for language minorities in the school and community.**
  - ☐ When planning to implement a bilingual program, set up community meetings in different languages to provide interested parents, parent-teacher groups (such as the PTA), district administrators, and community members with more information.
    - ✓ Include research information and presentations by schools with established bilingual programs if possible.
    - ✓ Include parents, especially language minority parents, from the very beginning so that they are aware of the goals, structures, and benefits of the program as well as the commitments they must make for successful implementation.
    - ✓ Prepare an informational packet on the benefits of native language instruction, the features of a bilingual program, and a summary of the research on the effectiveness of such programs.
  - ☐ Make sure that staff members and parents are confident and well-informed about the benefits of native language instruction and support so they can dispel the fears and opposition of others when called on to defend instructional issues that support the use of students' native languages.
  - ☐ At site council and PTA meetings, invite bilingual parents and community members to talk about the benefits of bilingualism and cross-cultural proficiency.
  - ☐ Work with your PTA and local service organizations to purchase children's books or collect primary language magazines from doctors' offices that can be sent home.

Figure 3.3. Literacy Survey for Parents

Survey families to find out what forms of literacy occur in the home. Provide this list of questions for teachers to ask parents early on in the school year. They can also use the discussion to encourage parents in ways they can support their children's literacy at home.

1. What does your child like to read at home?

2. How much time each week does your child spend reading on his or her own?

3. Does your child read documents for others (leases, mail, advertisements)?

4. What does your child write (draw) at home? Does your child write for pleasure (for example, poems and stories)?

5. Does he or she participate in writing family letters to friends and relatives?

6. Does your child read and/or write during religious education?

7. With whom does your child read and write?

8. Do you subscribe to newspapers or magazines in your home? Do you share information that you read with your child?

9. What language is primarily used in the home? What language is used with your child when reading and writing at home?

10. Does your child have a library card? Have you been able to take your child to the public library?

11. What does your child like to do at home?

12. What are some of your child's favorite stories, songs, or nursery rhymes?

13. Is a tape recorder available if your child brought home a taped book?

14. Is a VCR/DVD available if your child brought home a video?

15. Tell me about the type of schooling your child has received. Nine-month school cycle? Year-round? Certified teacher?

16. Has your child received instruction in his or her native language in previous grades? To what extent? All day? A few hours each day?

17. Is there anything else you would like to share about your child?

Figure 3.4. Literacy Letter to Parents

Adapted and modified from New York State Education Department, 2001.

Dear Parent(s),

Below is a brief list of suggestions that can be useful for assisting in your child's language and reading development. You can support your child's school success in the following ways:

Reading

- One of the most important things you can do is to read to your children every day, and as often as possible, in your native language. Literacy in the native language helps in developing proficiency in the second language, and what children learn in their native language will transfer to English. When you read with your children, you are giving them experiences that they need to be successful in school.

- You can read to your child, ask your child to read to you, or listen to a tape-recorded reading together. If you do not speak English and your child reads a book to you in English, or if both of you listen to an English book on tape, your child can then explain the story to you, and you can both discuss it as you look at the pictures.

- Ask your children to read aloud to you so they can practice reading. Choose books that are not too hard so that they will be successful reading and want to read more. Encourage them to reread the books they love.

- Visit the public library with your children. Choose books for yourself and your children. As often as possible, read stories to your children in your native language and about your native culture. The public library is located at

  _____.

- Keep many types of reading materials (books, magazines, newspapers, etc.) in your native language and in English in your home.

- Encourage your older children to read to your younger children, and allow your children to see that you also enjoy reading.

- Make reading together a fun time. Ask your children questions about what they have read or what you have read to them. You can ask questions such as, "What is happening in the story? What do you think will happen next? What did you like best about the story?" When you ask questions like these, you can help your children become excited about reading and more responsible for their own learning.

- Select a quiet place in your home for reading where your child is comfortable and away from distractions.

Writing

- Find different opportunities for your children to write in your native language and in English. Encourage them to write in a journal or diary; leave notes for family members; write shopping lists for you; write down recipes; write thank you notes, birthday cards, and letters to family and friends; or even write a book! When you encourage your children to draw and write, you are teaching them to express themselves in writing.

- Show your children that you and other adults use writing for many purposes. This can include writing letters, making out checks, writing notes, and making shopping lists.

- Make a writing box or basket for your children to encourage them to practice writing. Keep writing materials, including paper, pencils, pens, and crayons, around for your children during play time.

- Ask your children to read aloud what they have written. When you show interest in their writing, this encourages them to write more.

Talking

- Take your children to places in the community that offer learning experiences. Talk to your children about what they are seeing. Provide them with the names of new objects of attention, concern, or interest. Answer questions they may have. When you talk to your children, you are helping them to think and explore new ideas. This way they are learning to use language for many reasons. There are many interesting places in our town that you may want to take your child to. My favorites are _____.

- Tell your children stories you already know—stories about your family, funny stories, and stories and songs you liked to hear when you were a child. If you and your child are more comfortable using another language, then sing and talk in your first language. This will build your child's listening and speaking skills, as well as passing along important cultural information.

- Discuss things that happen in school every day. Talk to your children about their favorite subjects and teachers, and about any special events that go on. Listen closely to what your children say and show them that you've heard them. This keeps them talking to you.

- Select television programs that you and your child can watch together and discuss.

- Limit the amount of time your children watch television and instead encourage them to read, write, listen to music, or talk with family members or friends.

Thank you for taking the time to read this. If you need additional reading books at home or if you have any questions, please feel free to call your child's teacher at _____.

Sincerely,

Figure 3.5. Library Letter

Visit Your Local Library!

Dear Parents,

Libraries have books, videos, music, newspapers, computers, and more. The most amazing thing is that you can use them all for free! Most libraries have good children's sections with books in English and other languages. Remember, children love trips to the library—especially during the long summer! Here are a few thoughts for getting started:

- To get a free library card, bring in one proof of identification that has your current address, such as a driver's license, phone bill, or water bill (anything with your address on it). With this library card, you can check out books for children and adults for two weeks at a time. When you're done with those books, you can bring them back and exchange them for more.

- If it's your first time in the library, ask a librarian to give you a tour of the library. It's okay to ask, because that's part of their job.

- If you ask, a librarian will also help you find books that you or your child might like.

- Children can also get their own library cards. It makes them feel special.

- Libraries provide activities like speakers, story times, and movies. Many events are especially for children.

- Let your child choose his or her own books.

- Libraries may also have books on tape or CD, Internet access, movies, games, computers you can use, homework help, and more. Visit your library and ask!

- There are summer reading programs at the library. This is important because can lose their reading skills over the long summer.

- Set a good example by taking care of the books and returning them on time.

- Remember: If you forget to return books and materials on time, you may need to pay a small fine.

Library Address:

Library Hours:

Building the Vision

As you answer each of the following questions, think about what might be done to facilitate change. Seek staff, parent, and community input in identifying goals that will promote native language instruction and support based on your school's vision, resources, and population.

1. How will you share the research on native language instruction and support with all staff?

2. What are your staff's and parents' beliefs about bilingualism and about programs that promote bilingualism?

3. How will your school's vision be determined regarding the use of native language instruction and support?

4. Which strategies and suggestions in the Leadership Challenge will be appropriate for your school? How will you share the strategies and suggestions with all staff?

5. How can your school best use your resources and personnel to provide instruction and support in students' native languages?

6. How will you empower your staff to design a new language program, determine student groupings, or decide on the mode of language use?

7. How could the staff be organized to provide first language instruction?

8. What professional development training do teachers need to improve native language instruction practices? How will you determine their needs?

9. How will you fund materials that support primary language instruction?

10. How can your school actively involve parents and the community in extending the primary language?

11. What are the priorities for improving your school's primary language practices? What initial goals will your school implement to improve the use of primary language?

4

Student Assessment

> *Pupils do not come to school with identical experiences and they do not have identical experiences at school. We cannot, therefore, expect assessments to have the same meaning for all pupils. What we must aim for, though, is an equitable approach where the concerns, contexts, and approaches of one group do not dominate.*
>
> (Gipps, 1994, p. 156)

Chapter Highlights: This chapter explores the components of student assessment that are unique to ELLs—identification, placement, exit, and monitoring. It then examines standardized testing and standards-based assessment in relation to ELLs. The importance of authentic assessment is highlighted, with an emphasis on performance assessments, portfolios, and self-assessments. In the Leadership Challenge, you will be able to identify specific ways that you and your staff can promote effective assessment practices for English learners.

What Principals Should Know

Critical Questions

1. What components of student assessment are unique to ELLs?
2. What are the considerations for standardized testing and standards-based assessment?
3. Why is authentic assessment important for ELLs?

Essential Vocabulary

Alternative assessment: Approaches for finding out what students know or can do other than through the use of multiple-choice testing (O'Malley & Valdez Pierce, 1996, p. 237).

Anecdotal records: Informal written notes on student learning products or processes, usually jotted down from direct observation (O'Malley & Valdez Pierce, 1996, p. 237).

Authentic assessment: Procedures for evaluating student achievement or performance using activities that represent classroom goals, curricula, and instruction, or real-life performance (O'Malley & Valdez Pierce, 1996, p. 237).

Benchmarks: Anchor papers used in defining exemplary performance on the levels of a scoring rubric. May also be a set of objectives, as in benchmark objectives, that define what is expected of a student in a particular area at a certain grade level (O'Malley & Valdez Pierce, 1996, p. 237).

Cloze test: Reading test that consists of passages from which words are omitted at regular intervals; also provides an indication of overall language ability (Snow, 2000, p. 115).

Content bias: Test content and procedures reflecting the dominant culture's standards of language function and shared knowledge and behavior (August & Hakuta, 1997).

FEP: Fluent English proficient.

Inter-rater reliability: Technical measure of the degree of agreement between two raters rating the same assessment item (e.g., a student writing sample) using the same scale (Snow, 2000).

LEP: Limited English proficient.

Linguistic and cultural biases: Factors that adversely affect the formal test performance of students from linguistic and cultural backgrounds, including timed testing, difficulty with English vocabulary, and the near impossibility of determining what bilingual students know in their two languages (August & Hakuta, 1997, p. 115).

NEP: Non-English proficient.

Norming bias: Small numbers of particular minorities included in probability samples, increasing the likelihood that minority group samples are unrepresentative (August & Hakuta, 1997, p. 115).

Performance assessment: Assessment tasks that require students to construct a response, create a product, or demonstrate applications of knowledge (O'Malley & Valdez Pierce, 1996, p. 239).

Portfolio: A collection of student work showing student reflection and progress or achievement over time in one or more areas (O'Malley & Valdez Pierce, 1996, p. 239).

Self-assessment: Appraisal by a student of his or her own work or learning processes (O'Malley & Valdez Pierce, 1996, p. 240).

Critical Question #1:
What Components of Student Assessment
Are Unique to ELLs?

Assessment and Effective Schools Research

Research studies have found that effective schools use systematic student assessment to inform efforts to improve student achievement and take a holistic approach in assessing the needs of ELLs (Carter & Chatfield, 1986; Goldenberg & Sullivan, 1994; Slavin & Yampolsky, 1992). Researchers agree that effective schools for English learners must do more

> *Accurate and effective assessment...is essential to assure that ELL students gain access to instructional programs that meet their needs.* (O'Malley & Valdez Pierce, 1996, p. 4)

than simply assess students to identify them as being limited in English proficiency. The assessment system should include plans and criteria for student placement in and exit from appropriate language programs, diagnosis of individual students, and monitoring of progress in content and language areas (August & Lara, 1996; Cheung, Clements, & Mieu, 1994; Kane & Khattri, 1995). Assessments should also be used to provide accountability for student and school attainment of standards and goals (Ascher, 1990; Lapp, Fisher, Flood, & Cabello, 2001), assist in identifying variables (programs, staffing, curricula, materials) that might be contributing to students' lack of success (Cummins, 1986), and most importantly, upgrade and inform teaching and learning based on best instructional practices (García, 1994c). LaCelle-Peterson and Rivera (1994) state that any adequate assessment system that includes ELLs must be (1) comprehensive, assessing that all students are learning both in language and academic areas; (2) flexible, permitting students to show their progress in language and academics in a variety of ways; (3) progress-oriented, tracking student progress on established goals from year to year, rather than by comparison with other students; and (4) student-sensitive, bringing in the experience and expertise of educators who know ELLs' needs and learning characteristics.

Multiple Measures and Multiple Contexts

An effective assessment process for ELLs must incorporate information about students in a variety of contexts obtained from a variety of sources through a variety of procedures and measures (August & Pease-Álvarez, 1996; Genesee & Hamayan, 1994; Ortiz & Wilkinson, 1990). The use of multiple indicators and multiple contexts is critical because linguistically

> *Every assessment is an assessment of language.* (American Educational Research Association [AERA], American Psychological Association, & National Council on Measurement in Education, 1985, p. 120)

diverse students who have not had "substantial" exposure to English may, on any assessment given in English, in reality be assessed on their English proficiency rather than their knowledge of content (AERA et al., 1985). Because bilingual students have two language systems that overlap with each other and yet are distinct, a second language learner's strongest language may actually vary from context to context, depending on the affect, interaction, or topic (Valdés & Figueroa, 1994). Ascher (1990) explains:

> In any given moment or circumstance, any bilingual will have a temporarily stronger language. A bilingual student may have relatively greater fluency with the formal or informal style in either language; or may dream and speak, but not read or write, in one of the languages. Often, too, bilingual students switch back and forth from one language to another as they speak and think. These variations arise from such circumstances as their age of arrival in the U.S., the language(s) spoken at home and in the neighborhood, the frequency of television watching, and, of course, the language(s) emphasized in their classrooms....What is important about all these linguistic patterns for testing is that we do not yet know how to measure the extent to which one of the languages of a bilingual student influences the other, or even how to describe bilingual competence. (pp. 1–2)

Consequently, developing bilingual students may know the information but not be able to express that knowledge. Also, if students do not have adequate reading and writing skills, it is questionable as to whether the tasks they are asked to perform will even have consistent meaning (Gipps, 1994). Therefore, children cannot be assessed exclusively by approaches that consider performance in only one language and only one way (Moll & Diaz, 1987). Multiple assessments are necessary to validate inferences that are made about student progress (Linn, 1993; Wiggins, 1992) and to provide opportunities for students to demonstrate their competence of specific skills or content in different ways (Gardner, 1993). Through multiple assessments, both formal and informal (see Figure 4.1), ELLs can be provided with many opportunities to demonstrate their knowledge in a manner that best reflects their present communication abilities.

Figure 4.1. Formal and Informal Assessments

Lapp et al., 2001, p. 10.

Type	Purpose	Procedure
Formal Assessment		
Standardized testing	To measure a student's performance in a variety of skills and compare those scores to students in other geographic locations	Administered at set intervals; students answer questions from booklet on standard forms
Criterion-referenced tests	To indicate attainment of mastery on specific instructional objectives, usually by answering a percentage of questions correctly	Administered with lesson plans; students read items and answer on separate paper
Informal Assessment		
Observations	To assess a student's use of language in a variety of instructional settings	Observe and record student's use of language, often written in logs or journals
Skills checklists	To track a student's development by noting which skills have become or are becoming part of a repertoire	Set up a checklist of desirable skills in language arts and periodically observe the student to determine which have been attained
Portfolio assessment	To document in a variety of ways how a student has developed as a language user	Teacher collects or student selects samples of work, including "published" writing, taped oral readings, and conference notes
Conferencing	To provide opportunities for the teacher and student to discuss development	Student and teacher meet at set times to review performance and discuss instruction that may be required for student to progress
Peer reviews	To involve students in the evaluation process and to build their evaluative and interactive skills	Students are given guidelines for evaluation; two or more meet to discuss one another's work; peer's grade is factored into final grade
Self-assessment	To empower students by making them responsible for and reflective of their own work	Students continually evaluate their performance and progress via checklists, interactions, inventories, conferences, and portfolios

Identification and Placement

Since federal law requires all school districts to identify students who are ELLs, initial assessments are usually used to determine new students' level of English proficiency and whether to place them in special language-related programs (see Figure 4.2). States and local districts use a variety of methods to make these decisions and to monitor the progress of the students (August & Lara, 1996; Cheung et al., 1994; Fleischman & Hopstock, 1993). These methods include home language surveys, registration and enrollment information, observations, interviews, referrals, grades, classroom performance, and testing. Some districts establish "Welcome Centers" or "Newcomer Centers" where new language minority students are assessed in a multilingual, welcoming, and sensitive setting. An intake center can also serve as an information center for parents regarding adult education, health services, transportation, housing, and legal information.

Initial identification begins with screening for a native language background, which is usually done at enrollment by having parents of all students who are new to the district complete a home language survey. This survey asks parents about the languages used at home and usually consists of the following questions:

- What language did your son or daughter learn when he or she first began to talk?
- What language does your son or daughter use most frequently at home?
- What language do you use most frequently to speak to your son or daughter?
- What is the language most frequently spoken at home?

If the home language survey indicates that a language other than English is used in the home, then the student is assessed for English language proficiency. Although the intent of the survey is simply to identify students whose primary or home language is a language other than English, it is important to keep in mind that some parents indicate that English is spoken in the home when actually it is not. They may indicate this out of fear (especially if they are undocumented immigrants), misunderstanding, or a desire for their children to be placed in mainstream classrooms (Clements, Lara, & Cheung, 1992; De Avila, 1990). As such, a teacher referral system should be in place if further information or observation indicates that the student's home language is not English (for example, observation of the child speaking a non-English language or having difficulty in understanding or producing English, or indication from the parent or child that the language spoken in the home is non-English). See also Figure 4.3, p. 112.

The most common method used by school districts to determine students' language proficiency is a test of oral language proficiency in English; districts also administer written English proficiency tests to students who meet specified oral language scores. Commercially available or state-approved language proficiency tests are used for both of these purposes. Some states have developed their own English language assessments; others are using commercial instruments such as the Stanford English Language Proficiency Test, the Language Assessment Scale (LAS), the IDEA Proficiency Test (IPT), the English Language Development Assessment, and the Maculaitis Assessment of Competencies II. The Stanford, LAS, and IPT are the most commonly used commercial assessments (Center on Education Policy, 2006).

Initial and annual assessment in language proficiency should involve reading, writing, listening, and speaking assessments, with a holistic view of the integrated information. Students are usually placed in language support programs (see Chapter

5) if they score non-English proficient (NEP) or limited English proficient (LEP), with fluent English proficient (FEP) being the goal. However, educators need to be aware that standardized language proficiency tests have limitations (such as single performance sample, lack of familiarity with testing procedures, acculturation factors, and anxiety) that can sometimes lead to inappropriate program placement and exit. Also, many commercialized tests measure a minimum level of language proficiency, not the complex academic language skills that students must have to succeed in school. Freeman and Freeman (1998) comment

> Generally, tests are usually administered when students first enter a new school system. The students may be confused. They are often undergoing some degree of culture shock, and they may not understand the purpose of the test. The test tasks they are asked to complete are not meaningful…[and] not consistent with the principles for success. They test parts of language; they test language out of context; they have no meaning or function for the students;…they fail to draw on background knowledge and strengths of the students; and they are used to label students. The tests don't provide the kind of information that effective teachers need to make decisions about how to integrate English language learners into their classrooms. (pp. 251–252)

Figure 4.2. Procedures for Identification, Assessment, Placement, Evaluation, and Exit of ELLs

Adapted and modified from New Mexico State Department of Education, 2003.

Step	Process	Results
Step 1:	Identification of Primary or Home Language Other Than English	
	Administer Home Language Survey. Initial identification of student's home language must occur upon enrollment.	Determines who is to be assessed for English language proficiency skills.
	PHLOTE definition: A "PHLOTE" student is a student with a "primary (first learned) or home language other than English." A PHLOTE student may be FEP (fluent English proficient) or an English language learner/limited English proficient (ELL/LEP) who is unable to speak, read, write, or understand the English language at levels comparable to his or her grade-level English-proficient peers, as determined by measures of proficiency for language minority students, and who also cannot meaningfully participate in the curriculum. **Home language survey:** The home language survey (HLS) is used to determine if there is a primary (first learned) or home language influence other than English. An HLS must be completed *for each student* either by the student's parents or legal guardian upon enrollment. If a teacher notices that the student is using or responding to a language other than English, a teacher language observation form may be used to identify the language or languages to which the student has been exposed.	
	If there is one (or more) positive response on the home language survey, then the district must continue the identification process by administering an approved language proficiency assessment in both English and the home language (if possible).	

Step 2:	Assessment of English Language Proficiency and Home Language Proficiency	
	■ Use language proficiency test to formally assess language proficiency skills (listening, speaking, reading, writing, and comprehension) of PHLOTE students. ■ If possible, assess language proficiency skills in native language. ■ Test annually all ELL/LEP students. Any PHLOTE student who scores below the "fluent English proficiency (FEP)" level in any skill area measured by the English language proficiency assessment should be identified as an English language learner. ■ Test new students within 10 days of enrollment. ■ Select trained personnel to administer, score, interpret, and use test data. Personnel administering the native language assessment should be fluent in the native language. ■ Record and review student language proficiency and academic performance for placement. ■ File scores in cumulative folders. ■ Disseminate test results to the student's teachers, parents, and other appropriate school staff.	■ Determines the level of the student's English and native language proficiency in all skill areas. Needed for student placement, program planning, and implementation of the program. ■ Establishes baseline data on student language proficiency in order to monitor student progress in the program.
Step 3:	Program Placement/Program Model	
	■ Notify parents of student placement within 30 school days of the first day of the school year, thereafter, within 10 days of enrollment for new students. ■ Place ELLs in an appropriate language program according to the students' language proficiency and educational needs. Level of support is dependent upon student's needs. ■ Serve ELLs in a language program model that is scientifically research-based.	■ Placement in an approved language program model.
Step 4:	Student Evaluation	
	■ Assess all students' academic and language progress annually as part of the comprehensive assessment system. ■ Review individual progress to address individual instructional needs. ■ Reclassify students based upon academic achievement data and English language proficiency. ■ Reclassify or exit student from the ELL service program when he or she attains the FEP level and meets exit criteria and procedures. ■ Continue to monitor each FEP student as part of the program for two additional years after he or she exits the ELL services program. ■ Re-enroll students whose progress can be associated with a decline in English language proficiency into an ELL services program.	■ Student continues in or exits the program. ■ The language program must ensure monitoring of student performance for two years after a student exits the ELL services program. During these two years, the student may be reclassified back to an English language learner status based on the following identified criteria: • Academic achievement on the state assessment test below average • Language proficiency assessment results verify ELL status • Student improvement team referral • Student grades

Step 5:	Program Evaluation	
	■ Analyze and evaluate longitudinal data on an annual basis: 　● Assess proficiency in English language and home language 　● Review academic achievement, rates of attendance, dropouts, parent involvement, school safety 　● Compare ELL students' performance with non-ELL students as part of the comprehensive assessment system ■ Review and revise program as needed to address individual instructional needs ■ Report and disseminate results to all stakeholders: parents, teachers, community entities, federal and state agencies	■ Program is modified and continuously refined to ensure that students are succeeding.

Criteria for Exiting Students from ELL Status		
Factors in Determining ELL Participation in the Regular Program	**Required to Meet Title VI of The Civil Rights Act of 1964**	**Required to Meet NCLB Title III Requirements (2001)**
■ Ability to keep up with their non-ELL peers in the regular educational program ■ Ability to participate successfully in essentially all aspects of the school's curriculum without the use of simplified English materials ■ Dropout and retention rates are similar to those of their non-ELL peers ■ Monitoring and evaluation of academic performance of current and former ELL students	Procedures and criteria for transition from ELL services: ■ Language proficiency in speaking, reading, writing and comprehension of English and in subject matter to enable the student to participate independently in the academic program ■ Ability to satisfy district transition criteria, which must include standardized test scores and English proficiency measured through comprehension, speaking, reading, and writing; ■ Documentation of progress of former ELL students ■ Continued monitoring of former ELL students' progress	■ Description of the progress made by students in learning the English language and in meeting state academic achievement standards ■ Description of the number and percentage of students in the programs and activities attaining English proficiency by the end of each school year, as determined by a valid and reliable assessment of English proficiency ■ Description of the progress made by students in meeting challenging state academic achievement standards for each of the two years after such students are no longer receiving ELL services.

Figure 4.3. SOLOM Teacher Observation:
Student Oral Language Observation Matrix

California State Department of Education, 1994.

Student: _____   Date: _____

Language Observed: _____   Grade Level: _____

Social Domain: ☐   Academic Domain: ☐

SOLOM Phases:	Phase I: Phase II: Phase III: Phase IV:	Score 5–11 = Score 12–18 = Score 19–24 = Score 25 =	non-English proficient limited English proficient limited English proficient fully English proficient	

Based on your observation of the student, mark an "X" across the block in each category that best describes the student's abilities.

Category	Level 1	Level 2	Level 3	Level 4	Level 5
A. Comprehen-sion	Cannot understand even simple conversation.	Has great difficulty following what is said. Can comprehend only "social conversation" spoken slowly and with frequent repetitions.	Understands most of what is said at slower-than-normal speed with repetitions.	Understands nearly everything at normal speed, although occasional repetition may be necessary.	Understands everyday conversation and normal classroom discussions without difficulty.
B. Fluency	Speech is so halting and fragmentary as to make conversation virtually impossible.	Usually hesitant; often forced into silence by language limitations.	Speech in everyday communication and classroom discussion is frequently disrupted by the student's search for the correct manner of expression.	Speech in everyday conversation and classroom discussions is generally fluent, with occasional lapses while the student searches for the correct manner of expression.	Speech in everyday conversation and in classroom discussions is fluent and effortless, approximating that of a native speaker.
C. Vocabulary	Vocabulary limitations so extreme as to make conversation virtually impossible.	Misuse of words and very limited vocabulary; comprehension quite difficult.	Student frequently uses the wrong words; conversation somewhat limited because of inadequate vocabulary.	Student occasionally uses inappropriate terms and/or must rephrase ideas because of lexical inadequacies.	Use of vocabulary and idioms approximates that of a native speaker.

D. Pronunciation	Pronunciation problems so severe as to make speech virtually unintelligible.	Very hard to understand because of pronunciation problems. Must frequently repeat in order to make himself or herself understood.	Pronunciation problems necessitate concentration on the part of the listener and occasionally lead to misunderstanding.	Always intelligible, though one is conscious of a definite accent and occasional inappropriate intonation patterns.	Pronunciation and intonation approximate those of a native speaker.
E. Grammar	Errors in grammar and word order so severe as to make speech virtually unintelligible.	Grammar and word-order errors make comprehension difficult. Must often rephrase and/or restrict self to basic patterns.	Makes frequent errors of grammar and word order that occasionally obscure meaning.	Occasionally makes grammatical and/or word-order errors that do not obscure meaning.	Grammatical usage and word-order approximate those of a native speaker

Multifaceted Approach

Effective schools for ELLs must do more than identify students as being limited in English proficiency. Because low-level proficiency on an English proficiency test is not an indicator of ability or even of achievement, a multifaceted approach is necessary. Although

> *The key to effective programs…is an ability to make instructional decisions based on data, not assumptions.* (CEEE, 1996, p. 25)

assessing ELLs is a complex and time-consuming task, teachers must have adequate information to plan effective instruction and provide appropriate educational services to the students. Additional information not only assists in making appropriate placement decisions, but it also helps put assessment results in context and helps teachers know and understand the backgrounds and needs of their students (August & Pease-Álvarez, 1996; Genesee & Hamayan, 1994; Hamayan, 1993). Additional information should be gathered from assessments, family members, previous educational providers, and the students themselves. Data from various sources would include information about the following:

- Native language and languages spoken in the home, literacy in the home, parents' and siblings' educational backgrounds, language development histories, health histories
- Levels of oral proficiency in both English and the native language
- Literacy levels in both English and the native language
- Previous schooling and educational experiences including type of educational experiences (consistent, interrupted; rural, urban; type of program, such as bilingual or ESL) and years of schooling

- Academic data such as achievement test scores, classroom grades, teacher observations, cognitive development, giftedness, and exceptional learning characteristics
- Level of acculturation

Researchers also agree that placement decisions should not be based on English performance alone (Hamayan, 1993; Saville-Troike, 1991). When appropriate, ELLs should also be assessed in their primary language to better determine their academic achievement and to ensure appropriate program placement (August & Pease-Álvarez, 1996; Genesee & Hamayan, 1994; Saville-Troike, 1991). Hamayan (1993) emphasizes that if students have mastered the academic concepts and skills in their first language, academic assessments only in English will result in underestimates of their academic achievement and in improper placement decisions. Mace-Matluck, Alexander-Kasparik, and Queen (1998) state, "Assessment of native language literacy is a crucial factor in the intake process, because prior schooling in the home country does not guarantee students' proficiency in academic language" (p. 109). Rather, it is the level of first language literacy and content knowledge that are strong predictors of academic success in English. Assessing native language proficiency could range from formal assessments (commercial native language proficiency tests) to informal assessments (student observations, student and parent interviews, student writing samples in the native language, running records on student readings in a grade-level native language book until an appropriate level is discovered). When appropriate data are collected and analyzed, placement decisions are based on students' needs, not assumptions. Once students are assessed and placed, it is important that teachers observe students carefully to confirm that the placement is appropriate. When students are placed in language instruction programs, districts are required to annually notify the parents or guardians of each ELL student no later than 30 days after the beginning of each school year, or within two weeks of enrollment for students who are identified after the start of the school year.

Questions for Reflection

What information is initially collected on ELLs? Are multiple measures of language proficiency and academic achievement used? Is native language proficiency assessed?

What additional information is needed? Who should be involved in this process?

How is the information used for placement and instructional decisions? What are the criteria for placement? How are the criteria used to determine different levels of support?

Is the placement information provided and fully explained to classroom teachers?

What organizational structures need to be implemented for better data collection and analysis to occur?

Exit and Monitoring

As with placement decisions, certain legal standards apply when exiting students from language support programs. According to the September 27, 1991, Office for Civil Rights policy update (Williams, 1991), ELLs "must be provided with services until they are proficient enough in English to participate meaningfully in the regular educational program" (p. 6). Factors that should be examined to make this determination include the following:

1. Whether they are able to keep up with their non-LEP peers in the regular educational program;
2. Whether they are able to participate successfully in essentially all aspects of the school's curriculum without the use of simplified English materials; and
3. Whether their retention in-grade and dropout rates are similar to those of their non-LEP peers. (Williams, 1991, p. 6)

Standards that should be met for exiting students include the following:

- First, exit criteria should be based on objective standards, such as standardized test scores, and the district should be able to explain why it has decided that students meeting those standards will be able to participate meaningfully in the regular classroom.
- Second, students should not be exited from the LEP program unless they can read, write, and comprehend English well enough to participate meaningfully in the recipient's program. Exit criteria that simply test a student's oral language skills are inadequate.

- Finally, alternative programs cannot be dead end tracks to segregate "national origin" minority students. (Williams, 1991, p. 6)

When determining whether a student has met exit criteria, information about the student in a variety of contexts obtained from a variety of sources through a variety of procedures and measures should be collected and analyzed. One test score on a language proficiency test should not determine whether a student should be exited. Considerations for exit (see Figures 4.2 and 4.4) might include a combination of the following data and information:

- Documented success of grade-level outcomes (performance assessments, portfolios, teacher observation, grades)
- English language proficiency level on language proficiency test
- English language state assessment profile scores
- Native language proficiency level on language proficiency test
- State assessment results
- Standardized achievement test results
- Criterion-referenced test scores comparable to those of native English speakers
- Reading at or near grade level

Once students are exited, their progress should continue to be monitored and documented for two years. If a child is not being successful without the program, services should resume.

Figure 4.4. Sample Exit Form

Recommendation for Exit
Based on the multiple evidence checked below, it is recommended that this student be exited from second language support services and be monitored for two years following the date of exit.

Student Name:
Date of meeting:_____ Members present:

Criteria used to exit student from services (check *all* that apply):	Must be able to answer yes to both questions.
☐ Documented success of grade-level outcomes (teacher evaluation and grades) ☐ English language assessment information ☐ Native language assessment information ☐ State assessment scores proficient or above ☐ Standardized achievement scores ☐ Criterion-referenced test scores comparable to native English speaking peers ☐ Reading level at or near grade level ☐ Individual Outcome Plan goal(s) met ☐ Other (explain):	1. Will the student be able to keep up with his or her non-ELL peers in the regular educational program? 2. Will the student be able to participate successfully in all aspects of the school's curriculum without the use of simplified English materials or support? **Exit Meeting Summary:**

By reviewing multiple indicators of the above criteria and signing, all agree student should be placed in the regular classroom with no ESL support/modifications. The student will be monitored for two years to ensure success. If the child is not being successful, he or she will be recommended for reclassification.	
Parent signature(s):	Teacher signature(s): (Teachers may request reconsideration of placement during the year)

Two-Year Monitoring Evaluation (attach copy of grade card for each year)	
First year follow-up comments (check each quarter):	Second year follow-up comments (check each quarter):

Recommendation: ___ No reentry ___ ESL support ___ Other program (specify)
Date of notification letter for reentry:

☐ This student has been monitored for at least two years after the date of exit and is fully integrated into and successful in the regular school instructional program.
Date: _____ ESL Teacher Signature: _____

Whether assessment is used for initial placement, monitoring, or exit, Hargett (1998) suggests asking two "what" questions to guide the process when selecting appropriate assessment strategies: (1) "What information about a student is needed?" and (2) "What will that information be used for?" (p. 3) Then it's a matter of matching the right assessment strategy to the school's questions about the student. The right strategy might be a test, a scoring rubric, or teacher observations, but the "assessment tasks must represent the kind of information the school wants to know about the student" (Hargett, 1998, p. 4) as represented in Figure 4.5.

Figure 4.5. Requirements a Test Should Meet

Hargett, 1998, p. 4.

Questions	Requirements
Can the student participate in the oral language of a mainstream classroom?	The tasks must simulate the oral language of a mainstream classroom.
Can the student read and write English at levels similar to his or her mainstream grade mates?	Ask the student to read or write something at that level.
Does the student need an ESL or bilingual program? If the student needs an ESL or bilingual program, what should his or her placement be?	Give tasks that represent a range of difficulty, from grade-level performance to little or no English proficiency.
Does the student read and write the native language at grade level?	Staff need to know what that language's grade-level expectations are; tasks should require the student to read and write something at that level.
Are the student's academic skills near grade level in the native language?	Give tasks that represent that language's grade level standards in the academic areas of interest.
What specific aspects of English grammar or vocabulary does the student lack?	Tasks should pinpoint specific grammatical structures or vocabulary.
Is the student progressing in oral or written English?	Tasks should cover a range of difficulty, spanning at least the student's initial ability level and the level he or she is expected to reach after instruction.

Cultural Variables in Assessment

Cultural differences also play a role when planning and interpreting assessments. Because of cultural bias, certain tests indicate students' knowledge of the mainstream culture and ways of demonstrating knowledge (Estrin & Nelson-Barber, 1995). Content bias occurs when the content and procedures of an assessment reflect the language structure and shared knowledge of the dominant culture or when test items do not include activities, words, or concepts familiar to language minority students (Medina & Neill, 1990). Garcia and Pearson (1994) state, "It is most severe when test tasks, topics, and vocabulary reflect the culture of mainstream society to such an extent that it is difficult to do well on a formal test without being culturally assimilated" (p. 344). For example, students' performance may be affected when they are not familiar with the format of tests (multiple-choice, fill-in-the-bubble answer sheets, or certain testing conditions) or when test items have different answers in different cultures (e.g., color of fruit), contain culturally foreign scenes or items (e.g., ice hockey for a student who is not familiar with the sport), or contain culturally inappropriate topics (e.g., disagreeing with a teacher).

Because the interactive, collaborative classrooms common to the United States are foreign to many cultures, response styles and interactive patterns of culture groups also affect assessment. For example, some students avoid participating in whole-group discussions because of their cultural backgrounds; others are not comfortable with public, individual displays of their learning and would prefer to respond in whole or small group formats (Cloud et al., 2000). While native English speaking students are usually comfortable with guessing when they are not sure of an answer, some ELLs will not respond if they are not certain that their answer is accurate (Cloud et al., 2000). In addition, students who are still acquiring English need more time to process the language; this means more time to respond on a test as well as more time to respond to a question posed in class.

Questions for Reflection

How often are your ELLs assessed for English language proficiency? For native language proficiency? How are results used to drive instruction?

What criteria other than language proficiency tests are used for exiting students?

How are students monitored after they are exited from the program? Have criteria been predetermined for resuming services?

To what extent are cultural variables considered in assessment?

Critical Question #2:
What Are the Considerations for Standardized Testing and Standards-Based Assessment?

Standardized Testing

The *No Child Left Behind* (NCLB) *Act* of 2001 calls for the assessment of all students on their attainment of high academic standards. Although the intent is to hold schools and districts accountable for the achievement of all students, researchers and policy makers are torn between their concerns with norming bias and overall fairness of the tests, and the importance of including ELLs in mainstream assessments through appropriate testing accommodations. Some feel that the overall test results for the school, district, or state are more comprehensive and that there is more attention and pressure to improve services to ELLs when these students are included (Zehler, Hopstock, Fleischman, & Greniuk, 1994). Rivera and Stansfield (1998) state, "Inclusion in the testing program helps to remind districts and schools that students will need to receive at least the same quality and the same amount of content instruction as is given to other students" (p. 67).

However, others feel that standardized tests pose a dilemma for ELLs and shouldn't be required until students reach a minimum level of English proficiency. Heubert and Hauser (1999) state

> The central dilemma regarding participation of English language learners in large scale assessment programs is that, when students are not profi-cient in the language of assessment (English), their scores on a test given in English will not accurately reflect their knowledge of the subject being as-sessed (except for a test that measures only English proficiency). (p. 214)

The National Center for Research on Evaluation, Standards, and Student Testing (Abedi & Dietel, 2004) indicates that the language demands of state assessment tests negatively influence accurate measurement of ELLs' performance because the tests measure achievement *and* language ability. Cummins (2000) maintains that high-stakes testing can "(1) significantly disadvantage ELL students with respect to the perception of their ability and progress; and (2) provide essentially meaningless data unless the results for ELL students are disaggregated in a sophisticated way that links progress to factors such as stages of English proficiency development, length of residence, program type, and socioeconomic status" (p. 157). Gottlieb (2000) notes that the most important factor in determining whether ELLs are qualified to take standardized tests should be a predetermined threshold of literacy in English, not ar-bitrary criteria and variables such as years in the United States or years of bilingual or ESL services. Another challenge in making adequate yearly progress for the NCLB mandate is the instability of the ELL subgroup. High-achieving ELLs are redesignated as fluent English proficient and exit the ELL subgroup, often resulting in flat subgroup scores or sometimes even declining scores due to the continuous addition of new ELLs, who are typically low achieving (Abedi & Dietel, 2004).

Additionally, ELLs "(a) are often unfamiliar with the type of standardized testing usually required in U.S. schools; (b) may have different learning and testing styles; and therefore (c) may be unable to demonstrate the extent of their knowledge at a single sitting on one designated testing day" (Navarrete & Gustke, 1996, p. 5). Most standardized tests use multiple-choice items requiring a high level of English language proficiency that ELLs may not have; as such, they often do not reflect what students know (O'Malley & Valdez Pierce, 1996). ELL students also need more time to complete tests because they have to process both language and content information of test questions. Furthermore, ELLs may not have received the same curriculum as that assessed on the test (Abedi, 2003).

Reliance on standardized tests as a measure of ELLs' cognitive development and academic progress is also criticized due to the lack of reliability and validity of such tests on the English learner population (Abedi, 2003; August & Hakuta, 1997; Valdés & Figueroa, 1994). Concerns for ELLs that result from the "mainstream bias" of formal testing include norming bias (small numbers of ELLs in the sample making it unrepresentative), content bias (content is reflective of dominant culture), linguistic and cultural biases (timed tests, difficulty with vocabulary, and difficulty assessing knowledge of bilingual students), and examiner bias (August & Hakuta, 1997; Garcia & Pearson, 1994). For example, the standardized tests that most states currently use were developed for the assessment of native English speakers and are often not normed or field-tested on populations that include English language learners.

Translated tests are not necessarily the answer either. Besides the fact that some students are not literate in their native language, translated tests are often ineffective and unreliable. Ascher (1990) explains

> Translated tests are always different tests, unknown and unfair. While it is not difficult to translate a test, it is extremely difficult—if not impossible—to translate psychometric properties from one language to another. A word in English is simply not the same word in terms of difficulty in Spanish, Hmong, Russian, or Chinese. (p. 3)

Test Accommodations for Assessment

The intent of accommodations on large-scale assessments is to level the playing field for ELLs when measuring their performance, without altering the validity of the test. In other words, accommodations should make language less of a factor, but should not give ELLs an unfair advantage. Based on a review of research, Abedi (2001) recommends the following:

- Some accommodations are more effective than others. Providing extra time, a glossary of key terms on the test *plus* extra time, or reducing the language complexity of the test questions resulted in substantially higher test scores for ELL and non-ELL students. *Providing a glossary without extra time did not increase ELL performance, possibly due to information overload.*

- Translating test items from English to other languages may not be a successful accommodation when ELLs are taught in English....[T]he language of the assessment should match the student's primary language of instruction.
- Modify test questions to reduce unnecessary language complexity....Reducing language complexity helps to narrow the performance gap between native English speaking students and ELL students.
- Customized dictionaries are a viable alternative to providing traditional dictionaries as accommodations. A traditional dictionary may provide ELL students with an unfair advantage on certain types of tests. (p. 4)

In another review of research studies, Abedi (2003) cites the effects of certain accommodations on ELL test performance:

- Effectiveness of accommodation in reducing performance gap between ELL and non-ELL vary considerably by types of accommodations and student background (p. 20).
- Extra time...may lead to higher scores for English learners (Hafner, 2001; Kopriva, 2000) (p. 21).
- Students with intermediate self-reported English reading proficiency did benefit from a published dictionary; the poor readers did not (Thurlow, 2001) (p. 21).
- English learners showed significant performance improvement using a customized dictionary (Abedi, Lord, Kim, & Myoshi, 2000) (p. 21).
- Abedi, Courtney, and Leon (2002) found computer testing to help improve ELL performance (p. 21).

High-stakes Decisions

Another issue regarding standardized tests is the possible misuse of them for high-stakes decisions such as school funding, grade-level promotion, graduation, or identification for special education programs, where second language learners could receive inappropriate instruction. Critics point out that, when used as the primary indicators of ability or growth, standardized tests result in inaccurate comparisons between ELLs and other students, create questionable guidelines about the placement and identification of ELLs for special services, and inadequately reflect their achievement. Low test scores on standardized tests create difficulties with all types of assessment, from tests for English language proficiency that are used to place students in English language support programs to intelligence tests, which are often used for special education placement. Low test scores for ELLs are often a product of the cultural conditions not considered in testing, not necessarily of student achievement or ability levels. Katz (2000) states that standardized testing results place "disproportionate numbers of immigrant children, poor children, and children of color into lower tracks and special-needs programs and prevent them from participating in gifted and talented programs" (p. 144).

Because the guidelines for assessment and identification of students with special needs have been designed for English speaking students, ELLs are at risk for either over-referral or under-referral to special education programs. Lipsky and Gartner (1997) believe that the use of standardized tests has led to an overrepresentation of English learners in special education programs; in fact, much of the literature is concerned with avoiding inappropriate referrals for these students (Baca & Almanza, 1991). Meeting the needs of ELLs should first focus on prevention and early intervention. However, if an ELL is referred for a special education evaluation, a culturally and linguistically nonbiased evaluation must comply with state and federal regulations. In addition, an assessment of the child's native language skills is strongly advised so that any significant problems can be identified and addressed. See the following for additional guidance. Overall, it's understandable how formal test results for English learners can be challenged, thus indicating the need for standardized measures to be complemented with other indicators that show how ELLs are learning. Schools must pursue alternative ways of ensuring that these students are meeting state standards.

Building Staff Knowledge: ELLs with Disabilities

Echevarria et al., 2004; Müller & Markowitz, 2004; National Association for Bilingual Education (NABE) & ILIAD Project, 2002.

Prevention of Failure for ELLs

Preventing school failure for ELLs involves two primary elements: (1) creating environments that are conducive to ELLs' success, and (2) using effective instructional strategies.

Positive School Climate Factors for All Students
- Strong administrative leadership
- High expectations for student achievement
- Challenging curricula and instruction
- Safe and orderly environment
- Ongoing, systematic evaluation of student progress
- Shared decision making that involves community, parents, and staff

Positive School Climate Factors Specifically for ELLs
- Teachers have shared knowledge base about the following:
  - ✓ Second language acquisition

- ✓ Relationship of native language proficiency to development of English proficiency
- ✓ Assessment of proficiency in native language and English
- ✓ Sociocultural influences on learning
- ✓ Effective first and second language teaching methodology
- ✓ Informal assessment strategies, especially in literacy and language development
- ✓ Strategies for working with culturally and linguistically diverse families
- ▪ School supports linguistic and cultural diversity:
  - ✓ Language programs supported by staff, parents, and community
  - ✓ Staff understand native language instruction is foundational to high levels of English proficiency
  - ✓ Language development is the shared responsibility of all teachers
  - ✓ Curriculum reflects students' cultures, backgrounds, and languages
  - ✓ All parents are viewed as capable advocates and valuable resources

Effective Instruction
- ▪ Teachers use strategies known to be effective with ELLs:
  - ✓ Provide comprehensible input
  - ✓ Draw upon students' prior knowledge
  - ✓ Provide multiple opportunities to review concepts
  - ✓ Provide basic instruction within context of higher-order thinking and problem solving
  - ✓ Provide opportunities for application of concepts
  - ✓ Use collaborative learning activities for student engagement and use of conversational and academic language

Early Intervention

Implement early intervention strategies as soon as learning problems are noted.

Clinical Teaching
- ▪ Use sequential instruction where teachers teach initial concepts, reteach using different strategies for students who need it, and assess to identify student strengths, weaknesses, and causes of difficulties
- ▪ Assess conversational and academic language proficiency to decide the language(s) of instruction and student goals for language instruction
- ▪ Use assessment data and documentation of interventions to improve student performance

Peer and Expert Support/Teacher Assistance Team (TAT)
- ▪ Use building-based support teams (four to six teachers, along with the teacher who requests assistance) to develop strategies and implement recommendations
- ▪ ESL teachers can demonstrate strategies and help coordinate ESL and content instruction
- ▪ Screen for potential reading problems

Alternative Programs and Services
- Consider a variety of alternatives to address needs not attributable to disabilities:
  - ✓ Small-group or individualized instruction
  - ✓ Cross-age tutoring
  - ✓ More modeling and practice
  - ✓ Explicit teaching of learning strategies
  - ✓ Modified assignments
  - ✓ Parent conference and involvement
  - ✓ Family and student support groups
  - ✓ Assessment of medical needs (hearing, vision, nutrition)
  - ✓ Primary language support
  - ✓ More intensive English language development

Referral to Special Education

Refer only after prevention and early intervention efforts have occurred.
- Questions to ask:
  - ✓ Is the child in a positive climate?
  - ✓ Have effective instructional strategies for ELLs been used?
  - ✓ Did clinical teaching/TAT recommendations resolve the problem?
  - ✓ Did other general education alternatives prove successful?
  - ✓ Can the team document that the student's problems are not the result of a lack of academic support, poor study habits and time management, lack of opportunity to learn, limited English proficiency, environmental disadvantage, cultural differences, or other special factors (socioeconomic status, mobility, interrupted schooling, etc.)?
- Use qualified professional assessment personnel:
  - ✓ Knowledgeable about first and second language acquisition, effective instruction for ELLs, and influence of culture and socioeconomic status on student performance
  - ✓ Bilingual professionals if possible
- Assessment:
  - ✓ Assess in native language and English (depending on school history)
  - ✓ Use equivalent instruments in native language and English
  - ✓ Use formal and informal assessments
  - ✓ Use valid and reliable instruments free of racial and cultural bias
  - ✓ Use native language assessments that have been developed and tested on students who are similar in language, culture, and background
  - ✓ Obtain current language proficiency information in both languages
  - ✓ Observe in various contexts (classroom, playground, home)
  - ✓ Acquire information about student's performance and functioning levels within classroom
  - ✓ Use materials and procedures that measure the extent to which a child has a disability, not the child's English language skills
  - ✓ Obtain parental input about student's performance in home and community
  - ✓ Use curriculum-based assessment and dynamic assessment
  - ✓ Determine if suspected disability is manifested when student is using native language; disability cannot occur in only one language

Linking Standards to Assessment

With the increased accountability in meeting state standards, standards must be the critical element in guiding curriculum and instruction, and the foundation upon which assessment is based. The need for alignment of all of these factors is particularly critical for ELLs:

> *A state and national vision that strives to help the educational community set high standards for all students…is a goal that educators and families must embrace. But what a school does with those standards is what is crucial.* (Miramontes et al., 1997, p. 177)

> Assessment has to mirror curriculum if it is to be a valid account of what students know and are able to do. If assessment is an expression of the curriculum and the curriculum, in turn, maximizes the opportunity to attain designated…standards, there is continuity in the education program for students. Anchoring curriculum, instruction, and assessment in the…standards increase the validity of the educational program. (Gottlieb, 1999, p. 3)

The literature has pointed out that for linguistically diverse learners, meeting content standards is a more complex and cognitively demanding task than it is for native English speaking students (McKeon, 1994). In addition to meeting the standards, ELLs are often faced with understanding and processing the English language while making sense of the content to be assessed. Also, their previous schooling experiences may have had different curricular sequences, content objectives, and instructional methods from their current school. Overall, ELLs may need more time to meet state standards, which may require the development of additional benchmarks to assess their progress in meeting the standards (August & Hakuta, 1997).

Navarette and Gustke (1996) state that when linking standards to assessment in a way that considers the needs of English learners, it is important to support the view that all students can learn to high standards, to make sure that standards address language proficiency as well as academic achievement, and to make certain that the standards are interpreted broadly enough so that a variety of assessment strategies can be used. In fact, ELLs should be assessed for both content knowledge and language development to evaluate the progress that they are making in English and to provide information for interpreting their performance in the academic content areas (Hamayan, 1993; Tinajero & Hurley, 2001). Because they are acquiring English language skills at the same time that they learning content, additional language arts standards should be considered in assessing students' progress. Teachers of English to Speakers of Other Languages (TESOL) has developed ESL standards for pre-K–12 students. These standards acknowledge the central role of language in the achievement of content and highlight the learning styles and particular instructional and assessment needs of English learners who are still developing English proficiency. These standards (TESOL, 1997) specify three goals for second language learners:

Goal 1: To Use English to Communicate in Social Settings

Standard 1: Students will use English to participate in social interaction.

Standard 2: Students will interact in, through, and with spoken and written English for personal expression and enjoyment.

Standard 3: Students will use learning strategies to extend their communicative competence.

Goal 2: To Use English to Achieve Academically in All Content Areas

Standard 1: Students will use English to interact in the classroom.

Standard 2: Students will English to obtain, process, construct, and provide subject matter information in spoken and written form.

Standard 3: Students will use appropriate learning strategies to construct and apply academic knowledge.

Goal 3: To Use English in Socially and Culturally Appropriate Ways

Standard 1: Students will use the appropriate language variety, register, and genre according to audience, purpose, and setting.

Standard 2: Students will use nonverbal communication appropriate to audience, purpose, and setting.

Standard 3: Students will use appropriate learning strategies to extend their sociolinguistic and sociocultural competence. (pp. 9–10)

Besides the ESL standards that TESOL has designed to guide the instruction and assessment of English skills and knowledge for ELLs, states have developed their own ESL standards, which are often modeled after the TESOL standards.

Questions for Reflection

Are assessments in place that reflect whether ELLs are meeting content and language standards? To what extent are language standards assessed?

To what extent are assessment results disaggregated? Are standardized assessments coded in such a way that their performance can be linked to student variables such as native language proficiency, type of program, years in the program, and years exited from the program?

Critical Question #3:
Why Is Authentic Assessment Important for ELLs?

Authentic Assessment

Both researchers and practitioners support the use of authentic alternative assessments with ELLs (Fradd & Hudelson, 1995; Gottlieb, 1995; McNamara & Deane, 1995; O'Malley & Valdez Pierce, 1996; Pearson & Berghoff, 1996). O'Malley and Valdez Pierce (1996) define alter-

> *Traditional assessment techniques are often incongruent with ESL classroom practices.* (Hurley & Tinajero, 2001, p. 33)

native assessment as "any method of finding out what a student knows or can do that is intended to show growth and inform instruction and is an alternative to traditional forms of testing, namely, multiple choice tests" (p. 1). An alternative assessment is criterion-referenced and typically authentic because "it is embedded in classroom instruction and reflects real-life tasks, involves the learner in his or her own assessment, and has as its purpose to inform instruction" (Valdez Pierce, 2001, p. 66). Researchers agree that authentic assessment practices reflect a view of instruction that is more sensitive to the natural growth of English learners, provide a much more accurate picture of ELLs' progress and academic potential, and are more likely to promote effective instructional practices (Cummins, 2000; Valdez Pierce & O'Malley, 1992). The following principles help to provide guidelines for authentic assessment. Assessment should

- Help teachers find out what students know and can do, not what they cannot do (Cooter & Flynt, 1996).
- Grow out of authentic learning activities (Cooter & Flynt, 1996; Ruddell & Ruddell, 1995).
- Be tied to teachers' instructional goals (Ruddell & Ruddell, 1995), have a specific objective-linked purpose, and help teachers make instructional decisions (Cooter & Flynt, 1996).
- Be an integral part of instruction based on everyday classroom activities (Tinajero & Hurley, 2001).
- Take into consideration the diversity of students' cultural, linguistic, and special needs (Ruddell & Ruddell, 1995).
- Be collaborative, providing opportunities for students to evaluate their own work (Ruddell & Ruddell, 1995).
- Be multidimensional, based on a variety of observations, in a variety of situations, using a variety of instruments (McLaughlin & Vogt, 1996; O'Malley & Valdez Pierce, 1996; Ruddell & Ruddell, 1995).
- Be longitudinal and ongoing (Cooter & Flynt, 1996; Ruddell & Ruddell, 1995; Tinajero & Hurley, 2001).

Authentic assessments include performance assessments, portfolios, and student self-assessments (O'Malley & Valdez Pierce, 1996). A combination of all three assist in evaluating ELLs' language development and academic progress at all levels of proficiency by providing opportunities for ongoing assessment of student progress, integration of assessment and instruction, assessment of learning processes and higher-order thinking skills, and a teacher-student collaborative approach to assessment (Valdez Pierce & O'Malley, 1992). A combination can also be used to link both content and language standards to assessment (see Figure 4.6).

Performance assessment is defined as "assessment tasks that require students to construct a response, create a product, or demonstrate applications of knowledge" (O'Malley & Valdez Pierce, 1996, p. 239). Performance assessment examples (see Figure 4.6) are oral reports, writing samples, individual and group projects, exhibitions, and demonstrations. To be authentic, the criteria for scoring performance assessments (usually rubrics) are made public and discussed (Herman, Aschbacher, & Winters, 1992). Navarette and Gustke (1996) provide the following framework of six essential elements and related questions for selecting and designing a performance assessment system for ELLs:

1. **Connect Standards to Assessment.** Is the assessment linked to high content and performance standards that describe what all students should know and be able to do? Are the standards clear to the students and teachers involved?

2. **Link Instruction, Learning, and Assessment.** Does the assessment reflect both the content taught and the instructional approaches used?

3. **Enhance Performance Assessment Practices.** Is the assessment sensitive to the linguistic challenges faced by diverse students? Are promising practices in assessing linguistically diverse students considered in the design process?

4. **Ensure Meaningful Multiple Assessments.** Does the assessment system provide for meaningful multiple measures, providing students with opportunities to demonstrate their abilities and knowledge multiple times and over several tasks?

5. **Create Clear Scoring Criteria.** Are the scoring criteria clear and appropriate, providing usable and interpretable scores?

6. **Prepare Educators to Be Skilled Judges of Student Performance.** Do educators have the necessary training, background, support, and resources to use the assessment system in a reliable and valid manner for linguistically diverse students? If not, what type of training needs to be provided? (p. 9)

Portfolio assessment is defined as "a collection of student work showing student reflection and progress or achievement over time in one or more areas" (O'Malley & Valdez Pierce, 1996, p. 239). Because portfolio assessment is one of few assessment methods that accommodate the varying abilities of students, it is highly important for ELLs, especially those who are in the early stages of second language development. Oosterhof (1999) links portfolios to performance assessments in the following way:

> To some extent, the content of portfolios can be thought of as a series of performance assessments. To this exten t, the procedures for producing a performance assessment apply to designing portfolios....Portfolios, however, go beyond assessing students. They represent an instructional system and integrate assessment into student learning. (p. 184)

Portfolio entry examples (see Figure 4.6) are writing samples, reading logs, drawings, audio or videotapes, teacher and student comments on progress, and solutions to math problems that demonstrate problem-solving ability. The scoring criteria for portfolio assessment can include scoring guides, rubrics, checklists, or rating scales (O'Malley & Valdez Pierce, 1996). Portfolio assessment can be used to combine

> *The greatest advantage of using portfolios comes from the information they can provide on how ELL students are benefiting from instructional activities.* (O'Malley & Valdez Pierce, 1996, p. 54)

the information from both alternative and standardized assessments, and incorporates student reflection and self-monitoring as a key element of the process (Valdez Pierce & O'Malley, 1992). Portfolio contents can include performance-based assessments, scores on norm-referenced tests, results of state assessment tests, language proficiency tests, or other information that provides a picture of student progress.

Self-assessment is defined as "appraisal by a student of his or her own work or learning processes (O'Malley & Valdez Pierce, 1996, p. 240). Self-assessment and self-regulation are highly effective in helping students to improve their learning (Rudd & Gunstone, 1993; Smolen, Newman, Wathen, & Lee, 1995; Zimmerman & Martinez-Pons, 1990). Student self-assessment is an important element in authentic assessment and can and should be incorporated in performance and portfolio assessment.

Figure 4.6. Performance and Portfolio Assessments

Type	Information	Examples	
Performance Assessment			
Oral Language Assessment	Can take various forms depending on their authenticity regarding classroom activities, ■ Define the purpose first, ■ Administer appropriate language level assessments ■ Find authentic opportunities which the student has not prepared for ■ Assess social and academic proficiency over time	■ directed dialogues ■ incomplete story/topic prompts ■ oral interviews ■ picture cues ■ story retellings ■ simulations/situations	■ standardized language proficiency tests ■ student self-evaluations ■ Student Oral Language Observation Matrix (SOLOM) ■ teacher observation checklists
Reading Assessment	■ Focus on reading comprehension, not isolated reading skills ■ Assess reading proficiency in both languages	■ anecdotal records ■ cloze tests ■ individual reading inventory ■ miscue analysis ■ rating scales ■ reading comprehension checklists	■ reading logs ■ reading skills checklists ■ reading strategies ■ running records ■ story retellings ■ student self-assessments
Writing Assessment	■ Use developmentally appropriate prompts ■ Provide choice of topics ■ Check for cultural bias ■ Explain scoring criteria ■ Provide model papers	■ anecdotal records ■ checklists ■ dialogue journals ■ writing samples scored holistically with rater scales or with weights assigned to categories	■ student self-assessments
Portfolio Assessment			
	■ Collection of documents will depend on purpose of the assessment, ■ Most useful when each piece reflects progress toward learning goals	■ anecdotal records ■ checklists ■ conferencing forms ■ literacy development checklists ■ dialogue journals ■ reading logs ■ research papers ■ running records (miscue analysis)	■ self-assessments ■ taped oral readings ■ test results (formal and informal) ■ videotapes ■ writing samples ■ writing samples of problem-solving processes

Questions for Reflection

What assessments need to be designed and implemented to meet the learning needs of ELLs?

Are assessments in place that reflect whether ELLs are meeting grade-level outcomes and making appropriate progress?

Do you have assessments that reflect whether ELLs are sustaining growth over time? That indicate whether they are closing the achievement gap?

Leadership Challenge: What Principals Should Do

Critical Question

How will you promote and encourage systematic and appropriate assessment practices for ELLs?

Directions: As you read the following list of suggestions, check the items that best align to your school's vision, program goals, resources, and needs of your students. Items from the Principal's Survey in Chapter 1 are designated in bold font.

Vision and Leadership: Standards 1, 5

- **Have knowledge and understanding about the elements of effective programs.**
- **Communicate the vision.**
- **Examine current practices.**
- **Promote and maintain best practices.**
- **Advocate for equity.**
  - ☐ When developing the schoolwide vision and school goals, consider your school's assessment practices.
    - ✓ Are the beliefs, values, and commitments about student learning evident in assessment practices?
    - ✓ Does the assessment system have clearly articulated expectations and criteria? Does it shape a common vision of what students should know and be able to do?
    - ✓ Are high standards emphasized, and do multiple forms of assessment permit ELLs to demonstrate high standards?
    - ✓ Are authentic assessments used?
    - ✓ Are assessments culturally appropriate?

✓ Are assessment results used for diagnosis, to refine curriculum and instruction, and for program evaluation?

✓ Is the use of ELL data an essential component of school planning?

✓ Is there an effective system in place for data collection on ELLs?

✓ Is there a well-developed articulation plan for sharing ELL student assessment information?

✓ Is there a system in place for regularly informing ELL parents of student progress?

✓ Is the school culture supportive of efforts to improve assessment practices and achievement for ELLs?

✓ What should be added to the assessment practices? What should be eliminated?

Positive School Culture and Instructional Program: Standard 2

◆ **Recommend implementation of effective programs/practices.**

◆ **Ensure sustained attention to ELLs.**

◆ **Provide procedures for early data collection on ELLs.**

◆ **Monitor ELL students' language and academic development.**

☐ Develop/refine a comprehensive plan for the assessment of ELLs.

✓ Include alternative assessments that focus on content and application of content. Use various methods such as performance-based and portfolio evaluation that builds on students' strengths and backgrounds.

✓ Ensure that assessment for the purposes of identification, placement, and exit of ELLs involves the use of multiple measures.

✓ Evaluate the school's current procedures and tools for language assessments: formal L1 and L2 language assessment instruments (e.g., LAS, IPT, Woodstock-Muñoz), teacher observation rating scales (e.g., SOLOM), language interviews and checklists, informal classroom observations.

✓ Make sure that assessment for the purposes of identification and placement include some type of formal and/or informal native language proficiency assessment.

✓ Determine additional information that needs to be acquired on new students, how it will be acquired and shared, and how it will inform placement and instruction. This should include previous schooling and types of schooling information, as well as literacy in the home.

✓ Articulate clear criteria for placement (initial English language proficiency tests, native language assessments) and exit (language proficiency, standardized test scores in reading and content areas, reading levels, performance-based and portfolio assessments, writing proficiency, grades, teacher recommendation, parent input) of ELLs.

✓ Determine which academic assessments will be considered: standardized test scores, informal reading assessments, writing samples scored on a rubric, criterion-referenced tests.

✓ Include procedures in which assessment information is shared between grade levels, with next year's teachers to inform their instructional plans, and with current teachers for ELLs who are moving from one level of language support to another.

✓ Maintain records of ELLs' educational program(s) and years of schooling in English so that disaggregations can be made to examine their performance and the effects of the programs that serve them (LaCelle-Peterson & Rivera, 1994).

☐ Consider the use of additional assessment instruments:

✓ Acculturation Quick Screen: Measurement of ELLs' relative level of acculturation to the mainstream public school culture of the United States; helps distinguish between "culture shock" and a learning disability (Crosscultural Development Education Services).

✓ Snapshot Assessment System for Migrant, Language-Minority and Mobile Students: Content-area assessment tool for native language knowledge in language arts, mathematics, and science (K–6) (Mid-continent Regional Educational Laboratory).

☐ Establish a multidisciplinary assessment team that includes bilingual/ESL teachers to determine whether ELLs' difficulties are the result of language differences, cultural differences, opportunity to learn, or disabilities. Explore information with resource people who are familiar with the student's culture and language.

♦ **Foster a school climate that values cultural and linguistic diversity.**

☐ Monitor assessment tools to assure that they are culturally and linguistically responsive and unbiased.

☐ Ensure that teachers understand the relationship between first language and second language in both oral and written performance. ELLs often use different discourse styles and patterns.

✓ ELLs' writing patterns may differ from that of mainstream students. For example, Spanish speaking students often do not use English linear logic (beginning, middle, end) to write, but rather use a divergent pattern. When students write in English, they should be explicitly taught to use English discourse patterns, but when they write in Spanish, they should be taught to use and be assessed by the discourse patterns in Spanish (Escamilla & Coady, 2001).

✓ Assessments, such as writing rubrics that measure the output of ELLs, should be sensitive to the stages of second language acquisition and where individual students are in that process (use of punctuation, grammar, verb tenses). See Chapter 2.

☐ Allow students to respond to certain assessments in the language of their choice and ensure that some portfolio artifacts are in the students' native languages (e.g., writing samples).

◆ **Promote instructional approaches that foster content acquisition.**

◆ **Restructure the school to be a professional learning community.**

◆ **Hold high expectations for all students and make the achievement of ELLs a priority.**

◆ **Place high priority on training for all school staff to help them serve ELLs more effectively.**

◆ **Develop structures to strengthen curriculum and instruction.**

☐ Provide staff development on unique ELL assessment issues such as identification, placement, exit, evaluation of language proficiency, evaluation of students' content knowledge and skills, and cultural variables. Staff awareness of ELL assessment needs helps to prevent teachers recommending students for remedial or special education programs due to a lack of appropriate assessments or a misunderstanding of assessment issues (McKeon, 1994).

☐ Provide ongoing training, support structures, and meaningful opportunities (study groups, in-service training, workshops, conferences) that promote knowledge and implementation regarding the following:

✓ Appropriate assessments and their purposes.

✓ Connecting standards to assessment and assessment to instruction.

✓ Development of multiple and meaningful assessment tools that are valid, reliable, and free of biases.

✓ Development of explicit and understandable scoring criteria, ratings, and checklists.

✓ Time and opportunities for teachers to collaboratively score and interpret assessments, analyze data, and adjust instructional plans.

✓ Collaboratively choosing samples of student work representative of specific levels of performance (benchmarking).

✓ Administering, maintaining, and managing assessment records.

✓ How to inform students about the expected standards of achievement and how they will be assessed.

✓ Practice for students on the desired performance criteria.

✓ How to grade ELL students.

✓ How to distinguish between language difficulties and learning problems.

☐ Design and implement an assessment portfolio system that includes ELLs.

✓ Include ESL/bilingual teachers in deciding about the goals and content of the portfolios—what information is needed and how it can be provided.

✓ Develop scoring criteria and standards of performance aligned to state standards. Decide on common goals for student learning and how they will be assessed, develop scoring rubrics and checklists, and agree on standards of performance that should be demonstrated. Articulate benchmarks for ELLs.

✓ Provide staff development on the implementation of portfolios, scoring criteria, and benchmarks. Training should include a discussion of second language proficiency and its effect on student achievement. Efforts should be made to attain inter-rater reliability.

✓ Establish guidelines for administration; a standardized collection of student work; and the time, place, and manner in which standardized prompts will be given. Score the portfolios and report the results. Decide who will receive the information about the results and how often.

✓ Assess the effectiveness of the program and modify the scoring criteria based on feedback and results of the scored portfolios.

✓ Study the effects of the program on ELLs to determine whether improved information is available due to portfolio implementation (Gómez, 1999).

☐ Provide information to all teachers about "testing modifications" that your state allows and make sure your teachers use these modifications as needed when testing students in the classroom.

☐ Help teachers reduce unnecessary language complexity when creating their own tests:

✓ Eliminate unfamiliar or infrequent words.

✓ Shorten long nominal phrases.

✓ Change complex phrases to simple phrases.

✓ Change passive verbs to active verbs.

✓ Replace conditional clauses with separate sentences or change the order of the conditional and the main clause.

✓ Remove or rephrase relative clauses (Abedi, 2003).

☐ Remind teachers about assessment information when creating their own tests:

✓ Use pictures to enhance test items.

✓ Provide extra time.

✓ Provide a customized dictionary or glossary with extra time.

✓ Preteach "test language" and vocabulary.

✓ Multiple choice can be multiple guess.

✓ Manipulatives and other hands-on items lend themselves as assessment tools.

✓ Remember to ask, "Am I testing reading comprehension or content concepts?"

◆ **Assist teachers in increasing their certainty about the goals for student achievement.**

□ Together, determine ELL program goals and grade-level goals and how the goals for both will be measured.

✓ Develop authentic assessments for student outcomes based on state standards in each content area.

✓ Develop authentic assessments for specific outcomes in oral language, reading, and writing for second language proficiency (also native language proficiency in bilingual programs).

✓ Align ELL outcome plans and progress reports to identified student outcomes and assessments.

✓ Use English (and native language in bilingual programs) outcomes as criteria for moving through levels of support in the program and for exit criteria.

✓ Clearly communicate standards and expectations to students to foster student self-assessment.

◆ **Promote and monitor effective teaching and learning for ELLs.**

◆ **Provide substantial feedback to teachers on their teaching.**

□ Provide pressure, support, and leadership to classroom teachers in using effective assessment practices for ELLs.

✓ Monitor the work of individual teachers through discussion, checking lesson plans, evidence of student work, and assessments. Check the alignment of curriculum standards and determine whether teachers are teaching to the standards and how each teacher's ELLs are achieving.

✓ Monitor the work of the study groups. Are they evaluating current assessment techniques for ELLs? Are they examining, developing, and critiquing rubrics? Are they documenting evidence of ELL learning? Are they using student data to revise lesson plans and differentiate instruction?

✓ Ask grade-level teams to create products as a result of their study groups: statements of student outcomes by units of instruction, creation of common assessments and rubrics, team action plans based on analysis of data.

School Management: Standard 3

◆ **Facilitate ample opportunities for collaborative planning and design of curriculum and lessons.**

◆ **Allocate appropriate funding for materials, translation, and professional development.**

☐ Set up a comprehensive computerized data system on student performance. Ensure that teachers use the data system to review information on individual students and make informed decisions about instruction.

☐ Implement "electronic portfolios" in which student work is scored, scanned, and stored in a computer file. The portfolio can be maintained as a part of the student's permanent portfolio for future review.

☐ Allocate appropriate funding for staff development activities on alternative assessments and provide time for assessment-related training and collaboration .

☐ Provide professional materials for study groups. Examples include:

✓ O'Malley, J. M., & Valdez Pierce, L. (1996). *Authentic assessment for English language learners: Practical approaches for teachers.* New York: Addison-Wesley.

✓ Genesee, F., & Upshur, J. A. (1996). *Classroom-based evaluation in second language education.* New York: Cambridge University Press.

✓ Hurley, S. R., & Tinajero, J. V. (2001). *Literacy assessment of second language learners.* Needham Heights, MA: Allyn and Bacon.

✓ Valdez Pierce, L., & O'Malley, J. M. (1992). *Performance and portfolio assessment for language minority students.* (NCBE Program Information Guide Series, No. 9). Washington, DC: National Clearinghouse for Bilingual Education. (ERIC Document Reproduction Service No. ED346747). Available: http://www.ncela.gwu.edu/pubs/pigs/pig9.htm

✓ Müller, E., & Markowitz, J. (2004, March). *Synthesis brief: English language learners with disabilities.* Alexandria, VA: NASDSE, Project Forum. Available: http://www.nasdse.org/publications/ells.pdf

School and Community: Standards 4, 6

◆ **Take strong steps to work with ELLs' parents.**

◆ **Ensure that all communication to parents is provided in their native languages.**

☐ Access state websites for parent notification letters in various languages. Examples of letters for a variety of programs in multiple languages can be found at websites for Illinois (http://www.isbe.state.il.us/bilingual/htmls/parent_notification.htm) and New Jersey (http://www.state.nj.us/njded/bilingual/resources/letter/).

- [ ] Clearly communicate program and grade-level goals to parents. Discuss how these goals will be measured. Ensure that the goals are provided in parents' native languages.
- [ ] Ensure that grade cards and progress reports are provided in parents' native languages.
  - ✓ Add a student self-evaluation component that involves parents to grade cards and progress reports.
  - ✓ Provide information on students' progress in language proficiency.

- **Actively solicit bilingual parents, family members, and community volunteers to be involved.**

- **Advocate for language minorities in the school and community.**
  - [ ] Provide information so that the parents of ELLs understand the purpose and use of various assessments, including information about state assessments, achievement tests, classroom assessments, and diagnostic tests—how they are used, how their child is progressing, and what their roles are. Ensure that teachers regularly inform ELLs' parents about student progress.
  - [ ] When scores of state assessments are shared with parents and community members, explain that the scores are the result of a combination of a student's English language proficiency and academic knowledge, and that the academic achievement level in English does not accurately reflect ELLs' academic achievement level in their primary languages.
  - [ ] Actively solicit parent involvement in assessment activities. Set up specific procedures so that parents are able to view their children's portfolios. This enables parents to see examples of strengths and weaknesses of their child's progress. For example, portfolios or samples of student work could be sent home for parents and students to review together using guidelines such as those in Figure 4.7 (Cloud et al., 2000).

Figure 4.7. Guidelines for Parent-Student Conference on Student Work

Adapted from Cloud et al., 2000, p. 161.

Please review the attached work with your child and answer the following questions together. Thank you for helping your child to think about and share his or her work with you.

General guidelines:

- Always be supportive and positive.
- Avoid negative judgments or statements.
- Focus on what your child has done, not on what he or she has not done.
- Let your child do most of the talking.
- Listen carefully and make comments that build on what your child says.

Questions you might ask:

- What is this piece of work about?
- What parts do you like the most? Why?
- What parts were difficult?
- What parts were easy to do?
- What would you do differently if you were to do it again?

Please write your impressions of your child's work: _____

_____

_____

Child's Name: _____ Parent Signature: _____

Building the Vision

As you answer each of the following questions, think about what might be done to facilitate change. Seek staff, parent, and community input in identifying goals that will promote an effective assessment system based on the school's vision, resources, and population.

1. How will you share the research on assessment for ELLs with all staff?

2. What is the school's vision about assessment practices?

3. What are the parents' beliefs about assessment?

4. How will the school look and how will student achievement levels improve if your staff's beliefs about effective assessment practices are implemented?

5. Which strategies and suggestions in the Leadership Challenge will be appropriate for the school? How will you share the strategies and suggestions with all staff?

6. What are the priorities for improving the school's current assessment practices? What initial goals will the school implement to improve the assessment system?

7. How will you keep the vision and goals foremost in everyone's mind and tied to school activities?

8. What resources are needed to support school goals? How will assessment goals affect funding decisions? What information is needed?

9. What professional development training do teachers need to improve assessment practices? How will you determine their needs?

10. How can the school actively involve parents and the community in the assessment process?

11. How will the progress and impact of assessment goals be monitored?

5

Supportive Schoolwide Climate and Organizational Structures

Every child needs to feel welcome, to feel comfortable. School is a foreign land to most kids (where else in the world would you spend time circling answers and filling in the blanks?), but the more distant a child's culture and language are from the culture and language of school, the more at risk that child is. A warm, friendly, helpful teacher is nice but isn't enough. We have plenty of warm friendly teachers who tell the kids nicely to forget their Spanish and ask mommy and daddy to speak to them in English at home; who give them easier tasks so they won't feel badly when the work becomes difficult; who never learn about what life is like at home or what they eat or what music they like or what stories they have been told or what their history is. Instead, we smile and give them a hug and tell them to eat our food and listen to our stories and dance to our music. We teach them to read with our words and wonder why it's so hard for them. We ask them to sit quietly and we'll tell them what's important and what they must know to "get ready for the next grade." And we never ask them who they are and where they want to go.

Mary Ginley (Nieto, 1999, pp. 85–86)

Chapter Highlights: This chapter explores the research on the components of a supportive schoolwide climate, programming options, and effective organizational structures. In the Leadership Challenge, you will be able to identify specific ways that you and your staff can promote an effective school context for English language learners.

What Principals Should Know

Critical Questions

1. What are the components of a supportive schoolwide climate for English learners?
2. What program approaches are best for ELLs?
3. What factors contribute to effective parent involvement?

Essential Vocabulary

Culturally relevant curriculum and instruction: The selection of culturally relevant content, examples, modes of presentation, grouping structures, learning activities, reinforcers, motivational devices, and the like to promote understanding and learning (Cloud et al., 2000, p. 204).

Developmental bilingual education (also known as maintenance or late-exit bilingual education): A program that uses two languages, the student's primary language and English, as a means of instruction. The instruction builds upon the student's primary language skills and develops and expands the English language skills of each student to enable him or her to achieve competency in both languages (U.S. General Accounting Office, 1994).

Dual language program (also known as two-way immersion or two-way bilingual education): A bilingual program that allows students to develop language proficiency in two languages by receiving instruction in English and another language in a classroom that is usually made up of half native English speakers and half native speakers of the other language (Christian, 1994).

English as a second language (ESL): The field of English as a second language; courses, classes, and programs designed for students learning English as an additional language (TESOL, 1997).

English language development: Instruction designed for English language learners to develop their listening, speaking, and writing skills in English (NCELA, 2002).

Pullout ESL: Students are pulled out of their regular classrooms for specified periods of instruction to develop their English language skills.

Transitional bilingual education (also known as early-exit bilingual education): An instructional program in which subjects are taught in two languages—English and the native language of the ELL students—and English is taught as a second language. English language skills, grade promotion, and graduation requirements are emphasized. The primary purpose of these programs is to facilitate ELL students' transition to an all-English instructional environment while they receive academic subject instruction in the native language to the extent necessary. Transitional bilingual education programs vary in the amount of native language instruction provided and the duration of the program (U.S. General Accounting Office, 1994).

Critical Question #1:
What Are the Components of
a Supportive Schoolwide Climate for ELLs?

School Climate and Effective Schools Research

Research indicates that a supportive schoolwide climate is one of the important attributes of effective schools for ELLs (August & Hakuta, 1997; Berman et al., 1992; Berman et al., 1995; Carter & Chatfield, 1986; Lucas et al., 1990; Moll, 1988; Tikunoff, 1983; Tikunoff et al., 1991). A supportive schoolwide climate refers to the beliefs, assumptions, and expectations that teachers, students, and parents bring to the environment. In studies of effective schools (August & Hakuta, 1997; García, 1997a; Lucas et al., 1990), the following aspects have been identified as contributing to a supportive climate for ELLs:

- School leaders make the education of language minority students a priority.
- Value is placed on students' linguistic and cultural backgrounds.
- High academic expectations for student achievement are communicated to language minority students.
- School staff members share a strong commitment to empower language minority students through education.
- ELLs have integral involvement in the overall school operation.
- Parents of language minority students are encouraged to become involved in their children's education.

Value on Linguistic and Cultural Background

Acquiring a second language is not only cognitively challenging, it also has emotional, social, and political implications (Snow, 1990). Language is more than words—it is a part of one's personal, ethnic, and cultural identity,

> *The more students are affirmed in their identities, the more successful they will be.*

and learning a second language involves alterations in one's identity (Brown, 1992). This is particularly important when considering the needs of newcomers as they are going through the acculturation process and experiencing culture shock. Being in a new country and not being able to communicate disrupts a student's way of thinking, acting, and feeling. Newcomers may go through a range of emotions—feeling frustrated, angry, depressed, lonely, or homesick—which may result in physical ailments such as headaches, stomachaches, sleeplessness, or aggressive or withdrawn behavior. ELLs may also experience rejection from others, prejudice, and embarrassment. In addition, the classroom environment or program structure can create social and psychological distance among groups. As a result, the student may resist learning and experience emotional "blocks" or "trauma" when trying to speak English (Cummins, 1992).

However, in a culturally supportive school, educators are sensitive to ELLs' social/emotional factors, and value the linguistic and cultural backgrounds of their students (Berman et al., 1992, 1995; Lein et al., 1997; Lucas et al., 1990; Minicucci & Olsen, 1992; Moll, 1988; Ogbu & Matute-Bianchi, 1986). Carrasquillo and Rodriguez (1996) note that cultural differences in language and learning styles should not be seen as deficiencies, but instead should be used to facilitate learning. In exemplary schools with supportive climates, educators celebrate diversity and encourage students to enhance their native language skills (Lucas et al., 1990; Moll, 1988); build on their differences in language or culture (Sleeter & Grant, 1994); and acknowledge equal prestige to both the native and second languages during instruction and when eliciting student responses (Carter & Maestas, 1982). Jiménez (2001) found that the Latina/o students he worked with thrived when their specific backgrounds and national origins were recognized and when the challenges they faced in becoming proficient bilinguals were acknowledged. Furthermore, Gonzalez (1992) adds that "in order to motivate the children to become personally involved in their learning, teachers need to include many of their cultural and linguistic characteristics in the curriculum" (p. 32). August (2006) found that culturally meaningful material also facilitates comprehension.

High Expectations

In addition to learning English, ELLs need to develop content knowledge and the higher-order thinking skills that will be required of them in future schooling and employment. High expectations for all students, an element often cited in the effective

> *Teachers' attitudes and behaviors can make an astonishing difference in student learning.* (Nieto, 1999, p. 167)

schools literature, are particularly important for ELLs, of whom less is often expected (McLeod, 1996). Research has found that second language learners' success is often predetermined by teacher expectations (August & Hakuta, 1997) and that students achieve more when their teachers perceive them as able and interested in learning (Onosko, 1992). Teachers' expressions of high expectations for student success is a feature that is found in both effective bilingual and ESL classrooms (Berman et al., 1995; Carter & Chatfield, 1986; Tikunoff, 1985; Tikunoff et al., 1991). Teachers in effective schools communicate high expectations for all students, display strong demand for students' academic performance, and deny the cultural deprivation argument (Carter & Chatfield, 1986; Carter & Maestas, 1982; García, 1991a; Lein et al., 1997; Lucas et al., 1990).

Having high expectations of children does not mean making harsh demands on them. As Scheurich (1998) points out,

The belief is that high expectations remedy the supposed deficits that the children bring to school with them and the negative effects of low teacher expectations for some children. There is, also, a kind of harshness that sometimes accompanies this—that children should not be coddled or spoiled but should be pushed to achieve or taught the discipline of achievement. In contrast, in these highly successful schools, the focus on high expectations is based on the revolutionary belief that the natural condition of all children is high performance...and that this high performance is not based on pushing children but on providing loving, facilitating conditions that deliver learning in a way that fits, supports, engages, and energizes the child. (pp. 460–461)

In effective schools for ELLs, high expectations are reflected by continuously reinforced messages that high levels of learning and achievement are expected of all students (Berman et al., 1995). Examples include the kinds of learning events that teachers ask students to engage in (recall of information versus higher-order thinking) and how teachers use language with their students (frequency of interaction, type of interaction, and seating arrangements) (Schinke-Llano, 1983). Effective teachers ask many questions, including a high number of high-level questions, to all students (Gersten & Jiménez, 1994) (see Figure 5.1). In turn, students are more likely to perform well when asked and expected to answer higher-order questions (Henze & Lucas, 1993). High expectations are also reflected by how well the staff know and understand the communities from which their students come and the kind of comments that they make about them (Samway & McKeon, 1999). High expectations are also conveyed through personal relationships in which staff communicate to the students, "This work is important; I know you can do it; I won't give up on you" (Howard, 1990).

High expectations for ELLs are important not only within the classroom but also within the school. In high-achieving schools, principals communicate their expectations of high performance to everyone in the school (Cotton, 2003). A shared vision and common goals for all students include viewing English learners as highly capable students who are able to take on challenging work (Carter & Chatfield, 1986; Minicucci & Olsen, 1992; Moll, 1988; Stedman, 1987). Goldenberg and Sullivan's study (1994) credited school climate changes to the identification of schoolwide goals and high expectations for students, followed by consistent, visible, multiple, and long-term efforts to work toward the goals.

Building Staff Knowledge: Asking High-Level Questions

Materials: High-Level Question Cues (Figure 5.1, p. 148)
Time: 15 minutes

Highlight the following information: Research has found that second language learners' success is often predetermined by teacher expectations (August & Hakuta, 1997) and that students achieve more when their teachers perceive them as able and interested in learning (Onosko, 1992). Research has also found that expectations are reflected by the types of questions that teachers ask all students (Gersten & Jiménez, 1994). In turn, students are more likely to perform well when asked and expected to answer higher-order questions (Henze & Lucas, 1993).

Activity: Discuss in groups:
- Why do we ask students lower-level questions?
- Why don't we ask more high-level questions?
- What do we need to do to make sure we ask students higher-level questions?

Have each group briefly report out to the rest of the staff. Have each team set a goal for peer observations in terms of asking higher-level questions. Provide copies of the High-Level Question Cues (Figure 5.1, p. 148) on cardstock for each teacher to use to help prompt higher-level questions in the classrooms. In grade-level teams, have teachers collaboratively write high-level questions for their read-alouds or shared reading selections.

Follow-up: When observing classrooms, provide specific feedback to teachers on how often they ask higher-level questions and of whom. This can easily be done by recording the students' names with two columns, one for tallying each time the student is asked a question and a second for tallying each time the question was a high-level question. Discuss other examples of indicators of low and high expectations.

Figure 5.1. High-Level Question Cues

Level	Cue Words	Sample Questions
Evaluation: Development of opinions, judgments, decisions; making choices; assessing value	■ assess ■ choose ■ convince ■ decide ■ defend ■ determine ■ evaluate ■ explain ■ grade ■ judge ■ prioritize ■ prove ■ rank ■ rate ■ recommend ■ support	■ Do you agree with _____? ■ What choice would you have made? Why? ■ What do you think about _____? ■ How would you decide about? ■ Is _____ the right thing to do? Why or why not? ■ Explain why _____. ■ Based on what you know, how would you explain _____? ■ Why did the author write this story? ■ Why did the character choose _____? ■ Rank _____ according to _____. ■ How would you prove or disprove _____? ■ Would it be better if _____? ■ Would _____ have an effect on _____? Why or why not? ■ Which _____ seems best? ■ Would you recommend _____? Why or why not? ■ What information supports your view?
Synthesis: Combination of ideas to form a new whole; generalization from given facts or several areas	■ change ■ combine ■ compose ■ conclude ■ create ■ design ■ develop ■ imagine/make up ■ invent ■ plan ■ predict ■ rearrange ■ retell ■ rewrite ■ solve ■ suppose ■ what if?	■ What changes would you make to _____? ■ What ideas can you add to _____? ■ Add a new ending to _____. ■ Decide what you would do if _____. ■ How would you create or design a new _____? ■ Design a different way of _____. ■ Use your imagination to_____. ■ Pretend you are _____ and _____. ■ What solutions would you suggest for _____? ■ How would you improve _____? ■ What would you predict from _____? ■ List the events in sequence. ■ Rewrite or retell as a _____ (different character, version, ending). ■ How would you solve _____? ■ Suppose you could _____. What would you do? ■ What might happen if _____?
Analysis: Separation of a whole into component parts; seeing patterns or hidden meanings	■ analyze ■ arrange ■ categorize ■ classify ■ compare ■ contrast ■ decide ■ deduce ■ discover ■ divide ■ examine ■ explain ■ select ■ separate ■ summarize	■ What are the parts or features of _____? ■ Outline or web _____. ■ Classify _____ according to _____. ■ How does _____ compare and contrast with _____? ■ What things are different? ■ What things are similar? ■ Which events are fact? Which are opinion? Why? ■ What kind of person is _____? ■ What lesson did _____ learn from _____? ■ What evidence do we have for _____? ■ Sort this into _____ categories. ■ What are the parts of _____? ■ What is the relationship between _____? ■ What caused _____ to act the way he or she did? ■ Why do you think _____? ■ What evidence can you find for _____?

Involvement in Total School Organization

The research on effective schools shows that students, mainstream or ELLs, are more academically successful when they are in positive and challenging learning environments that integrate students rather than segregate them (Lindholm-Leary, 2005). Effective schools make the ELL program an integral part of the school organizational structure (McLeod, 1996), with English learners mixed with English-only students in a carefully planned manner to maximize educational and social success (Berman et al., 1995; McLeod, 1996; Tikunoff et al., 1991).

> *Interacting with English speaking peers provides ELLs with language practice, promotes an inclusive community feeling, and prevents social isolation and alienation by promoting the belief that these students are a part of a diverse mainstream, not a separate element of the school.* (McLeod, 1996)

If the program is isolated, ELLs often feel stigmatized and marginal (Cloud et al., 2000), but well-integrated programs help them feel a part of the school and give all students a greater appreciation of other languages and cultures.

Exemplary schools use creative ways to include ELLs in the regular educational program and to meet their language and content needs. Rather than being segregated from English speaking students all day, ELLs are integrated whenever possible in academic and social contexts, providing them with opportunities to learn conversational English from their peers (Berman et al., 1995; McLeod, 1996). Cooperative groupings help students to successfully participate in classroom activities, learn from each other, and feel valued (Berman et al., 1995; Schunk & Hanson, 1985; Slavin, 1987). Wong Fillmore, Ammon, McLaughlin, and Ammon (1985) note that all learners, especially Hispanic students, profit from opportunities to interact with their English speaking peers. The educational program in exemplary schools addresses the needs of all students, and English language proficiency is only one of many criteria used to group students, not the only one. Examples of creative structures include the following (Berman et al. 1995; McLeod, 1996):

- ELL programs are integrated into the total school program through developmental, ungraded "wings" (early childhood, primary, middle, and upper) to accommodate the many newcomer students with wide ranges of educational backgrounds and to allow for different grouping strategies.
- Students and teachers are divided into "families" for each grade level, with additional families for newcomer immigrant students.
- Teachers work in instructional teams where students are kept with the same teachers for several years (see Leadership Challenge for more detailed information).

Questions for Reflection

What are your teachers' beliefs about the ELLs in their classrooms? Do your beliefs align with the teachers' beliefs?

How is respect for students' languages and cultures valued, embraced, and celebrated in your school?

Are students encouraged to build on their native language skills and cultural identities, or are they made to feel that they must "take on a new identity" in order to be educated?

Does the school diminish or promote student potential? Do staff exhibit high academic expectations for all students?

Are high quality curricula accessible to your ELLs?

How are your second language learners an integral part of your school?

Critical Question #2:
What Program Approaches Are Best for ELLs?

Program Models

English learners need language instruction educational programs that allow them to progress academically while they are acquiring English language skills. In fact, the recent research synthesis of Genesee and colleagues (2005) noted the importance of a language program specifically designed for ELLs:

> ELLs are more successful when they participate in programs that are specially designed to meet their needs (ESL, bilingual, etc.) than in mainstream English classrooms and when the program is consistent throughout the student education. A program that is enriched, consistent, provides a challenging curriculum, and incorporates language development components and appropriate assessment approaches is also supported by the findings of the research in this corpus. (p. 377)

A wide array of programs with a variety of titles and definitions exists for English learners (see Figure 5.2, p. 151), all of which include both academic content and English language development components. The effectiveness of the various program models has long been a controversial topic, and although one program model may be better than another in a particular situation, researchers agree that "there is no one right way to educate English-language learners; different approaches are necessary because of the great diversity of conditions faced by schools" (August & Hakuta, 1997, p. 174). The specific model a school district implements will depend on school demographics (type, number, and concentration of ELLs), student characteristics (age, academic background, and English proficiency level) and available resources (ability to find qualified personnel, availability of classroom space) (Rennie, 1993).

Figure 5.2. Program Models

Zelasko & Antunez, 2000.

Characteristics of the Major Program Models for ELL Students				
Typical Program Names	Native Language of LEP Students	Language of Content Instruction	Language Arts Instruction	Linguistic Goal of Program
Language(s) of Instruction: English and the Native Language				
Two-way Bilingual Education, Bilingual Immersion, or Dual Language Immersion	Ideally, 50% English speaking and 50% LEP students sharing same native language	Both English and the native language	English and the native language	Bilingualism
Late-exit or Developmental Bilingual Education	All students speak the same native language	Both; at first, mostly the native language is used. Instruction using English increases as students gain proficiency	English and the native language	Bilingualism
Early-exit or Transitional Bilingual Education	All students speak the same native language	Both at the beginning, with quick progression to all or most instruction using English	English; native language skills are developed only to assist transition to English	English acquisition; rapid transfer into English-only classroom
Language(s) of Instruction: English				
Sheltered English, Specially Designed Academic Instruction in English, Structured Immersion, or Content-based ESL	Students can share the same native language or be from different language backgrounds	English adapted to the students' proficiency level, and supplemented by gestures and visual aids	English	English acquisition
Pull-out ESL	Students can share the same native language or be from different language backgrounds; students may be grouped with all ages and grade levels	English adapted to the students' proficiency level and supplemented by gestures and visual aids	English; students leave their English-only classroom to spend part of their day receiving ESL instruction	English acquisition

Programs are primarily defined by the amount of native language instruction, the mix of students' linguistic backgrounds, and the goals of the program. Most existing programs can be placed into two categories based on the languages that are used to provide instruction, English as a second language and bilingual education. ESL programs primarily use English, and bilingual programs use the native language. However, within the models, a variety of native-language instruction and/or support can be used, as well as various approaches to fostering English language development.

In ESL models, instruction is provided using English. These models feature some form of English language development and may teach grade-level content. Description of the primary ESL models follows:

- **Pullout ESL:** Students are pulled out of their classrooms for specified periods of instruction to develop their English language skills. The main focus is on communication, grammar, and vocabulary. Academic content is addressed through mainstream classes, where native-language support from a bilingual paraprofessional might be provided.

- **Sheltered instruction/structured immersion/content-based instruction/also known as sheltered English or "Specially Designed Academic Instruction in English" (SDAIE):** Students are provided with grade-level standards-based instruction in English in ways that provide comprehensible and accessible input. Instruction also promotes English language development. Sheltered instruction requires the use of differentiated and scaffolded instructional strategies that make the content comprehensible (see Chapter 2) such as the use of visuals, graphic organizers, gestures, modeling, demonstrations, and hands-on activities. Sheltered instruction can be used as an instructional strategy or a program model (Genesee, 1999). It can be used in various formats and at different times such as during literacy blocks or sheltered content classes, and through ESL classes, team teaching, or sheltered instruction in the mainstream classroom.

In bilingual education programs, content instruction is provided through both English and the students' native language while the students develop English proficiency (see Chapter 3). All bilingual programs include an English language development component. The models include the following:

- **Transitional bilingual education (TBE)/also known as early-exit bilingual education:** Students receive academic instruction in their native language while making the transition to English-language instruction. This model uses native language instruction for academics so that students do not fall behind in their subjects, but the goal of the program is to exit students as quickly as possible to all English "mainstream" classrooms.

- **Developmental bilingual education (DBE)/also known as maintenance or late-exit bilingual education:** Students receive academic instruction in their native language (usually five years or more) while making a gradual transition to English-language instruction. The goals of the program are fluent bilingualism and academic proficiency in both the native language and English with some native-language instruction maintained for an extended time after they have become fully English-proficient.

- **Two-way immersion (TWI)/also known as two-way bilingual education or dual-language immersion:** This model combines developmental bilingual education for language-minority students and foreign-language immersion for English speaking students. Ideally, half of the students are native English speakers and half are second language learners who speak the same language. Both groups of students receive academic instruction in both languages, with the goal being to develop academic proficiency in both languages. Models are sometimes referred to as 90–10, 80–20, 50–50, referring to the percentages of academic instruction through the minority language and the majority language (see Chapter 3).

In examining the research on various program models, Genesee and colleagues (2005) state

> [R]esearch was consistent in showing that ELLs who received any specialized program (bilingual or English as a Second Language) were able to catch up to, and in some studies surpass, the achievement levels of their ELL and English speaking comparison peers who were educated in English-only mainstream classrooms. (p. 375)

Also, students who participated in programs with extended instruction using their first language (two-way immersion and late-exit programs) outperformed students who received only short-term instruction using their first language (early-exit programs) (Cazabon et al., 1998; Fulton-Scott & Calvin, 1983; Lindholm, 1991), and students who were in an assortment of programs or who had not been in a specialized program had low levels of achievement and the highest dropout rates (Genesee et al., 2005; Thomas & Collier, 2002).

Programming and Customized Learning Environment

No single approach or program model works best in every situation. Researchers recommend that schools identify the conditions under which one approach or some combination of approaches is best suited and then adapt

> *Effective schools used a combination of approaches to meet students' needs.*

programs, instructional approaches, and use of primary languages that would best serve their students, meet their goals and needs, and match local resources and conditions (Berman et al., 1995; Genesee, 1999). Bilingual education is often not possible in schools because of the prevalence of different languages, a lack of bilingual personnel, or lack of support from the state. Instead, students are often placed in ESL programs. However, ESL programs that focus on language development and give little attention to subject-area curricula have been found to be the least effective programs. One solution has been the integration of language and content (Chapter 2), which has shown to be more effective than approaches that teach English in isolation (Thomas & Collier, 1997, 2002).

Effective schools described in the literature organized comprehensive programs of language and academic development for ELLs, often using a combination of bilingual, sheltered, and ESL approaches to meet the various needs of their students (Berman et al., 1995; McLeod, 1996; Texas Education Agency, 2000). All schools used students' primary languages for developing literacy skills, delivering content, or both. Teachers also used high-quality sheltered instruction. Rather than relying on segregated or pullout ESL classes as the main way of helping students acquire English, the schools used innovative ways to organize time and teaching resources, grouping and regrouping students during the day for different instructional purposes (Berman et al., 1995; McLeod, 1996). They also provided carefully planned transitions to mainstream classes, with added support for students through after-school tutoring or extended school year programs. Teachers met regularly to collaboratively plan and develop instruction, coordinating both horizontally and vertically (Berman et al., 1995; McLeod, 1996; Texas Education Agency, 2000).

Based on their research findings and the findings of other researchers, Thomas and Collier (1997) offer the following recommendations regarding programming decisions:

- Action 1: Don't "water down" instruction for English language learners and don't completely separate them from the instructional mainstream for many years, but also don't dump them into the mainstream unassisted until they are ready to successfully compete with native English speakers when taught in English.

- Action 2: Provide opportunities for parents to assist their children using the parents' first language, the one they know best and the one in which they can best interact with their children at a higher cognitive level.

- Action 3: Provide continuing cognitive development and academic development while your students are learning English by means of the use of their first language in instruction for a part of each school day.

- Action 4: Use current approaches to instruction, emphasizing interactive, discovery learning and raising the cognitive level of instruction in all classrooms by avoiding "drill and kill" programs that may have positive short-term effects but which fail to allow students to sustain their achievement gains across time and to reach full parity with native speakers of English.

- Action 5: Improve the sociocultural context of schooling for all of your students, English learners and native-English speakers alike.

- Action 6: If you can, try to move away from an emphasis on all-English instruction and move away from less effective forms of bilingual education.

Try to move toward one-way and two-way developmental bilingual education (mainstream, enrichment bilingual education, rather than remedial approaches) as the program alternatives that may allow your students to eventually reach full educational parity with native speakers of English in your school.

- Action 7: If, for pragmatic and practical reasons (e.g., a low-incidence language or shortage of bilingual teachers), you must use all-English instruction, select and develop its more effective forms. Specifically, try to move your school away from its least effective form, ESL pullout, and move toward the use of ESL taught through academic content and current approaches to teaching as a more efficacious alternative that helps students develop academically and cognitively to a greater degree.

- Action 8: If you are now implementing transitional bilingual education at the elementary school level, try to move toward an alternative that is even more effective in the long-term—one-way or two-way developmental bilingual education.

- Action 9: If you are now implementing two-way bilingual education, work on more fully developing a valid and effective implementation of this approach.

- Action 10: If you're concerned about cost-effectiveness, be aware that it is most cost-effective to teach the grade-level, mainstream curriculum (not a watered-down version) to English language learners and language minority students who are proficient in English using a bilingual teacher, teaching a mainstream bilingual class.

- Action 11: Think "enrichment" rather than "remediation" when you design programs for English language learners. Your English learners are not "broken" and they don't need fixing. (pp. 77–79)

See Building Staff Knowledge on p. 156 for activities to examine program models with your staff.

Questions for Reflection

Do the organizational structures of your school support cross-cultural interaction?

Has your school considered a combination of second language approaches to meet the needs of your students? Are your students grouped in ways that maximize learning?

What support is provided to students who are transitioning to mainstream classes?

Building Staff Knowledge:
Examining Program Models

Adapted from York-Barr, Sommers, Ghere, & Montie, 2001.

Materials: Information and research about the program model(s) you are proposing and a table card in six different colors.

Time: 90 minutes

Activity: Assign one color to six different subgroups of staff. Write on a large sheet of poster paper: "What program model(s) will improve our current programming for ELLs?" Post the question so that it is visible to all staff. Each group should have a recorder who will take notes and report on the ideas that are recommended by the various "colors."

- **White = Data:** What does the research say? How effective has this program been and under what specific circumstances?
- **Yellow = Optimism:** What are the positive aspects of this program? Who will benefit as a result of implementing this?
- **Black = Caution:** What are the downsides to this program? What are the negatives as a result of implementing this?
- **Red = Emotion:** How will people react to this program? Who will be upset by this?
- **Green = Growth:** How will this affect student achievement? What will students and staff learn as a result of this? How will students and staff change and grow as a result of this?
- **Blue = Process:** What information will the staff, the board, and the community need in order to understand this program? Who could put the process together? How will we introduce this idea to the staff and other stakeholders?

After each individual or group has had time to reflect upon their questions, each "color" should report their findings to the entire group. The recorder should make notes of the findings.

Follow-up: Engage in further discussions about implementation, combining programs, prioritizing goals, and establishing timelines. Ask the following questions:

- Which program or combination of programs corresponds with our vision for ELLs?
- What are our beliefs about our current practices?
- What should our goals be to improve programming for ELLs?
- What commitments are we willing to make?

Critical Question #3:
What Factors Contribute
to Effective Parent Involvement?

Benefits of Parent Involvement

Compelling research evidence has emphasized the positive effects of parental involvement on children's academic achievement
(Carrasquillo & London, 1993; Delgado-
Gaitan, 1991; Epstein, 1990; Quelmatz,
Shields, & Knapp, 1995). Researchers have
established a positive correlation between
parents' active participation in their children's
learning and the children's sustained gains in
academic achievement (Bermúdez &
Márquez, 1996; Carrasquillo & London, 1993;
Ochoa & Mardirosian, 1996; Shartrand, Weiss, Kreider, & Lopez, 1997). In addition,
positive effects of parent-school partnerships have been found with both low- and
middle-income populations as well as with populations of different racial and ethnic
groups (Dauber & Epstein, 1993; Delgado-Gaitan, 1990; Epstein & Dauber, 1991;
Hidalgo, Bright, Sui, Swap, & Epstein, 1995).

> *There is considerable evidence that parent involvement leads to improved student achievement, better school attendance, and reduced dropout rates, and that these improvements occur regardless of the economic, racial, or cultural background of the family."*
> (Inger, 1992, p. 1)

The benefits of a positive relationship between schools and parents include increased family participation in the schools, increased student attendance, decreased
dropout rates, positive parent-child communication, improved student attitudes and
behavior, and more parent and community support of the school (Carrasquillo &
London, 1993; Inger, 1992). English language learners are more likely to succeed
when their parents participate in their education by helping with homework, attending school events, conferring with teachers, serving as volunteers, or participating in
school governance (Bermúdez & Márquez, 1996; Tse, 1996).

Barriers to Parent Involvement

Although the research repeatedly documents that successful programs for ELLs
maintain ongoing and guided parental involvement (Genesee, 1999), barriers such as
the following prevent parent participation in the educational system:

- Lack of knowledge about school systems in the United States and about
  the role that family members are expected to play or can play in schooling
  in the United States
- Parents believing that they should not interfere with the role of educators

- Failure of the school to communicate with parents in a language they understand, and lack of access to a person at the school who speaks the parents' language
- Parents feeling powerless when they cannot resolve problems or advocate for their children because they are not fluent in English
- Parents feeling judged regarding their occupation, economic status, or group membership (ethnicity or social class)
- Scheduling of activities at times and places that are not convenient or accessible to parents
- Isolation from the community at large due to limited English, undocumented status, fear of violence, lack of access to safe and reliable public transportation, or lack of child care
- Lack of activities and information relevant to parents and their children
- Parents' negative educational experiences, such as discrimination and humiliation for speaking Spanish when they were in school

(Boethel, 2003; Epstein & Dauber, 1991; Lucas, 1993; Nicolau & Ramos, 1990; Ritter, Mont-Reynaud, & Dornbusch, 1993)

Although three-fourths of children of immigrants are born in the United States and are U.S. citizens, many have undocumented parents who are apprehensive about interacting with public institutions such as schools because they fear deportation or immigration-related consequences (Capps, 2005). Sometimes parents are unable to participate in their child's education because they have more pressing personal needs due to their recent arrival, such as language issues, searching for safe and affordable housing, or needing help for trauma or culture shock (Violand-Sánchez, Sutton, & Ware, 1991). Some are hesitant to participate in school activities that involve spoken English (calling to report the child's absences, parent-teacher conferences, volunteering). In some cultures, parents are not expected to take an active role in the educational system, or the role is very different from the one expected in the United States. For example, some Latino parents believe that the roles of the home and the school are very distinct and that one should not interfere with the other. The parents often see their role as providing basic needs and making sure the students are respectful and well-behaved. However, they view the teacher as one who provides knowledge, a highly respected role that they cannot and should not interfere with, and the school system as "a bureaucracy governed by educated non-Hispanics whom they have no right to question" (Nicolau & Ramos, 1990, p. 13).

Barriers to School Involvement

Since a large percentage of underachieving students come from minority backgrounds, many from non-English speaking homes, the problem of underachievement is compounded because teachers rarely understand the cultural or linguistic backgrounds of families and have limited communication with them (Samway & McKeon, 1999). Ochoa and Mardirosian (1996) cite examples in which low parent participation is, in many ways, related

> *The families of language minority students are usually not involved in the school, due to educators' perceptions that these parents do not care about their children or would not help them even if contacted.* (Carrasquillo & Rodriguez, 1996, p. 55)

to low expectations of students' academic success. Parents are often perceived as being uninterested, and students are frequently perceived as being "disadvantaged," having deficits in their family environment or abilities (Díaz, Moll, & Mehan, 1986). August (2006) found that language minority parents have the desire and often the ability to help their children succeed academically, but schools often "underestimate and underutilize parents' interest, motivation, and potential contributions" (p. 9). Although many immigrant parents come from cultures where it is not proper to intervene in the school's business or question teachers' methods, when they are given opportunities to be involved, their families are just as involved as other families (Kohl, Lengua, & McMahon, 2000).

One of the most promising ways to increase student achievement is to involve students' families (Chavkin, 1993; Henderson & Berla, 1994). Researchers suggest that educators need a supportive belief system about family and community involvement and strategies for how to make connections with family and community. Nicolau and Ramos (1990) state that educators must discard the deficit model of working with families and operate on an enrichment model based on the idea that parents truly want the best for their children. They must tell parents that they are as important as the school, and they must tell students how important their homes and communities are. Educators also need to understand that they must be more proactive in partnering with marginalized parents on the parents' terms (Lopez, 2001), believe that they are the most important factor in making the connections happen, and display caring attitudes to facilitate that relationship (Noddings, 1995). The principal must also play a key role in parent and community involvement by providing strong leadership and administrative support (Espinosa, 1995).

Moll, Amanti, Neff, and González (1992) propose that parent involvement start with a strengths perspective, with educators viewing students and parents as "funds of knowledge," validating their life experiences as worthy of inclusion in the classroom curriculum. In this model, educators focus on students' languages and cultures as strengths and resources, instead of viewing them from a deficit perspective. "Funds of knowledge" include essential knowledge and information about students' languages, cultural practices, and families. In order to develop and use these "funds," teachers need to gather information about their students and their environments, parents, and communities. Teachers then use this information to build on and validate students' knowledge and culture and to develop lessons that help create a meaningful and culturally relevant curriculum for ELLs.

Eliminating Barriers

Joyce Epstein, director of the Center on School, Family, and Community Partnerships at John's Hopkins University, has identified six types of involvement that can help families, schools, and communities come together to support children's education. Effective partnership programs between schools and communities formulate plans and specific goals that address these types of involvement:

> *These parents care deeply about their children and would like to help if they are invited, made to feel welcome, and are specifically told what to do to improve their children's educational performance.* (Carrasquillo & Rodriguez, 1996, p. 55)

1. **Parenting:** Families must provide for the health and safety of children and maintain a home environment that encourages learning and good behavior in school. Schools provide training and information to help families understand their children's development and how to support the changes they undergo.

2. **Communicating:** Schools must reach out to families with information about school programs and student progress. This includes the traditional phone calls, report cards, and parent conferences, as well as new information on topics such as school choice and making the transition from elementary school to higher grades. Communication must be in forms that families find understandable and useful. For example, schools can use translators to reach parents who don't speak English well. Communication must also go both ways, with educators paying attention to the concerns and needs of families.

3. **Volunteering:** Parents can make significant contributions to the environment and functions of a school. Schools can get the most out of this process by creating flexible schedules so more parents can participate and by working to match the talents and interests of parents to the needs of students, teachers, and administrators.

4. **Learning at Home:** With the guidance and support of teachers, family members can supervise and assist their children at home with homework assignments and other school-related activities.

5. **Decision-making:** Schools can give parents meaningful roles in the school decision-making process and provide parents with training and information so they can make the most of those opportunities. This opportunity

should be open to all segments of the community, not just people who have the most time and energy to spend on school affairs.

6. **Collaboration with the Community:** Schools can help families gain access to support services offered by other agencies, such as health care, cultural events, tutoring services, and after-school child care programs. They also can help families and community groups provide services to the community, such as recycling programs and food pantries (Epstein, 1997).

Effective schools for ELLs have high expectations for parental involvement. They work to overcome the obstacles and make it a priority to actively encourage and facilitate parents' involvement in their children's schooling (Lucas, 1993). Educators view ethnically and linguistically diverse parents as concerned individuals who are willing and able to be involved in their children's education. Research studies have shown that schools can increase parent and community involvement and build trust through the following methods:

- Build on the cultural values of families
- Make a strong commitment to home-school communication (bilingual staff, telephone calls, written communication in parents' home languages, translated meetings) with an emphasis on personal contact with families (face-to-face communication and home visits)
- Provide a warm environment for families
- Provide adult English classes, family literacy programs, and formal parent support activities
- Invite, encourage, and persevere in getting parents to volunteer and become actively involved in their children's learning
- Facilitate accommodations for family involvement (transportation, translators, child care, other services)
- Communicate information about parent expectations (for example, that parents are to expected to attend parent-teacher conferences)
- Establish shared governance and advocacy groups
- Provide staff development on the cultural characteristics of the families
- Make referrals to community agencies, services, and resources.

(Berman et al., 1995; Boethel, 2003; Delgado-Gaitan, 1991; Espinosa, 1995; García, 1991b; Henderson & Mapp, 2002; Lucas et al., 1990; McLeod, 1996; Nicolau & Ramos, 1990; Stedman, 1987)

Communication is a key factor in encouraging and soliciting parent involvement in effective schools (see Figure 5.3). Parents are often not able to visit the school due to transportation or work schedules, so schools must go beyond written communication and telephone contact. Written communications, even when they are translated, are often written at a high literacy level, assume that all families are literate, and are less effective than personal conferences. Home visits or visits at a neutral site, such as a community center, demonstrate the school's commitment to parent communication, provide face-to-face communication with parents, give insight into the child's needs and influences, establish positive and personal relations with the family, and assist in understanding parental concerns (Inger, 1992; Sosa, 1997). The first meeting with parents should be held outside of the school in a less threatening environment; should primarily be a social event, with business goals reserved for following meetings; and should involve extended family members when appropriate (Nicolau & Ramos, 1990; Procidano & Fisher, 1992; Sosa, 1997).

Calderón and Carreon (1999) recommend family support teams who help "families feel respected and welcomed in the school and become active supporters of their children's education" (p. 182). In this model, parents learn strategies and ways they can facilitate literacy when reading with their children in their primary language. A study of literacy practices in Latino families found that when mothers were given explicit instruction on using literacy activities with their children at home, they reported engaging in substantially more activities directly related to their children's schooling (Melzi, Paratore, & Krol-Sinclair, 2000). August (2006) reported that participating in more home literacy experiences is related to superior literacy outcomes.

Schools in studies by Berman and colleagues (1995) and McLeod (1996) established formal parent outreach committees and employed community liaisons for outreach services. Bilingual aides called home when students were absent; translated written materials to be sent to parents; interpreted at parent-teacher conferences; made home visits; and helped families acquire medical care, clothing, and other services. Some schools entered into partnerships with families and agencies to ensure that the health and social service needs of their students were met. Services included food assistance, clothing, health and dental care, counseling, substance abuse prevention, and gang prevention. The schools also involved parents in school governance committees and invited parents to serve in other capacities; had designated parent centers where parents could hold meetings, work on projects for teachers, and socialize; and offered parent workshops on parenting topics, study skills, gang awareness, communication skills, college awareness, and English classes.

Questions for Reflection

What are your staff's beliefs about the parents of ELLs? How are they valued?

How do the parents feel about the school? Do they feel welcomed and valued? What are the parents' needs?

Are effective strategies for parental engagement in place? If so, are they working? If not, what needs to be done?

What are the students' needs? What parent activities could have a direct impact on student achievement?

Figure 5.3. Parent Survey

Parent Names:

1. What are the most convenient times for you to come to the school or a meeting?

2. What times are best for you to participate in school activities?

     (Please mark with an X the time slots and days that fit your schedule.)

	Monday	*Tuesday*	*Wednesday*	*Thursday*	*Friday*
Morning 8:00 a.m.–12:00 p.m.					
Afternoon 12:00 p.m.–5:00 p.m.					
Evening 6:00 p.m.–10:00 p.m.					

3. Do you need child care for your other children when you visit the school?
        Yes   No
4. Do you need transportation to the school?
        Yes   No
5. Would you like a family member to come with you?
        Yes   No
6. Do you need an interpreter?
        Yes   No

(Please mark with an ✓ those items you are interested in.)

What would you like to know more about?	**What would you like to do?**
☐ bilingual/ESL education ☐ what your child learns in school ☐ how to help your child with math and reading ☐ volunteering to help in the classroom ☐ how U.S. schools are different from your native country's schools ☐ community services (health, dental, counseling, housing, transportation)	☐ visit your child's classes ☐ talk to the teacher about your child ☐ talk to other parents about the school's programs ☐ volunteer to help in the classroom ☐ attend parenting classes ☐ participate on a parent committee

Building Staff Knowledge:
Needs Assessment

Materials: Needs assessment chart

Activity: Examine the comprehensiveness of school programs that promote an effective school climate. In small groups, generate a list of staff, student, and family needs. After the first column is complete, discuss what is in place or needs to be in place (programs, supports, resources) to fully respond to the identified needs. The lists that are generated will provide a good starting place for your family school committee. Many of the suggestions in the Leadership Challenge will help to provide ideas for the committee.

Staff, Student, or Family Need	Programs We Have/What We Have Done	Has This Made a Difference?	Programs We Need/What We Need To Do
Need for staff understanding about cultures			
Culture shock of students and parents			
Students with interrupted schooling			
Non-English speaking parents			
Parents without transportation			
Welcoming school climate			
Parents' lack of knowledge about school system			
Lack of high expectations for ELLs			
Literacy training			

Follow-up: The school-community committee should discuss what has happened after the needs assessment was completed. The staff should then prioritize the list of suggested issues and needs and set goals together for an action plan and how to assess the impact of the action steps.

Leadership Challenge:
What Principals Should Do

Critical Question

How will you promote and encourage a positive schoolwide climate and effective organizational structures in your school?

As you read the following suggestions, check the items that best align to your school's vision, program goals, resources, and student needs. Items from the Principal's Survey in Chapter 1 are designated in bold font.

Vision and Leadership: Standards 1, 5

- **Communicate the vision.**
- **Examine current practices.**
- **Advocate for equity.**
  - ☐ When developing the schoolwide vision and school goals, consider the climate and organizational structures of the school.
    - ✓ Are the beliefs, values, and commitments about student learning evident in valuing students' backgrounds, high expectations, and parent and community involvement?
    - ✓ Are district and school leaders strong advocates for the educational success of ELLs?
    - ✓ Do ELLs have adequate and appropriate opportunities to meet state standards? Have the same academic goals been set for ELLs as for mainstream students?
    - ✓ Do staff members display high expectations of ELLs and believe that they are capable of achieving academic success?
    - ✓ Are staff members sensitive to students' backgrounds? To what extent are students' linguistic and cultural backgrounds recognized and valued?
    - ✓ Is the curriculum connected to students' life experiences?
    - ✓ Are staff members representative of the major cultural groups of your students?
    - ✓ Are organizational structures based on students' needs? Do organizational structures facilitate student interaction and involvement with the whole school?
    - ✓ Does the current programming model maximize educational success for ELLs?
    - ✓ Are materials of high quality, culturally and developmentally appropriate, and accessible to ELLs?
    - ✓ Is the school culture welcoming and supportive of efforts to improve achievement for all students?

✓ What should be added to the school climate and organizational structures to increase ELL achievement? What practices should be eliminated?

◆ **Have knowledge and understanding about the elements of effective programs.**

◆ **Foster knowledge and understanding about the research.**

◆ **Advocate for programs.**

◆ **Promote and maintain best practices.**

☐ Actively seek external partners and research information to develop the best programming model for your ELLs. Ensure that there is a schoolwide commitment to providing all students with an equal opportunity to learn the same challenging content and high-level skills as native English speakers. Defend and promote programs that will provide the best opportunities for your ELLs.

☐ Share the research on effective schoolwide climate and organizational structures for ELLs with all staff. Engage the staff in evaluating the school's climate and organizational structures to support and enhance the education of ELLs. Ask, "What ELL needs are not being addressed by our school? What organizational structures or aspects of school climate do we need to implement to serve these students better?"

☐ Keep family and community on every agenda and encourage staff members to foster family and community relations on a daily basis.

☐ Organize a school-community committee of staff, parents, and community members for the main purpose of improving school climate and school-community relations.

Positive School Culture and Instructional Program: Standard 2

◆ **Recommend implementation of effective programs and practices.**

◆ **Promote instructional approaches that foster biliteracy development and content acquisition.**

◆ **Foster a school climate that values cultural and linguistic diversity.**

☐ Value bilingualism and diversity. Encourage teachers to acknowledge both the native and second languages during instruction and when eliciting student responses (Carter & Maestas, 1982).

☐ Have open and frequent discussions with staff to reflect on conscious or unconscious devaluing of students' identities. Determine whether there are policies, practices, or attitudes that send the message, "Leave your language and culture at home. It has no place at our school."

☐ Allow students to speak their native languages (Lucas et al., 1990). Encourage all staff to learn a second language (even if it's just a few phrases) and use it with the students.

☐ Make sure that all staff encourage beginning ELLs to continue writing in their native languages. They feel more comfortable in school and gain English skills faster than those who are not provided with this opportunity (Peyton, Jones, Vincent, & Greenblatt, 1994).

☐ Encourage teachers to use literature from the students' backgrounds. The use of culturally relevant literature affirms ELLs and helps all students to value and respect the cultures of others (Baruth & Manning, 1992).

☐ Make sure that all staff encourage ELLs to continue reading in their native languages. Provide books in the native languages of the children. Children use books in their first language more often have a greater feeling of security in their cultural backgrounds (Feuerverger, 1994).

☐ Use students' primary languages to promote a welcoming atmosphere. Some examples include the following:
   ✓ Post multilingual signs around the school (welcome signs at school entrances, cafeteria directions, library and office information, signs announcing school events).
   ✓ Put up bulletin boards with corresponding words in the various languages of the students.
   ✓ Ask bilingual students and parents to read school announcements over the intercom.

☐ Ensure that displays in hallways and classrooms reflect the cultural heritage of students.

☐ Monitor the culture appropriateness of textbooks.

☐ Encourage teachers to teach lessons that incorporate family origins and cultural heritages. Examples of such lessons include the following:
   ✓ Post a map on classroom bulletin boards on which students can place pushpins with their names on their families' countries of origin, or display student-created maps of their native countries.
   ✓ Have students interview family members, plan food festivals, or teach the class several words from another language (Shore, 2001).

☐ Have bilingual students and adults prepare bilingual videos acquainting new students and their families with the school. The videos can be about the school environment, daily procedures, special events (e.g., a tour of the school, riding the bus, cafeteria procedures, playground procedures, or going to the library).

☐ Create a nurturing and inclusive school environment through a variety of roles that staff, students, and parents can assume, such as the following:
   ✓ School concierge (older students) who answers morning questions

✓ School tour guides

✓ Bus greeters and bus buddies

✓ Cafeteria hosts and hostesses

✓ Student translators

✓ Bilingual peer mediators on the playground

✓ Language buddies in the classroom who help new students adjust by reading the lunch menu, giving a school tour, and so on (Gusman, 2001).

☐ Encourage teachers to help their classes understand and appreciate a new student's position by arranging for an adult to present a short lesson to the group in another language. The teacher can then help students process the experience in terms of how it feels to be educated in another language.

☐ Make sure that multicultural concepts are infused into the mainstream curriculum.

✓ The physical education teacher can teach multicultural games to all of the students, teachers, and recess supervisors.

✓ The music curriculum should include songs and musical elements that reflect the cultures of all of your students.

☐ Have teachers specifically integrate ELL and non-ELLs through specially coordinated classroom projects and school events, activities, or programs, such as the following:

✓ Field trips, plays, musicals, school events

✓ Peer-tutoring, cross-age shared reading, mentoring, pen pals, peer or cross-age dialogue journals

✓ Playground activities organized to specifically integrate ELLs and non-ELLs.

☐ Set up opportunities for cultural information to be shared at staff meetings for the purpose of clarifying students' behavior and sensitizing teachers to cultural differences. ELLs may experience culture conflict because the way they learn and communicate does not match the customs of the classroom. Examples of such conflict may include the following:

✓ A child may not participate because his or her culture does not support the patterns of interaction occurring in the classroom. Some children are not used to speaking in front of other students and may be hesitant to do so.

✓ Ways of expressing emotions (joy, excitement, frustration, fear) are different from culture to culture.

✓ Teacher praise can be misinterpreted by children from certain cultures. For many Latino and Asian children, instead of saying, "You should be proud of yourself," it would be more appropriate to say, "Your family will be proud of you" (McLaughlin, 1995).

- ◆ **Hold high expectations for all students and make the achievement of ELLs a priority.**
- ◆ **Provide substantial feedback to teachers on their teaching.**
  - ☐ Make sure that high-quality curricula is accessible to students, as much as possible, in their native languages and in English. Limited English proficiency should not be an obstacle to rigorous academic work. ELLs must be expected to achieve to high standards with challenging curricula focused on critical thinking, hands-on learning, exploration of process, and connections across disciplines. While students are learning English, they should also be reading high-quality literature; writing reports, newsletters, and stories; conducting scientific experiments; and participating in project-based work (McLeod, 1996).
  - ☐ Observe classroom practices to ensure that all teachers use techniques such as cooperative learning to set up cross-cultural interactions and that all teachers convey high expectations to students. Provide feedback to teachers about the following:
    - ✓ Balanced student roles, group dynamics, and interactions
    - ✓ Frequency and type of interaction
    - ✓ Seating arrangements
    - ✓ Student equity in the number and quality of higher-order thinking questions asked
  - ☐ Display school banners that convey high expectations in English and the other languages (Villareal, 2001).
- ◆ **Place high priority on training for all school staff to help them serve ELLs more effectively. Develop structures to strengthen curriculum and instruction.**
  - ☐ Arrange for ongoing staff development (both certified and classified) on the importance of valuing cultural and linguistic diversity, exhibiting high expectations, and encouraging parent involvement.
  - ☐ Facilitate coordination between bilingual or ESL programs and general programs. Bilingual/ESL and mainstream teachers should coordinate the purchase of materials for both programs, plan units of instruction together based on integrated thematic approaches, and participate jointly in field trips.
  - ☐ Provide time and structures for the staff to work together in planning instruction across grade levels and across content areas, both vertically and horizontally, and to share information about students and their families.
    - ✓ Make sure that bilingual/ESL and mainstream teachers meet regularly to discuss students' progress and to align their curriculum and instruction so that ELLs receive a comprehensive and coordinated educational program.

✓ Coordination of curriculum and regular, ongoing communication between ESL and mainstream teachers in schools with pullout programs is particularly crucial.

◆ **Assist teachers in increasing their certainty about the goals for student achievement.**

☐ Establish schoolwide goals and expectations for students followed by consistent, visible, multiple, and long-term efforts to work toward the goals (Goldenberg & Sullivan, 1994). Ensure that the ELL curriculum has clear instructional goals, clearly delineated assessment and accountability procedures that benchmark students' progress, and immediate and consistent measures such as after-school tutoring, small-group instruction or added tutoring during school hours, and one-on-one approaches when students are not meeting the benchmark.

◆ **Provide procedures for early data collection on ELLs.**

☐ During enrollment procedures, gather the following additional information to help facilitate communication with parents:

✓ Names and contact information for adults living with the child

✓ Names and contact information for parents and extended family members not living with the child

✓ Workplace address and phone numbers of caregivers

✓ English proficiency of parents and caregivers

✓ Languages spoken in the home

✓ Names and contact information of English speaking neighbors or relatives.

School Management: Standard 3

◆ **Influence and examine the organization of instruction.**

☐ Together with staff, investigate innovative ways to organize instruction and to protect and extend instructional time. Students could be organized in "larger-than-class groups" that include both ELLs and English proficient students such as "families," "houses," "wings," or paired classes. Within these groups, students can be grouped in different ways for instructional purposes, sometimes mixing different language and ability groups heterogeneously, and sometimes dividing them for instruction geared to their particular needs (Cloud et al., 2000; McLeod, 1996). Some examples follow:

✓ Linda Vista Elementary School divided its students into wings, which operated as four schools within the school. These wings were made up of students spanning two to three grade levels, with mixed levels of English proficiency and varied educational backgrounds. Within each wing, students were grouped by English language ability and native language for language arts and social studies, by mathematics proficiency for math classes, and heterogeneously for other classes. The daily schedule included a long block for language arts and shorter blocks for social studies and mathematics. During the final hour, called Afternoon Rotation, students participated in a science lab, science garden, art, music, and physical education (McLeod, 1996).

✓ Middle schools, divided students and teachers into "families" for each grade level, with additional families for newcomer students spanning all three grade levels. Within each family, students were clustered into strands for their core content courses. Spanish speaking ELLs were served within the structure through Spanish bilingual strands (McLeod, 1996).

✓ At Del Norte Elementary School, students studied language arts in a three-hour block Monday through Thursday mornings, and on Fridays they studied science. On Monday through Thursday, they studied math for almost two hours; on Fridays they studied social studies for two-and-a-half hours. They had a 45-minute Enrichment Time every day before lunch, in which they studied in small groups either Spanish as a second language, English as a second language, reading improvement, or reading enrichment. During the last 40 minutes of the school day on Monday through Thursday, students took classes in art, music, drama, or library research (McLeod, 1996).

✓ At Gladys Noon Spellman Elementary School, 90 minutes of uninterrupted instructional time were set aside each morning for reading and language arts. Each classroom teacher was teamed up with an instructional specialist. The team approach allowed for small group instruction and collaborative expertise (NAESP, 2001).

☐ Provide extended learning time for students outside of the daily class schedule with before- or after-school tutoring or reading programs, summer school programs, a year-round schedule, and so forth.

◆ **Hire bilingual staff with cultural backgrounds similar to those of the students.**

☐ Hire school personnel, reflective of the population served, who are bilingual (and biliterate, if possible) and are familiar with the students' cultures.

☐ Recruit parents who meet the educational and experience requirements to be employees.

◆ **Facilitate ample opportunities for collaborative planning and design of curriculum and lessons.**

☐ Provide opportunities for staff members to think critically about the "home culture" and to collaboratively plan how to incorporate that culture into daily literacy and content class activities and the homework assigned. Examples include the following:

✓ Provide time for teachers to collaboratively develop questions for students to answer with their parents' help. The questions should be related to class themes and to topics that parents will want to respond to.

✓ Provide time for teachers to collaboratively develop specific tasks that parents can do with their children on a regular basis. Parents will develop a routine of expecting the communication and of completing the specific tasks assigned. "Interactive homework" ideas can be found on the Internet.

✓ Encourage children to take home books, videos, and audiotapes in their native languages with accompanying parent questionnaires.

◆ **Allocate appropriate funding for materials, translation, and professional development.**

☐ Have your school librarian purchase books for students that address the newcomer experience and that reflect the culture of the student population. Examples include the following:

✓ Ada, A. F.(1993). *My name is María Isabel (Me llamo María Isabel)* (available in Spanish and English). West Lake, OH: Del Sol Books.

✓ Kuklin, S. (1992). *How My Family Lives in America.* New York: Simon & Schuster.

✓ Levin, E. (1997). *I hate English!* New York: Scholastic.

✓ Reiser, L. (1996). *Margaret and Margarita.*New York: Greenwillow.

☐ Purchase multicultural children's literature for your classrooms. There are many bibliographies of multicultural children's literature that can be used to form collections for classroom libraries.

✓ Hansen-Krening, Nancy. (Ed.). (1997). *Kaleidoscope: A multicultural Booklist for Grades K–8* (4th ed.). Urbana, IL: National Council of Teachers of English.

✓ Brown, D. (1994). *Books for a Small Planet: A Multicultural-Intercultural Bibliography for Young English Language Learners.* Alexandria, VA: Teachers of English to Speakers of Other Languages.

✓ De-Cou-Landberg, M. (1994). *The Global Classroom: A Thematic Multicultural Model for the K–6 and ESL Classroom* (Volumes 1 & 2). Reading, MA: Addison-Wesley.

✓ Kezwer, P. (1995). *Worlds of Wonder: Resources for Multicultural Children's Literature.* Scarborough, Canada: Pippin.

School and Community: Standards 4, 6

◆ **Take strong steps to work with ELLs' parents.**

☐ Establish a formal parent outreach committee.

✓ Conduct a needs assessment of your community through focus groups so you can address real, rather than perceived, needs of the parents.

✓ Use a needs assessment tool for staff as a guide to improve family involvement and promote staff discussions (one example is "Connecting Families and Schools," available from http://www.leadersroundtable.org/site/images/stories/PDF/connectingfamilyandschool.pdf).

✓ Develop a long-range plan for parent and community involvement as a part of your school improvement plan. Remember that there are many levels of parent involvement. Develop ways to assess the plan.

☐ Provide an accepting and friendly school environment in which parents feel welcome and valued.

✓ Train your classified staff in how they greet and treat ELLs' parents when they enroll their children.

✓ Invite parents to eat lunch with their children or visit their children's classrooms.

✓ Create classroom phone trees where bilingual parents call non-English speaking parents.

☐ Offer flexible scheduling and check for the best meeting times for parents (Guzman, 1990) (see Figure 5.3, p. 163). If a parent is holding two jobs or working a night shift, parent meetings or conferences should be planned accordingly.

☐ Provide the appropriate time and avenues for staff to learn about students' families. Teachers can then use this information to plan activities that will motivate parents to become more involved in their children's education.

✓ One principal took teachers on a bus tour of the neighborhoods of his students in order to help them gain a perspective on their lives (McLeod, 1996).

✓ Provide time, support, and information to staff to make home visits (Nicolau & Ramos, 1990), which are effective in developing trust and rapport with families (Espinosa, 1995) and enable staff to obtain additional information regarding the language, culture, and child-rearing practices.

☐ Plan first meetings with parents and extended families that are primarily social events and held at neutral sites (Nicolau & Ramos, 1990; Procidano & Fisher, 1992).

☐ Provide time for support staff to become involved with parents. Counselors, parent liaisons, or community aides can be responsible for making contacts with parents, making home visits, coordinating parent education programs, working with parents on attendance, translating when needed, and helping families obtain medical care, clothing, and other needed services. Some examples follow:

- ✓ A counselor paired Latina girls and their mothers with Latina professionals in the community. The professionals provided mentoring, support, and information, hoping that the mothers would support their daughters if they wanted to go to college (Berman et al., 1995).
- ✓ Workshops and programs could be provided for parents to strengthen their parenting skills, enhance parent networks, and minimize parental stress. Workshops could provide information on topics such as nutrition, discipline, and early learning activities (Valdés, 1996).

☐ Consult online resources such as the "Resources About Parent and Community Involvement" website at http://www.ncela.gwu.edu/resabout/ parents/for articles and materials your school can use to encourage parent and community participation.

☐ Investigate other online resources, such as the following:
- ✓ Samples of family-school compacts, found on the California State Board of Education Parent/Family website, under "Compacts." Available: http://www.cde.ca.govls/pf/pf/
- ✓ Caplan, J. G. (1998). *Critical Issue: Constructing School Partnerships with Families and Community Groups.* Pathways to School Improvement. Available: http://www.ncrel.org/sdrs/areas/issues/envrnmnt/famn comm/pa400.htm
- ✓ Harvard Family Research Project. (2005). *Taking a Closer Look: A Guide to Online Resources for Family Involvement.* Available: http://www.gse. harvard. edu/hfrp/projects/fine/resources/guide/
- ✓ Moles, O. C. (1996). *Reaching all Families: Creating Family-Friendly Schools.* Available: http://www.ed.gov/pubs/ReachFam/index.html
- ✓ Zelasko, N., & Antunez, B. (2000). *If Your Child Learns in Two Languages: A Parent's Guide to Improving Educational Opportunities for Children Learning English as a Second Language.* Available: http://www.ncela.gwu.edu/ pubs/parent/

◆ **Ensure that all communication to parents is provided in their native languages.**

☐ Provide frequent communication, both written and oral, in the languages and levels that parents understand. Translated communication demonstrates how the school values the home language. Keep *all* parents informed about school events, academic standards, and their children's progress.
- ✓ Tap into community volunteers and community-based organizations who may be willing to act as translators.

✓ Hire staff who can speak the parents' languages (Lucas et al., 1990; Sosa, 1990).

✓ Give parents a list of bilingual staff in the school and/or district whom they can contact about educational concerns.

✓ Have bilingual staff call parents who have limited literacy to provide important information to them.

✓ Use bilingual voice mail recordings. For important information that is mailed, place a telephone icon and phone number at the top of the mailing. When parents call the number, they will have access to a recorded message in their native language.

✓ Translate key information from newsletters into the native language (Power, 1999).

✓ Simplify forms that are sent home to families. Some parents may not have adequate literacy skills in their native language.

✓ Post the school's activity calendars in multiple languages.

✓ Provide bilingual parent handbooks.

☐ The most effective way to communicate with families is verbally in their native language. Avoid using children as interpreters for parents, which shifts power from the parents to the children and often subverts parental feelings of authority.

☐ Provide and discuss the following articles with staff: "Teacher Tips for Using an Interpreter" and "Handouts for Parents," both available from ESCORT (2001) at http:// www.escort.org/products/HSc9.pdf

☐ Organize a shared folder of information on your computer network that lists all interpreters, their contact information, and all available translated forms in various languages. Make the information available to all staff and encourage them to add new forms as they are created.

☐ Inform teachers about the Casa Notes website (http://casanotes.4teachers. org/). Casa Notes allows teachers to quickly customize typical notes that are sent home to parents or given to the students. Templates allow teachers to customize some of the content, choose a color scheme, and add a graphic. Teachers can select whether the notes should be in English or in Spanish.

♦ **Encourage ELL parents to participate in literacy-rich activities with their children.**

☐ Implement a family literacy program that can help family members develop their native language skills to higher levels, develop their English skills, and involve them in their children's education.

☐ Integrate important cultural interests and social issues into literacy content by asking parents for their suggestions for activities and ideas that parents and teachers can do together. Literacy instruction can then include culturally specific nursery rhymes, songs, and poetry.

☐ Explore the *AFT Toolkit for Teachers: Reaching Out to Hispanic Parents of English Language Learners* (available from http://www.colorincolorado.org/reachingout/toolkit.php) for workshop ideas, handouts, and activity sheets (in Spanish and English) to help parents contribute to the literacy development of their children.

☐ Inform teachers about the *School-Home Links Reading Kits* (available from http:www.ed.gov/pubs/CompactforReading), which contain multiple school-home activities for each grade. The activities are organized by reading and literacy skills appropriate for each grade and are available in Spanish and English.

☐ Consider purchasing *Parent Power: Energizing Home-School Communication* (Power, 1999). The resource kit (book and CD-ROM), which can be purchased with a multiple-user license, contains useful suggestions that elementary teachers and the school can use to work effectively with ELLs and their parents. The kit also contains essays, written in both English and Spanish, that address topics such as reading and writing at home, Internet use, and so on.

☐ Make sure that your staff members know that they should not tell the parents of ELLs to "speak only English at home," which devalues the home language and culture and creates problems in family communication. Children who lose proficiency in their first language are often unable to communicate with immediate and extended family members (Wong Fillmore, 1991b).

◆ **Actively solicit bilingual parents, family members, and community volunteers to be involved.**

☐ Develop a long-range parent involvement plan as an integral part of the school improvement plan. The plan should address the needs of language minority parents and involve some means for measuring the effectiveness of the plan.

☐ Take specific measures to invite ELL parents into the school and encourage them to be actively involved in their children's schooling. Show them ways that they can be involved and help their children to succeed in school.

✓ Invite parents and family members to serve as classroom volunteers.

✓ Invite parents for a visit during the school day.

✓ Invite ELL parents and family members to be guest speakers about their countries or cultures. They can share their experiences and show authentic materials from their cultures.

✓ Have parents extend invitations to other parents, preferably neighbor to neighbor. Ask parents who feel more comfortable with school involvement to bring three friends to a meeting.

☐ Address barriers to parental involvement, such as lack of transportation and child care for school functions (Guzman, 1990; Inger, 1993; Sosa, 1990).

- ✓ Solicit your parent-teacher organization's help in assisting parents to form carpools, providing routes and time schedules for public transportation, or contacting taxi and limousine companies to see if they will provide complimentary service at specific pick-up points during certain hours.
- ✓ Use paraprofessionals, teacher aides, volunteer parents, community service organizations, or high school service clubs to provide child care.

☐ Host parent involvement programs that provide information to parents about helping their children to succeed academically. Upon completion of the program(s), honor the parents at a parent recognition evening.

- ✓ Provide orientation sessions in different languages. Consider alternate, nonschool sites for the sessions, such as public libraries or shopping malls.
- ✓ Provide short orientation videos in different languages.
- ✓ Give workshops on acculturating parents to U.S. schools and the meaning of parent involvement (Procidano & Fisher, 1992). Topics might include helping their children with homework, volunteering in school, attending school activities, helping their children to become better in reading and math, and talking to school personnel (Valdés, 1996).
- ✓ "A Guide to Your Children's Schools: A Parent Handbook," available in English, Arabic, Bosnian, Russian, Spanish, and Vietnamese (http://www.isbe.state.il.us/bilingual/htmls/ellparents.htm) is a good resource for information about school systems in the United States.
- ✓ Provide information about your school: hours, school calendar, holidays, rules, curriculum, teacher expectations, language programs, and after school activities.
- ✓ Include information about parent rights regarding interpreters, free/reduced lunch applications, and NCLB.

☐ Make space for a "Parents' Room" or "Parents' Center" as a place for parents to meet, work on projects for teachers, and socialize. Provide books, articles, and other sources of information about parenting and literacy development. The room can also be the site for ESL or literacy classes for parents or for parenting seminars.

☐ Organize specific opportunities in which you and your staff have the opportunity to listen to parents' concerns, issues, and experiences. These discussions will provide valuable information for parental involvement and services.

☐ Have your counselor or parent-teacher organization start a program to pair new families that do not speak English with bilingual families who are familiar with the school system and can provide support and translation assistance. This will help new families to become more involved in their children's schooling and more familiar with resources and opportunities in the community. School personnel can help by sharing school information about policies, procedures, and upcoming events with the partner families.

◆ **Involve language minority parents in decision making.**

☐ Treat parents as contributors and collaborators (Guzman, 1990). Focus on their strengths, such as their language and culture.

☐ Actively seek a variety of approaches to solicit the input of language minority stakeholders. Traditionally active groups of parents will probably not reflect the views of all parents.

☐ When involving parents and families from different language backgrounds, consider meeting separately by language groups for part of the time to encourage more active participation and better attendance from language minority parents. Then, to counteract the segregation, have short joint meetings to share what has been discussed in each group (Miramontes et al., 1997).

◆ **Learn about the communities your students represent and attend language minority group activities.**

☐ Attend and encourage other school personnel to attend activities that provide greater visibility in the community—festivals, fund raisers, shopping (Cooper & Gonzalez, 1993).

☐ In teams composed of parents and educators, take "community walks." Walk through neighborhoods or housing projects getting to know people, asking about their concerns regarding the education of their children, and discussing what is going on at the school (McCollum, 1997). In this way, teachers will learn about their school community, and parents and teachers will interact.

◆ **Advocate for language minorities in the school and community.**

☐ Work with local community organizations and agencies to provide various forums for immigrant parents on various topics, such as the following:

   ✓ Forums on their legal rights concerning education and employment.

   ✓ Parent or family empowerment programs that help parents to take action to improve their lives and their children's lives (Valdés, 1996). These could address the challenges of poverty, single parenthood, or many other social topics.

☐ Work with local agencies, the public library, and social service organizations to provide parent outreach programs that help parents to enhance their own educational skills. Examples of such programs include the following:

   ✓ Literacy programs

   ✓ ESL classes for parents

   ✓ Workshops on writing skills or technology skills (loan out laptops, invite parents to school for computer training)

   ✓ Outreach services using buses outfitted with lending libraries and computer stations

☐ Establish formal systems for addressing students' nonacademic needs. Provide information and advocacy to help parents access needed services.

✓ Hire a bilingual social worker to assess student needs and develop a system of services such as health care information, child care, food stamps, and so on.

✓ Explore a partnership with medical universities in which medical interns serve as nurse practitioners at the school (McLeod, 1996).

✓ Establish student intervention teams (made up of the principal, parent liaison, nurse, school psychologist, school counselor, teachers, and/or community agency representative) to coordinate student social services.

✓ Work with community agencies to bring health care, dental services, social services, and mental health services onto school campuses. These services could include individual and group counseling, case management for families, and referral to community agencies.

✓ Inform parents of community resources and adult education programs.

Building the Vision

As you answer each of the following questions, think about what might be done to facilitate change. Seek staff, parent, and community input in identifying goals that will promote an effective assessment system based on the school's vision, resources, and population.

1. What qualitative and quantitative data will you use to determine your school's strengths and needs with regard to school climate? What are the most important issues?

2. How will you share the research on supportive schoolwide climate and organizational structures with all staff?

3. How will you share the previous strategies and suggestions with all staff?

4. Has your school clarified its vision about valuing students' language and cultures, demonstrating high expectations for all students, and encouraging parent and community involvement?

5. How do your current organizational structures align with the school's vision?

6. How does your current English language acquisition program align with the school's vision and improvement plan?

7. How will you empower staff to determine student groupings and organizational structures that support the academic achievement of ELLs?

8. How will the school best use resources and personnel to provide an effective schoolwide climate and context for ELLs?

9. How will the school increase parent and community involvement?

10. How will you fund materials and programs that foster a positive school climate?

6

Building the Context for Sustainable Change

> *Leaders matter....The habits that produce significant change in teaching and learning begin with significant change in what leaders think, say, and do. The implications of this are profound. It means, for instance, that leaders begin reform efforts by changing themselves before considering how others must change. It means that leaders carefully examine how their own assumptions, their own understanding of significant issues, and their own behaviors may be preserving current practices.*
>
> (Sparks, 2003, p. 1)

Chapter Highlights: This chapter concludes the book by reemphasizing the role of the principal as an advocate of change for ELLs and a leader of intellectual stimulation and reflection to promote best practices in an ELL-responsive school. The Leadership Challenge provides rubrics for exemplary practices that can be used for a needs assessment for your school.

What Principals Should Know

Critical Questions

1. How does the principal establish a school environment that facilitates change for ELLs?
2. How will the principal sustain the desired change for ELLs?

Essential Vocabulary

Professional learning community (PLC): The PLC conceptual framework can be grouped into three major themes that are evident in the policies, programs, and practices of the school or district. The themes are (1) a solid foundation consisting of collaboratively developed mission, vision, values, and goals; (2) collaborative teams that work interdependently to achieve common goals; and (3) a focus on results as evidenced by a commitment to continuous improvement (Eaker, DuFour, & DuFour, 2002, p. 3).

Critical Question #1:
How Does the Principal Establish a School Environment That Facilitates Change for ELLs?

Leading Learning Communities

In Chapter 1, the principal's leadership was discussed as a key component of the attributes of effective schools for ELLs. However, effective schooling practices will not occur without corresponding changes in teaching, learning, and curriculum. Establishing learning communities and providing for ongoing professional

> *Changing the school into a learning community involves the principal's support and active nurturing of the entire staff's development as a learning community.*

development targeted to enhance services to ELLs are two powerful strategies leaders should embrace.

According to Newmann and Wehlage (1995), "If schools want to enhance their organizational capacity to boost student learning, they should work on building a professional community that is characterized by shared purpose, collaborative activity, and collective responsibility among staff" (p. 37). Senge and colleagues (1999) assert that developing "leadership communities" is critical for successful school reform, and that principals must foster a broad-based leadership so that teachers also lead the reform. As such, principals must create the conditions that enable schools to become professional learning communities in an environment where staff can learn continuously. DuFour (2002) proposes that principals should function as "learning leaders" and that effective principals of professional learning communities

1. lead through shared vision and values rather than through rules and procedures;

2. involve faculty members in the school's decision-making processes and empower individuals to act;

3. provide staff with the information, training, and parameters they need to make good decisions;

4. establish credibility by modeling behavior that is congruent with the vision and values of their school; and

5. are results-oriented (DuFour & Eaker, 1998, pp. 184–194).

Collaboration

A critical element of professional learning communities is collaboration (Eaker et al., 2002). Current research on effective schooling for ELLs indicates that a collective and cooperative learning approach—one that targets teacher expertise, teacher reflection on practice, and collaboration with colleagues—is the key

> *When schools attempt significant reform, efforts to form a schoolwide professional community are critical.* (Louis, Kruse, & Raywid, 1996, p. 13)

to school improvement (August & Hakuta, 1997; Darling-Hammond, 1997; Stigler & Hiebert, 1999). The literature suggests several features that facilitate a collaborative process: meeting time with skilled consultants, meetings organized around perceived needs or areas of concern, evaluations of lesson delivery and student achievement, videotaping of lessons to allow for analysis and review, and follow-up and continuous feedback from trainers and colleagues (Calderón, 1994; Darling-Hammond & McLaughlin, 1995; Goldenberg & Gallimore, 1991a). Meetings of learning communities often include the presentation of research, how the research can be applied to teachers' particular needs, and structured time for teacher reflection and practice (Calderón, 1994; Leighton, Hightower, & Wrigley, 1995). In addition, teachers in learning communities conduct action research to investigate issues affecting student learning.

To foster effective collaboration, the principal must build time for collaboration into the school day and year, make the purpose of collaboration explicit, provide structures to facilitate that purpose, and provide training and support for staff to be effective collaborators (DuFour & Eaker, 1998). The exemplary schools for ELLs in Berman and colleagues' study (1995) facilitated teacher collaboration by organizing the school into smaller units ("schools within schools") in which the teachers frequently worked together, team teaching, providing common plan times for grade-level teachers, and building time into teachers' daily schedules for joint planning. Some schools implement flextime schedules in which schools lengthen the school day four days a week and dismiss students early on a fifth day in order to provide opportunities for joint planning and collaborative dialogue.

Examining the Mission

According to DuFour and Eaker (1998), establishing the foundation of a professional learning community involves examining the mission of the school by asking questions about the purpose: "Why do we exist? What are we here to do together? What is the business of our business? What is it we expect our students to learn, and how will we fulfill our collective responsibility to ensure that this learning takes place for all of our students?" (p. 58–62). These authors state that sometimes the all-inclusive statement that "all kids can learn," is accompanied by such qualifications as "based on their ability," "if they take advantage of the opportunity to learn," or "and we will accept responsibility for ensuring their growth" (pp. 59–60) (growth does not indicate the presence of high standards). However, the *No Child Left Behind Act* ensures that *all* children are held to high expectations and provided with a high quality education. Miramontes and colleagues (1997) concur:

> The typical approach…is to relegate the decision making to special programs people and to view the needs of [second language learners] as peripheral to the total school program. In a successful school community, however, teachers must make decisions about all students, regardless of special needs, on the basis of sound pedagogy, and within a perspective of high expectations for all. (p. 69)

In order to facilitate a mission statement that has an all-encompassing sense of purpose, DuFour and Eaker (1998) propose that the following two questions be asked:

- If we believe all kids can learn, exactly what is it that we will expect them to learn?
- If we believe all kids can learn, how do we respond when they do not learn? (p. 59)

Questions that also bring ELL needs to the forefront might include the following:

- Does "all kids" include those who are culturally and linguistically diverse?
- Does the ELL program in our school align with the vision of academic achievement for *all* students?

Developing the Vision and Shared Values

The next step involves examining the school's current vision and what it might become. DuFour and Eaker (1998) state that the vision should instill "a sense of direction" for the school and articulate "a vivid picture of the

> *You cannot have a learning organization without shared vision.* (Senge, 1990, p. 209)

organization's future that is so compelling that a school's members will be motivated to work together to make it a reality" (p. 62). In facilitating a vision that includes ELLs, principals need a "firm grasp of curricular issues" about the instruction of English learners and the "confidence to set high expectations and continuously uphold the vision" (Miramontes et al., 1997, p. 87).

The ongoing process of developing a vision statement operates from a research-based framework that includes background information about the school such as longitudinal achievement data, demographic trends, and external and internal factors affecting the district; research on effective schools; and research on school restructuring (DuFour & Eaker, 1998). Relevant background information as it pertains to English learners includes national, state, and local demographic trends, as well as research on effective schools for ELLs (see Chapter 1). Examining the vision through a research base can be accomplished by forming study groups that examine the research, visit schools that have already restructured, and collect data that challenge comfortable assumptions. Senge, Ross, Smith, Roberts, and Kleiner (1994) propose the school community ask the following questions when developing the vision:

- What would you like to see our school become?
- What reputation would it have?
- What contribution would it make to our students and community?
- What values would it embody?
- How would people work together? (p. 208)

Statements of shared values should be directly linked to the vision statement and should challenge people to clarify the "specific attitudes, behaviors, and commitments they must demonstrate in order to advance their vision" (DuFour & Eaker, 1998, p. 88). Value statements should focus on the question: "What are the specific commitments that we must make in order to move our school closer to the desired future we have identified?" (DuFour & Eaker, 1998, pp. 95–96). Commitments should be directly linked to the vision, limited to five or six statements, and stated as actions and behaviors rather than beliefs. Value statements might address commitments about classroom environment, school climate, student needs, student outcomes, instructional methods, methods of assessment, collaboration, professional development, and parent involvement.

Extending the Discussion

As the staff is determining the school's vision and shared values, the principal must continually advocate for the inclusion of English learners (Goldenberg & Sullivan, 1994; Minicucci & Olsen, 1992) and facilitate an ELL-responsive discussion, drawing attention to how the needs of these students uniquely shape the work of the school. Examples of questions to facilitate these discussions include the following:

> *Are your ELLs thriving or just surviving?*

- Is our vision based on sound principles of learning for English learners?
- How do we enable ELLs to learn English and meet the same academic expectations as other students?
- Who is responsible for educating ELLs? Who is responsible for their content knowledge and language development?
- What are our beliefs about bilingualism and about programs that foster bilingualism? What are our beliefs about use of the native language to facilitate learning?

- How is respect for cultural and linguistic diversity evident in our school?
- Is our vision reflected in daily learning opportunities? How do we organize our students and our time? How does our vision affect student grouping and other organizational structures?
- How does assessment reflect what students know and can do? What are our beliefs about authentic assessment?
- What do we believe about parent involvement? How do we involve parents as decision makers?
- What do we believe about parents who do not speak English? About undocumented immigrants? How do we involve parents who do not speak English?

Examining the Messages

Examine the messages that are sent about what is valued in your school or that fail to address issues of inequity by considering the following questions:

1. "Who's taking calculus?" Do the ELLs in your school have access to high-level and academically demanding content?

2. "Which classes meet in the basement?" Are programs for ELLs located in less desirable places? Are they segregated from the "regular" or "normal" students?

3. "Who's teaching the children?" Are ELLs being taught by experienced, well-prepared, and well-trained teachers? Does the faculty reflect the diversity of the student population in terms of race and ethnicity? Do staff members care about, mentor, and guide ELLs?

4. "How much are children worth?" Considering issues such as equity, access, resources, and funding, how does the "worth of children" differ for your district or school in regards to students' race, ethnicity, social class, and home address? (Nieto, 2002, pp. 6–10)

Examining the Data

After the vision statement has been written, schools need to collect baseline data to assess the current status of the school (Conley, 1996; Murphy & Lick, 2001). In addition to the data

> *It's hard to argue with your own data.* (Conley, 1996)

that are typically collected, the ELL-responsive principal should ensure the collection of a comprehensive picture of the school's English learners. Because standardized test scores and state assessments do not accurately represent success for ELLs, examining rubric-scored portfolios and performance assessments will provide important information about student learning (Pellegrino, Chudowsky, & Glaser, 2001). Coady and colleagues (2003) propose the following questions to guide the inquiry:

- How many or what percentage of students in the school have a home language other than English?
- What languages are spoken in their homes?
- What places of origin are represented?
- What educational backgrounds are represented? (Continuous or interrupted formal schooling, no prior schooling, schooling in the home country, rural or urban schooling, preschool, kindergarten?)
- Are some students literate in another language?
- Are ELLs the subject of many disciplinary referrals or actions in your school?
- How many or what percentage of students in the school are actually classified as ELL?
  - How many currently receive language services?
  - How are these students distributed across grade levels?
  - What are their levels of English proficiency?
  - What language services do ELLs currently receive?
  - In what types of classrooms do they receive literacy and content instruction?
  - What are their academic strengths and weaknesses? What is your evidence for this judgment?
- How many students (for whom English is a second language) have met exiting criteria and are now classified as English proficient?
  - How are these students distributed across grade levels?
  - What services, such as monitoring or transitional support, do exited ELLs currently receive?
  - How do they perform in mainstream classes? What is your evidence for this judgment?
  - What are their academic strengths and weaknesses? What is your evidence for this judgment?
- How does their achievement compare with the achievement of other groups of students and with the school/district as a whole?
- In what areas or skills do you see the greatest need for improvement among ELLs?
- In what areas or skills do you see the greatest need for improvement among other groups of students? (pp. 71–72)

Identifying Goals

Goals should be based on a shared vision and have the active support of a wide range of stakeholders who participate in achieving them. Written goals should be limited in number, focused on the desired outcomes, specific and measurable, monitored continuously, designed for short-term wins, and understood and accepted by all (DuFour & Eaker, 1998). Effective goals specify

- exactly what is to be accomplished
- the specific steps that will be taken to achieve the goal
- the individual or group responsible for initiating and/or sustaining each step toward achieving the goal
- the timeline for each phase of the activity
- the criteria to be used in evaluating progress toward the goal (DuFour & Eaker, 1998, pp. 101–102).

However, it is crucial to identify goals that will make a difference. Waters and colleagues (2003) state that the focus of change—"whether leaders properly identify and focus on improving the school and classroom practices that are most likely to have a positive impact on student achievement in their school"—determines whether or not leadership will have a positive or a negative impact on achievement (p. 5). The research presented in this book will assist you in selecting goals. Coady and colleagues (2003) suggest the following strategies for designing ELL-responsive goals:

1. **Rather than looking for reform models and strategies in the mainstream and adapting them to the needs of ELLs, consider reform models and strategies implemented with ELLs that can be used with or adapted for monolingual English and English-proficient students.**...When ELL pedagogies and materials designed for ELLs are shown to mainstream teachers, they often respond, "This would be good for all students, not just ELLs!" Many students benefit from the assessment and build-up of background knowledge and vocabulary, careful scaffolding of comprehension, and attention to language patterns.

2. **Consider strategies and reforms that explicitly address cultural and linguistic differences.** Consider the extent to which issues of language and culture are not limited to ELLs. Not all English speaking children speak the same type of English used by their teachers or written in their books.

3. **Consider reform strategies that view bilingualism and knowledge of other cultures as assets to be developed and shared.** Dual-immersion or two-way bilingual programs are examples of this approach. (p. 72)

Professional Development

Staff training and ongoing professional development are important components of any effective school for English language learners and "certainly of any effort to change and improve a school" (August & Hakuta, 1997, p. 184). Approaches draw from the research on effective professional development in general (Calderón, 1994; Lieberman, 1995; McLaughlin & Oberman, 1996), with emphasis on strong instructional leadership creating a climate of professional growth and accountability that supports teachers in their efforts to become proficient teachers of ELLs (Lucas, 1992).

> *Knowing the right thing to do is the central problem of school improvement. Holding schools accountable for their performance depends on having people in the schools with the knowledge, skill, and judgment to make the improvements that will increase student performance.*
> (Elmore, 2003, p. 9)

The principal can promote effective schooling practices for ELLs by ensuring that staff members are well trained and supported in the use of research-based methods, participating in study groups and other collegial learning activities with teachers, asking critical questions about ELLs' achievement, and consistently allocating time to discuss teaching and learning issues for English learners. Professional development cannot be a "one-shot process"; it must be collaborative, job-embedded, data-driven, results-oriented, and sustained over time (DuFour & Eaker, 1998; Murphy & Lick, 2001; Villareal, 2001). In a summary of the research about developing literacy in second language learners, August (2006) reports that teachers found professional development to be most beneficial when it provided hands-on practice with teaching techniques that could be applied immediately in their classrooms, in-class demonstrations with their own or a fellow teacher's students, or personalized coaching. Additional factors that improved the quality of instruction involved collaboration with special education teachers and specialists, as well as assistance from outside experts (August, 2006).

In considering what sort of training is most relevant, professional development is based on the best available research, exemplary practices, and theories of effective instruction that have contributed to the list of competencies and attributes of effective teachers of English learners (Carter & Chatfield, 1986; Pease-Álvarez et al., 1991; Tikunoff, 1983). Programs for ELLs are more successful when their teachers understand and have received training aligned to the program model in which they are teaching as well as the research-based principles of second language development (Genesee et al., 2005; Milk et al., 1992). Critical elements of teacher training in working with ELLs include the following:

- Understanding first and second language acquisition
- The role of the first language and culture in learning
- Knowledge of developmental language stages

- The nature of language proficiency
- Organization and effective delivery of instruction
- Methods for teaching content
- Reading and writing in a second language
- Familiarity with students' learning and cognitive styles
- Alternative assessment
- High expectations for students
- Sociocultural issues
- Facilitating parent involvement.

(Carrasquillo & Rodriguez, 1996; García, 1994a; 2001; Ladson-Billings, 1995; Ramirez, 1992; Wong Fillmore & Snow, 2000)

Special types of expertise frequently cited in portrayals of effective teachers of ELLs (Milk et al., 1992) include (1) using "comprehensible input"—content presentation methods that take into account students' languages and experiences; (2) eliciting students' use of the target language; (3) taking advantage of students' language resources; (4) infusing language development into content instruction; and (5) reflecting critically on professional practice. Of the 33 studies in August and Hakuta's work (1997), the training was predominantly in English language development strategies; use of sheltered instruction; and instructional strategies such as thematic units, vocabulary development, instructional pace, and cooperative learning. According to Genesee and colleagues (2005), educators need more than a wide variety of methods or activities; they need comprehensive frameworks for instruction such as the Five Standards for Effective Pedagogy (Tharp, Estrada, Dalton, & Yamauchi, 2000) and the Sheltered Instruction Observation Protocol model for integrating content and language instruction (Echevarria et al., 2000).

Research has also emphasized that an important component of effective professional development is training that is explicitly designed to prepare *all* teachers to work with ELLs to enable the students to attain the same rigorous content as their grade-level peers (Berman et al., 1995; Carter & Chatfield, 1986; Lucas et al., 1990; Minicucci & Olsen, 1992). All teachers need to know how to "make academic content accessible to LEP students; integrate language and content instruction; respect and incorporate students' first languages in instruction; and understand how differences in language and culture affect students' classroom participation" (Menken & Look, 2000, pp. 22–23).

Critical Question #2:
How Will the Principal
Sustain the Desired Change for ELLs?

Preparing English learners to achieve in school and to be successful beyond schooling is an urgent challenge in our schools. Adding to this challenge are the increasing numbers of second language learners, a large number of whom are not faring well in U.S. schools. The choice is either to continue to follow tradi-

> *When I look at the word 'advocacy' I visually see it come apart: 'ad-vo-ca-cy.' This makes me think of 'Adding Voice to a Cry.'* (Olsen & Jaramillo, 1999, p. 37)

tional practices, knowing that many of these students will be unsuccessful and that their failure will be inevitable, or to embrace practices that are more likely to result in success for them. Research has demonstrated that certain curricular, instructional, and schooling practices, when applied appropriately within supportive learning environments, can result in increased achievement for ELLs. However, creating the necessary changes in instruction, assessment, organizational structures, and school climate is not just a matter of professional development; it requires strong leadership.

Within a framework of successful schooling, research has shown that the principal's leadership is critical, with "a substantial relationship between leadership and student achievement" (Waters et al., 2003, p. 3). DuFour (2001) states that principals must "remember the words of Albert Schweitzer: 'Example isn't the best way to influence others—it's the only way'" (p. 16). You have taken important steps in making a difference for these students by reading the research information and best practices presented in this book, and by identifying school and classroom practices that will promote the achievement of second language learners in your school. Now the journey truly begins with regard to being a strong advocate for these students by leading your staff, parents, and community to a shared vision of and commitment to high academic achievement for all students. Now you must make the vision a reality by focusing on goals, implementing and improving school and classroom practices that are responsive to the needs of ELLs, initiating change, and stimulating improvements that support and align with your now-explicit vision.

In facilitating this framework of success, you add voice to the cry of ELLs by speaking out and acting on behalf of these students and challenging others to do the same. It will

> *Never, never, never give up.* (Winston Churchill)

mean examining all aspects of schooling from an advocate's viewpoint, educating others about what you know, forming questions, engaging staff in critical reflection, leading the design of new programs and supports, and keeping your knowledge and your staff's knowledge up to date with current research and exemplary practices occurring at other schools. As research continues to develop, you will need the best information available in order to design and implement an optimal program for your school's ELLs. However, keep in mind that the needs may change as your ELL population changes. Waters and colleagues (2003) identified intellectual stimulation—ensuring "that faculty and staff are aware of the most current theories and practices" and making "the discussion of these a regular aspect of the school's culture"—as having the second-highest effect size in their list of 21 specific leadership responsibilities that significantly correlate with student achievement. These practices include the following tasks for the principal:

- Keeps informed about current research and theory regarding effective schooling
- Continually exposes staff to cutting edge ideas about how to be effective
- Systematically engages staff in discussions about current research and theory
- Continuously involves staff in reading articles and books about effective practices (p. 12)

Fortunately, the knowledge base about exemplary practices for English learners, how they learn and how to structure schools to serve them, continues to grow. The more you keep current with this knowledge base, the more effective you will be in leading and educating others and using the ongoing research as a resource for staff discussion about current and future practices at your school. One way to stay current, besides attending conferences, is to get on the mailing lists of major organizations that produce materials and research and to subscribe to electronic newsletters. Informing others could involve staff memos, discussions at staff meetings, setting up a place in the professional library for the latest research and materials related to the achievement of ELLs, and suggesting or providing articles and books for your school's study groups. Rereading the chapters in this book and the suggestions at the end of each chapter as they relate to your needs and the needs of your school is a good place to begin. You will also want to explore the list of electronic resources (Appendix B) and the list of references at the end of this book. In addition, the Leadership Challenge found at the conclusion of this chapter may serve as a starting point for determining your school's progress toward realizing exemplary practices for these students. As you continue your journey of advocacy and leadership for English language learners, we urge you to continually seek new knowledge and consistently act in powerful and effective ways that reflect a commitment to addressing the needs of all learners!

Leadership Challenge:
What Principals Should Do

The following comprehensive reform rubrics can be used to stimulate an inquiry process, identify areas of strength and need, and/or measure your school's progress toward realizing exemplary practices for English language learners.

Figure 6.1. Comprehensive Reform Rubrics

Berman, Aburto, Nelson, Minicucci & Burkhart, 2000.

Dimension 1: Extent to which the school has a coherent vision for the education of all of its students that is shared by school staff, students, and parents.

Level 1	Level 3	Level 5 (Ideal)
The school might have a vision or mission statement but it is not coherent or is not fundamental to guiding the work of the school. Staff, students, and parents do not articulate a shared, common vision for the learning of all students.	The school has a clear and coherent vision but it is not shared by all stakeholders. The staff may be divided on the school's vision or parents and the school staff may have differing visions for the education of children.	All major stakeholders—school staff, parents, students, and community members—articulate a common, coherent, and shared vision of education for all students.

Dimension 2: Extent to which staff actions and behaviors demonstrate a common vision that includes a commitment to high expectations and standards for all students, including language minority students.

Level 1	Level 3	Level 5 (Ideal)
Staff do not share a common vision of high standards for all students. Students are divided into long-term achievement groups and teachers have lower expectations for language minority students. Staff believe school programs and services have minimal impact on student learning.	School staff are divided into factions, with some holding high standards for all students and others not holding high standards for all students, including language minority students. Not all staff believe individual or collective efforts can have an impact on student learning.	School staff have high expectations and believe that LEP and all students are fully capable of achieving academic success. The education of language minority students is a schoolwide priority. Staff show through their words, actions, curricula, and activities that they hold high standards for language-minority students. Staff believe their individual and collective efforts make a difference in student learning.

Dimension 3: Extent to which the school recognizes and values the cultural backgrounds of LEP and language minority students in all aspects of schooling.

Level 1	Level 3	Level 5 (Ideal)
School staff show little awareness of or respect for students' cultural backgrounds. There is no recognition of students' culture(s) in schoolwide events. Curriculum and instruction ignore students' cultural heritage. There is little or no attempt to reflect student and family cultural demographics in school staff.	Some staff members understand and respect the students' cultural backgrounds, but others do not. If multiple cultures are represented in the school, they are not equally recognized. There is little recognition of the students' culture(s) in schoolwide events. Curricula and materials tend toward an anecdotal treatment of the students' cultural heritage (holidays and heroes). Students are rarely encouraged to make connections between what they study and their own cultural backgrounds. Some staff are representative of student cultural characteristics.	The teachers and other staff understand and respect the students' cultural backgrounds. Many of the staff are from the students' home countries, and many speak the students' language(s), especially in schools where a majority of students are from one or two linguistic backgrounds. Aspects of the students' culture(s) are reflected in public displays and schoolwide events. Curricula, materials, and instructional activities make frequent connections with students' culture(s). The staff are representative of the major student cultural groups in the school.

Dimension 4: Extent to which high-quality curriculum goals and standards are defined for all students across core subject areas and standards are linked to assessment..

Level 1	Level 3	Level 5 (Ideal)
School does not embrace standards or does not articulate or implement them; or standards exclude LEP students. The school implements assessment requirements as dictated by external authorities (district, state, federal) but does not place much value on standards or assessments linked to standards.	Standards have been established in some, but not all, subject areas and grade levels; or standards are tied to assessment in some subject areas, but not all. LEP students are not expected to meet the same high standards as mainstream students. Multiple stakeholders at the school do not accept the standards.	School articulates and upholds rigorous curriculum standards connected to district, state, and national standards. Goals and standards are clear, well known to everyone in the school community, and upheld by multiple stakeholders. Content and performance standards are appropriate for LEP students and are linked to a student assessment system.

Dimension 5: Extent to which the curriculum is contextualized using the students' needs and experiences, curriculum is integrated across core subject areas, and students are engaged in authentic and meaningful tasks relevant to their context, culture, and life experiences.

Level 1	Level 3	Level 5 (Ideal)
The curriculum is generalized and not specific to school context (e.g., teachers rely primarily on textbooks and workbooks). The curriculum is fragmented and compartmentalized into distinct subject areas. There is little effort to demonstrate how schoolwork is linked to students' life experiences and culture.	Some curriculum units show integration of subject areas and some reflect students' backgrounds, but the connections are not well planned or not systematic. Students are encouraged to see some connections between the subjects they study and their life experiences. Materials are uneven across subjects or grades. Some teachers draw on multiple materials; some rely on standard texts.	Curriculum involves challenging learning activities, is responsive to students' needs and makes connections to students' life situations. Students are encouraged to make connections between their schoolwork and their life experiences. The curriculum is developmentally appropriate and draws on a variety of materials, including primary sources and the resources of students, families, and the community.

Dimension 6: Extent to which students and teachers are actively engaged in classroom learning, teachers employ a variety of instructional strategies, and grouping for instruction is tailored to students' learning needs.

Level 1	Level 3	Level 5 (Ideal)
Most class instruction is teacher-centered, with the teacher lecturing or using the recitation script and students acting as passive recipients of predetermined ideas and information. Grouping of students for instruction is inflexible or not based on students' needs or the educational task at hand, or the majority or all activities are done with the class as a whole. The language and learning needs of LEP students are not considered.	Instruction is active and student-centered some of the time, with students taking the initiative for some activities. Teachers use some variety in instructional activities but, more generally, most teachers lecture or make use of the recitation script much of the time. Grouping is sometimes matched to the students' needs but often is not consciously designed. Instruction and grouping sometimes take into account the language and academic needs of LEP students.	Instruction is active and student-centered. Teachers act as coaches and facilitators. They guide and support students in their individual and group efforts in challenging learning activities. Teachers use a variety of instructional strategies and provide for flexible grouping that is tied to students' learning needs and takes into account the language and academic needs of LEP students.

Dimension 7: Extent to which the use of technology in varied forms is integrated throughout the school for the furthering of learning goals and development of workplace skills.

Level 1	Level 3	Level 5 (Ideal)
The school has very little hardware or outdated hardware, or hardware is not readily accessible to students for classroom or laboratory use. Multimedia capabilities and software are limited. Students use computers only for tutorials or other computer-directed activities, or only use them on isolated occasions. Few teachers are familiar with how to use technology, and most are resistant to learning. The school has not made efforts to secure funding for improving the school's technology capabilities.	The school has some hardware available to some, but not all, students on a regular basis (e.g., computers in some classrooms or in a lab). Students may use technology for electives but not for core classes, or technology is used sporadically and not always tied to instructional goals. Students have limited access to the lab and to some software. LEP students have less access. Few teachers are appropriately trained in using technology for instructional purposes.	The school has an abundance of hardware to ensure consistent access by all students (e.g., computers in every classroom or in a lab). Video, multimedia, and Internet capabilities are available, as is a variety of software in the primary language(s) of LEP students. The school has a technology coordinator, or teachers are appropriately trained for technology use. Teachers use technology where appropriate as a tool for exploring the core curriculum as well as for the development of practical skills.

Dimension 8: Extent to which a comprehensive assessment system is used to examine student learning and refine curriculum and instruction to improve programs for all students, including language minority students.

Level 1	Level 3	Level 5 (Ideal)
Assessment and evaluation system arises from external requirements only. School makes no use of data for purposes of reflection on student achievement or program changes. Data are not disaggregated and examined to ensure educational equity or used for planning purposes. Key stakeholders do not value assessment as a way to measure student learning.	Assessments to measure learning against standards are available in some, but not all, curriculum areas. Assessment results are available to school staff for some, but not all, assessments. There may be gaps in assessing LEP students (measures, what is being measured, and timeliness of testing). The school has a limited number or type of data collection methods for assessing student and program needs and progress, but is currently developing or selecting more appropriate measures. A majority of, but not all, student and program components are assessed and evaluated. Findings are sometimes disaggregated or used to change instruction and programs or improve reform efforts. Some stakeholders value assessment; some do not.	All stakeholders at the school embrace standards and assessments to measure learning against standards. State or district assessments measure student progress in meeting content and performance standards. Multiple forms of assessment are used to determine how well students are meeting content and performance standards. Assessment results are accessible to the school staff and are used for individual diagnostic purposes to refine curriculum and instruction and program evaluation. Primary and English language proficiency and academic achievement for LEP students are assessed regularly. The use of data is a standard component of the school's planning.

Dimension 9: Extent to which LEP and language minority students have access to the same core curriculum as other students, are held to the same academic goals, and are taught by appropriately trained teachers.

Level 1	Level 3	Level 5 (Ideal)
There are serious gaps in the core curriculum available to LEP and language minority students. They are not expected to meet the same academic goals as mainstream students. There are few or no appropriate materials to support academic instruction in L1 or in sheltered classes. Few or no members of the instructional staff are appropriately trained to facilitate the learning of LEP students, and there are no plans to train or hire qualified staff.	LEP students are provided access to some, but not all, core curriculum areas. LEP and language minority students may not be expected to meet the same goals as mainstream students. Some, but not all, courses use materials that are appropriate for and understandable to LEP students. Some members of the instructional staff are appropriately trained to facilitate the learning of LEP students and the school is working to upgrade staff qualifications in this area.	All LEP and language minority students are provided with a full core curriculum (e.g., language arts, science, math, social studies, arts), and the school sets the same academic goals for language minority students as for mainstream students. Instruction is provided in a comprehensible manner, whether through the native language or sheltered instruction. Materials are of high quality and are appropriate for, and accessible to, LEP students. Instructional staff members assigned to teach LEP students are appropriately trained to facilitate student learning.

Dimension 10: Extent to which the school has implemented appropriate, varied, and flexible plans for the English language development of LEP students that provide coordination within the same grade as well as articulated sequences across grades, and that are supported by adequate, qualified staff so that LEP students may master academic English and transition successfully to mainstream instruction.

Level 1	Level 3	Level 5 (Ideal)
The school lacks a sequential planned program for development of academic English (and/or for L1 in programs intended to develop the primary language). There is at most a single pathway for English development and transition to mainstream instruction, with no flexibility to provide instructional support to accommodate differing student needs. There are few or no teachers who can deliver appropriate instruction for LEP students.	The school has elements of a sequential planned program for the development of academic English (and of L1 in designated programs), but there are gaps in the sequence or the program does not adapt to differing student needs. The program may not provide appropriate support during and after transition to mainstream instruction. There may not be sufficient, qualified staff to implement the program design.	The school has a planned, sequential program for the development of academic English, including support during and after transition to mainstream instruction. In response to differing student needs, there are multiple pathways for English language development. For programs designed to develop or sustain students' primary language, there is a planned sequence for development of L1 oral, reading, and writing skills, and teachers use L1 to advance content learning. Adequate, qualified staff are available to implement the program design.

Dimension 11: Extent to which staff (teachers, aides, and other instructional personnel) assigned to teach LEP and language minority students have knowledge of the students' language(s) and culture(s), understanding of language acquisition processes and ESL methodology, and professional preparation for teaching subject matter and/or language.

Level 1	Level 3	Level 5 (Ideal)
Few or no staff members assigned to teach LEP and language minority students are appropriately trained in techniques of instruction for LEP students. Most do not understand the learning difficulties created by limited English proficiency. The school has no interim measures to better accommodate the learning needs of LEP students. Teachers are not knowledgeable about the students' cultural backgrounds. There are no plans for hiring qualified teachers or training the existing staff.	Some staff members assigned to teach LEP and language minority students are appropriately trained to develop academic English proficiency (and L1 proficiency in designated programs) or to support students' learning of academic content. Some teachers understand the learning difficulties created by limited English proficiency. The school is working to increase the qualifications of the staff through professional development or new hiring.	All staff members assigned to teach LEP and language minority students understand the needs of students who are acquiring language while learning content. They are appropriately trained (as required) in developing students' academic English proficiency (and L1 proficiency in designated programs). They provide access to core curriculum either through sheltered instruction or the students' primary language, or by supporting their learning of content and language in mainstream instruction. Through training or experience, teachers are sensitive to students' cultural backgrounds.

Dimension 12: Extent to which the school organizes itself in ways that support the developmental needs of its students. Extent to which the school organization adapts to students' changing educational needs and ensures the integration of LEP students into the schoolwide culture.

Level 1	Level 3	Level 5 (Ideal)
The school is organized conventionally (e.g., grade-level divisions) with no apparent effort to change or increase the variety of organizational structures to meet student needs. The staff are unable to articulate an educational rationale for existing school structures. LEP students may be in segregated learning or social situations.	School has taken some strides toward systematically designing its organizational structure to meet student needs. School staff have some flexibility to modify school organization but are constrained in some areas. There may be some examples of innovative organization, but they do not pervade the school.	Staff have a sense of confidence that they can modify school organization to meet student needs and can articulate a rationale for the school's structure. The school creates structures that facilitate instructional interactions between small numbers of teachers and students. The school may include looped or continuum classes, where students remain with the same teacher over several years or may be divided into more personalized units such as houses, families, or academies.

Dimension 13: Extent to which time is effectively organized, protected, and extended in order to maximize student learning.

Level 1	Level 3	Level 5 (Ideal)
School is organized around traditional time blocks or otherwise uses time unconsciously or wastefully. In class, teachers spend excessive time on administrative tasks at the expense of learning time. At the school level, there are frequent administrative interruptions (assemblies or announcements) that disrupt classroom learning.	School uses some time optimization strategies, but time may not be organized, protected, or extended (e.g., time is extended but not protected), or the whole school is not involved in the extended time. Pullouts may exist, but the school has conscientiously taken steps to minimize their disruption of learning time.	Time is organized efficiently; time on task is protected and time is extended beyond the hours and days in a standard school schedule. School might have a year-round school, extended day, before- or after-school tutoring, some summer programs (not standard summer school), and policies that protect time in the classroom (e.g., longer time blocks for classes).

Dimension 14: Extent to which the school employs an inclusive decision-making process to guide school reform efforts.

Level 1	Level 3	Level 5 (Ideal)
Site decision-making body exists, but principal presents vision and dominates process. Site body has defined responsibilities and makes some schoolwide decisions, but there is little connection between what site body decides and teaching and learning schoolwide. Principal retains control and leadership over teaching and learning.	Site decision-making body includes some, but not all, key stakeholders (e.g., teachers, parents, other staff). It makes decisions about some important priorities. The principal shares decision-making authority with a core of committed staff or parents, but participation of others is sporadic.	Site decision-making body is representative of faculty, staff, parents, and students and is empowered to make decisions about a range of issues that affect teaching and learning, including staff development, budget, and curriculum. Principal facilitates and manages change, delegating authority to others in critical areas.

Dimension 15: Extent to which teachers work together across the school to further schoolwide goals of learning for all students.

Level 1	Level 3	Level 5 (Ideal)
Teachers are isolated from each other and work largely alone. Teachers in one class or program are not aware of the needs and expectations in another class or program that affect their students. There is no common paid planning time for teachers across grades, subject areas, or programs.	Some teachers collaborate on their own time, but the school day does not allow for it. LEP teachers might collaborate with each other but not with mainstream English teachers, and vice versa. There are limited opportunities for paid planning time for teachers.	All teachers working with a particular student or group of students interact to discuss their students and address issues and needs. Teachers have paid time for common planning during the school day and extended day (e.g., Saturday, summer). There is collaboration between LEP and mainstream English teachers.

Dimension 16: Extent to which the staff are engaged in continual professional growth that is appropriate to the learning needs of their students and the school's programmatic goals. Teachers are part of a community of learners.

Level 1	Level 3	Level 5 (Ideal)
School only has externally mandated training, training is isolated, or training consists only of one-shot workshops. Professional development is not seen as part of a school reform process.	School has isolated professional development activities, but they are not part of a coherent plan. Professional development is not built around student, program, or staff needs. Some, but not all, teachers are involved in professional development activities.	Teachers decide on their professional development activities and are encouraged to seek outside support as necessary. The staff development plan is coherent and ongoing, and is based on student, program, and staff needs, including information about language acquisition and about accommodating students' cultures for all teachers.

Dimension 17: Extent to which parents and community are actively engaged in school activities and work toward realizing the school's goals of student learning.

Level 1	Level 3	Level 5 (Ideal)
The school is passive in regard to both mainstream and special population parents and community members. There are no avenues to ensure the participation of LEP parents (no L1 community liaison, etc.). Parents and community members are generally not involved in providing classroom support or engaged in site decision making.	Participation by parents in school management and activities is limited to relatively few parents and community members or certain segments (e.g., only the Chinese or Anglo parents). The school addresses some elements of parent involvement but not others (e.g., may encourage parents' participation in activities with their children, but not provide for parents' educational needs).	School is proactive in ensuring strong participation in school management and activities by parents and community members representing all economic, language, and cultural groups in the student population. The school has avenues for communicating with parents and community members in their own language. Learning needs of parents and community members are addressed through English as a second language, GED, or other classes.

Dimension 18: Extent to which the school is engaged in partnerships with external entities that support and strengthen important aspects of schooling and students' lives.

Level 1	Level 3	Level 5 (Ideal)
The school does not seek out linkages to external agencies or garner support from the wider community. School may have evidence of sporadic donations or sponsorships, but the partnerships are not continuous or meaningful.	The school may have partnerships, but they are limited in number, of brief length, or are limited to only one aspect of schooling (e.g., only monetary sponsorship). Some staff members may be proactive in seeking outside resources and partnerships, but it does not pervade the school.	The school is proactive in identifying and integrating an array of resources from the wider community. The school has multiple partners engaged in significant and long-term efforts to assist the school in strengthening its programs or in providing support to families at the school. Partnerships are diverse (e.g., businesses, churches, social organizations) and comprehensive (e.g., monetary support, staff development, mentoring, decision making).

Dimension 19: Extent to which the school acknowledges and addresses the mental health, social services, and basic needs of students, parents, and community members.

Level 1	Level 3	Level 5 (Ideal)
School staff express no special awareness of the circumstances of families and their needs for basic necessities. School has no commitment to provide or link services to students and families. Services are limited to the school nurse for emergencies.	School staff speak knowledgeably about the circumstances of families and have a means of addressing most of their key health care and basic life needs. Staff are familiar with community and social service agencies and can make referrals for families. Some services are provided at or through the school, but staff acknowledge gaps in available services.	School staff understand the service needs of their families and the school offers or refers to a wide range of social and health services as needed, including health and dental care, mental health services, public assistance, employment, and so on. School may have services onsite or have well-developed relationships with community agencies for referral and follow-up.

Appendix A
ISLLC Standards

Standard 1: A school administrator is an educational leader who promotes the success of all students by **facilitating the development, articulation, implementation, and stewardship of a vision of learning that is shared and supported by the school community.**

Standard 2: A school administrator is an educational leader who promotes the success of all students by **advocating, nurturing, and sustaining a school culture and instructional program conducive to student learning and staff professional growth.**

Standard 3: A school administrator is an educational leader who promotes the success of all students by **ensuring management of the organization, operations, and resources for a safe, efficient, and effective learning environment.**

Standard 4: A school administrator is an educational leader who promotes the success of all students by **collaborating with families and community members, responding to diverse community interests and needs, and mobilizing community resources.**

Standard 5: A school administrator is an educational leader who promotes the success of all students by **acting with integrity, fairness, and in an ethical manner.**

Standard 6: A school administrator is an educational leader who promotes the success of all students by **understanding, responding to, and influencing the larger political, social, economic, legal, and cultural context.**

The Interstate School Leaders Licensure Consortium (ISLLC) Standards were developed by the Council of Chief State School Officers and member states. Copies of the standards, along with the detailed list of knowledge, disposition, and performance indications that support the framework, may be downloaded from the Council's website. Standards are in the process of being updated.

Council of Chief School Officers. (1996). *Interstate School Leaders Licensure Consortium (ISLLC) standards for school leaders.* Washington, DC: Author. Available: http://www.ccsso.org/content/pdfs/isllcstd.pdf

Appendix B
Electronic Resources

Information & Research

Barahona Center for the Study of Books in Spanish for Children and Adolescents: This is an essential starting point for schools interested in developing their library and classroom Spanish collections, with an extensive list of recommended books in Spanish. http://www.csusm.edu/csb/english/

Bilingual Books for Kids: This website offers a selection of bilingual Spanish/English materials, including books, musical and language-learning tapes, and games. http://bilingualbooks.com/

California Department of Education: English Learners: This site contains information on education issues, instructional resources, lesson plans, curriculum, and designing a standards-based accountability system for evaluating programs for ELL students. http://www.cde.ca.gov/sp/el/

California Tomorrow: A rich list of projects, publications, and resources that are useful in educating parents and building supportive communities. http://www.california tomorrow.org/

Center for Advanced Research on Language Acquisition (CARLA): CARLA is one of the U.S. Department of Education's Title VI National Language Resource Centers. It offers a number of resources to language teachers, including a battery of second language proficiency assessments and a working paper series. http://www.carla.umn.edu/index.html?go

Center for Applied Linguistics (CAL): CAL promotes and improves the teaching and learning of languages. This is an excellent site for information on model design, implementation, and general support information. A directory of Two-Way Programs is provided. The Center for Research on Education, Diversity and Excellence (CREDE) is located at the CAL site. http://www.cal.org/

Center for Language Minority Education and Research (CLMER): CLMER engages in a wide range of services, projects, and research initiatives to promote equity, excellence, and justice in schools and society, with a focus on underserved and underrepresented children, families, and communities. CLMER provides information and support on creating and developing high quality two-way programs. http://www.clmer.csulb.edu/clmer/

Center for Multilingual Multicultural Research (CMMR): The Center provides a base for those interested in multilingual education, English as a second language, foreign language instruction, multicultural education, and related areas, as well as the opportunity to come together for research and program collaboration. http://www.usc.edu/dept/education/CMMR/home.html

Center for Research on Education, Diversity and Excellence (CREDE): The website provides access to publications, research, and toolkits for administrators, teachers, and parents. http://www.credeberkley.edu/

Center for Research on the Education of Students Placed at Risk (CRESPAR): The site provides technical reports on areas such as effective reading programs, two-way immersion models, and transitional programs for ELLs. http://www. csos.jhu.edu/crespar/

Colorín Colorado: Packed with information, activities, and advice on turning children into confident readers, this bilingual website is rooted in the vast resources of Reading Rockets, public broadcasting station WETA's multimedia initiative, which provides information on teaching kids to read and helping those who struggle. It also includes downloadable resources for teachers and librarians to reproduce and distribute to parents in their own communities. http://www.colorincolorado.org/

Council of Chief State School Officers (CCSSO): CCSSO's website provides both general information on NCLB and information relating to specific implementation areas. Many of the sections link to CCSSO projects on the specific topic at issue. CCSSO maintains a 50-state database on many of these topics. http://www.ccsso.org

Culturally and Linguistically Appropriate Services (CLAS) Early Childhood Research Institute: The CLAS Institute collects and describes early childhood and early intervention resources that have been developed for children with disabilities and their families and the service providers who work with them. http://www.clas.uiuc.edu/

Directory of Two-Way Bilingual Immersion Programs in the U.S.: This is a comprehensive listing of two-way programs around the country. http://www.cal.org/twi/directory/

Dr. Mora's Cross-cultural Language and Academic Development CLAD Website: This is a comprehensive website on all aspects of second language learning and bilingual education. http://coe.sdsu.edu/people/jmora/Default.htm

Dual Language Education of New Mexico: This resource assists educators in designing and implementing dual language programs. Rubrics for accountability and assessment, advocacy, essential components, family and community involvement, model design, and teacher preparation and professional development for dual language programs are available on this site. http://www.duallanguagenm.org/index.html

Education Place Graphic Organizers: This website by Houghton Mifflin features 37 free, printer-friendly graphic organizers in English and Spanish, available for download. http://eduplace.com/graphicorganizer/

Education Resources Information Center (ERIC): ERIC provides a centralized bibliographic database of journal articles and other published and unpublished education materials. http://www.eric.ed.gov/

Edvantia: Help! They Don't Speak English Starter Kit: An excellent ESL teacher resource containing information on areas such as culture, instructional strategies, literacy, assessment, and home-school partnerships. The handbook can be downloaded for free from this website. http://www.edvantia.org/publications/index1.cfm?&section=publications&area=publications&id=515

The English Language Learner KnowledgeBase: This website is an online resource supporting educational professionals in the administration of their programs for ELL students. It brings together the theory and practice needed to create a quality program that meets the requirements of the Office for Civil Rights and Title III of the No Child Left Behind act. http://www.helpforschools.com/ELLKBase/index.shtml

Equity Assistance Centers (EACs): EACs provide training and advisory services to public schools in the areas of race, gender, and national origin equity to promote equal educational opportunities. Contact information for the 10 federally funded centers is available on this website. http://www.edgateway.net/pub/docs/eacn/home.html

Illinois Resource Center (IRC): The IRC has designed an electronic resource of locally and nationally relevant information that will assist educators in working with English language learners. A valuable resource on the site is an extensive list and description of suggested materials for bilingual programs and ESL programs. http://www.the centerweb.org/irc/

Illinois State Board of Education (ISBE): This website provides a wealth of resources for starting or improving a program. Among them are links to ISBE documents such as Home Language Survey and parent notification letters in 27 languages, a language proficiency handbook, a bilingual special education resource page, a Hmong dictionary of special education terms, and an e-kit, an electronic resource for educating English language learners. http://www.isbe. net/bilingual/default.htm

Innovative Practices in Language Instruction Educational Programs and School Improvement Efforts: This site features a selection of resources from NCELA's collection and the World Wide Web describing promising practices that districts can refer to learn more about innovative language educational programs and school improvement efforts. http://www.ncela.gwu.edu/practice/innovative/index.html

Intercultural Development Research Association (IDRA): IDRA is an independent nonprofit organization that conducts research; creates, implements, and administers innovative education programs; and provides teacher, administrator, and parent training and technical assistance. http://www.idra.org

James Crawford's Language Policy Web Site and Emporium: This website provides information and articles on language policy, bilingual research, and bilingual education. http://ourworld.compuserve.com/homepages/JWCRAWFORD/

Jim Cummins' ESL and Second Language Learning Web: Jim Cummins has written and presented many works on second language learning and literacy development. This website includes many of his writings and other sources. http://www.iteachilearn.com/cummins/index.htm

Kentucky Migrant Technology Project: The Educational Source: The website has a large collection of course materials online in both Spanish and English; translation guides for teachers, students, parents, and bus drivers; an ESL survival packet; translated school forms; ESL links; and a newcomer packet. http://www. migrant.org/index.cfm

The Knowledge Loom: The Knowledge Loom is a resource on best practices in teaching and learning. There is a searchable database of resources as well as interactive discussion centers where teachers can ask questions of experts in the field or post their own success stories and ideas about the implementation of best practices in real schools and districts. The website provides a spotlight section on culturally responsive teaching. http://knowledgeloom.org/index.jsp

Lee and Low Books: This website comes from an independent children's book publisher that specializes in multicultural themes. http://www.leeandlow.com/home/index. html

Little Explorers English Picture Dictionary: The Little Explorers Picture Dictionary and other illustrated (and some bilingual) illustrated dictionaries by Enchanted Learning are especially useful for teaching vocabulary. The website features illustrated dictionaries in 13 languages with over 1,300 illustrated dictionary entries. http://www.enchanted learning.com/Dictionary.html

The National Clearinghouse for English Language Acquisition and Language Instruction Educational Programs (NCELA): NCELA offers access to databases, classroom resources, research and many other reliable resources on language education for minority students, bilingual education, and English as a second language. http://www.ncela.gwu.edu/

Northwest Regional Educational Laboratory (NWREL): NWREL operates a technical assistance center serving the northwest states. The center provides information on educational programs and general school improvement to meet the needs of special populations of children and youth, including ELL students. http://www.nwrel.org/. The Equity Center provides additional useful information. http://www.nwrel.org/cnorse/index.html

Office of Language and Cultural Education (OLCE): OLCE offers information on program descriptions and teacher resources such as training modules and bilingual/ESL goals with suggested lesson plans and materials. http://www.olce. org/

Office of Superintendent of Public Instruction (OSPI), Washington: This site provides information on the programs operated by OSPI and a number of education links with information on culturally and linguistically diverse students and special education services. http://www.k12.wa.us/

Portraits of Success: This database was a national effort (1996–2000), supported by a number of experts in the field of bilingual education, to develop a database on successful bilingual education. http://www.alliance.brown.edu/pubs/pos/

Teaching Diverse Learners: This online resource provides both research and practical steps to enhance the capacity of teachers work effectively and equitably with English language learners. http://www.lab.brown.edu/tdl/index.shtml

U.S. Department of Education: This website offers a variety of important educational information for students, parents and families, teachers, principals, higher education administration, and others. It provides many links relevant to teaching culturally diverse students. http://www.ed.gov/index.jhtml

U.S. Department of Education, Institute of Education Sciences (IES): IES provides national leadership to advance the field of education research, making it more rigorous in support of evidence-based education. The Institute consists of the National Center for Education Research, the National Center for Education Statistics, and the National Center for Education Evaluation and Regional Assistance. http://www.ed.gov/about/offices/list/ies/index.html

U.S. Department of Education, Office for Civil Rights: This website provides education resources, civil rights data, and an A–Z reading room dedicated to the prevention of civil rights violations. http://www.ed.gov/about/offices/list/ocr/index.html

U.S. Department of Education, Office of English Language Acquisition, Language Enhancement, and Academic Achievement for Limited English Proficient Students (OELA): OELA administers Title III of the No Child Left Behind act (2001) and provides national leadership in promoting high-quality education for ELLs. This website provides links to grants, contacts, education resources, and research statistics. http://www.ed.gov/about/offices/list/oela/index.html

University of Texas at Austin, College of Education: This site provides links to bilingual education resources on the Internet. http://www.edb.utexas.edu/coe/depts/ci/bilingue/resources.html

Selected Resources for Developing ELL Programs

Assessment in ESL and Bilingual Education—A Hot Topics Paper: An overview of assessing language proficiency, review of assessment instruments, achievement testing, and special education assessments by Gary Hargett. An outstanding feature of this website is its section on what to look for when selecting an assessment instrument for ESL and bilingual students. http://www.nwrac.org/pub/hot/assessment.html

California English Language Development Content Standards: California's English language development standards supplement the English language arts content standards to ensure that ELLs develop proficiency in both the English language and the concepts and skills contained in the English language arts content standards. These are good resources for alignment of standards. http://www.cde.ca.gov/be/st/ss/index.asp

Dual Language Education of New Mexico Program Standards: This website provides a common definition of effective dual language programs; a tool in rubric format to use in designing, implementing, and evaluating an effective dual language program; and a framework for policy makers. http://www.duallanguagenm.org/standardspdf.html

ESL Standards for Pre-K–12 Students: This website highlights ESL standards for pre-K–12 students. Information on the following topics is included: why these standards are necessary, myths about second language learning, TESOL's vision of effective education for all students, general principles of language acquisition, and the three broad goals that have been established for ESOL learners. http://www.tesol.org/s_tesol/seccss.asp?CID=95&DID=1565

Evaluation and Assessment for Title VII Projects: This guide by the Evaluation Assistance Center-Western Region (EAC-West) contains information on a variety of topics, including creating appropriate goals and objectives for programs, determining student grades, identification of gifted and talented students, and identifying ELLs. http://www.ncela.gwu.edu/pubs/eacwest/handouts/

Evaluation and Assessment in Early Childhood Special Education: Children Who Are Culturally and Linguistically Diverse: This 1997 Individuals with Disabilities Education Act publication from the Washington State OSPI provides an overview of key issues relating to the evaluation of language minority students in special education. The following documents are included in the publication: Checklist of Language Skills for Use with Limited English Proficient Students and Profile of Language Dominance and Proficiency. http://www.k12.wa.us/SpecialEd/pubdocs/CLD.doc

Handbook of English Language Proficiency Tests: This EAC-West guide provides an overview of assessing English language proficiency, details regarding five different tests, and a checklist for selecting an appropriate test for a district's needs. http://www.ncela.gwu.edu/pubs/eacwest/elptests.htm

Identifying Limited English Proficient Students: This handout provides information on identifying ELL students and establishing transition and exit criteria. The handout also includes sample instruments for identifying ELL students. http://www.ncela.gwu.edu/pubs/eacwest/handouts/id-lep/backgrnd. htm

In the Classroom: A Toolkit for Effective Instruction of English Learners: This online toolkit is designed to make effective research-based lesson plans, activities, and curricula available to all teachers of ELLs, whether within bilingual education, ESL, or English-only settings. http://www.ncela.gwu.edu/practice/itc/index.htm

Informal Assessment in Education Evaluation: Implications for Bilingual Education Programs: This guide describes alternative assessment approaches and discusses how these approaches can supplement standardized tests. http://www.ncela.gwu.edu/pubs/pigs/pig3.htm

LEP Students and Title I: A Guidebook for Educators: This guidebook provides analysis and guidance on providing services to ELL students through a Title I program. http://www.ncela.gwu.edu/pubs/resource/lepguide

Myths and Misconceptions About Second Language Learning: What Every Teacher Needs to Unlearn: This article by Barry McLaughlin is a good starting point for discussion about second language learning. It would be valuable to use for a study group or staff meeting discussion. http://www.ncela.gwu.edu/pubs/symposia/reading/article6/mclaughlin93.html

A National Study of School Effectiveness for Language Minority Students' Long-Term Academic Achievement Final Report: Project 1.1: This is the final report of Thomas and Collier's five-year study of education services (1996–2001) provided for language minority students in U.S. public schools and the resulting long-term academic achievement of these students. http://credeberkley.edu/research/llaa/1.1_final.html

No Child Left Behind: A Desktop Reference: This guide outlines what is new under the No Child Left Behind act for each program supported under the Elementary and Secondary Act of 1965 and other statutes. http://www.ed.gov/admins/lead/account/nclbreference/index.html

A Portfolio Assessment Model for ESL: This guide provides detailed information on the design, implementation, and use of portfolios in assessment. http://www.ncela.gwu.edu/pubs/jeilms/vol13/portfo13.htm

Program Alternatives for Linguistically Diverse Students: This educational practice report by CREDE, edited by Fred Genesee, examines programs and approaches for educating ELLs. http://www.cal.org/crede/PUBS/edpractice/EPR1.pdf

Programs for English Language Learners: Resource Materials for Planning and Self-Assessments: This manual by the Office for Civil Rights includes information on legal issues, developing programs, and program evaluation. http://www.ed.gov/about/offices/list/ocr/ell/index.html

School Effectiveness for Language Minority Students: This National Clearinghouse for Bilingual Education (NCBE) document by Thomas and Collier presents a summary of an ongoing collaborative research study that is both national in scope and practical for immediate local decision making in schools. This summary is written for bilingual and ESL program coordinators, as well as for local school policy makers. http://www.ncela. gwu.edu/pubs/resource/effectiveness/thomas-collier97.pdf

Setting Expected Gains for Non and Limited English Proficient Students: This NCBE resource collection document by Edward De Avila provides essential information about expected gains on language proficiency tests. http://www.ncela.gwu.edu/pubs/resource/setting/index.htm

The Sheltered Instruction Observation Protocol: A Tool for Teacher-Researcher Collaboration and Professional Development: This document provides introductory information about the SIOP model for sheltered instruction. http://www.cal.org/crede/pubs/edpractice/epr3.pdf

Standards-Based Instruction for English Language Learners: This Pacific Resources for Education and Learning document by Joseph Laturnau explores the benefits of standards-based instruction for ELLs. http://www.prel.org/products/pc_/standards-based.htm

Success in Educating All Students: What Do Some Schools Do Differently? The purpose of this web-based pathway by the NCELA is to highlight the characteristics of schools that successfully educate linguistically and culturally diverse students to high standards. The characteristics that define these successful schools are described in the document. http://www.ncela.gwu.edu/pathways/success/

What Are the Defining Characteristics of Effective Instructional Programs for Language Minority Students? The purpose of this web-based pathway by the NCELA is to outline the attributes of effective programs for language minority students and English language learners. Links to references and related publications are provided. http://www.ncela.gwu.edu/pathways/effective/index.htm

Professional Organizations

Below is a list of professional organizations related to ESL and bilingual education. There are also state and regional associations that are affiliated with NABE and TESOL.

National Association for Bilingual Education (NABE): NABE is a national organization dedicated to addressing the educational needs of language minority students in the United States and advancing the language competencies and multicultural understanding of Americans. The organization offers annual conferences focused on bilingual education. The website offers access to the *Bilingual Research Journal* and *NABE News Magazine* and provides links to other resources. http://www.nabe.org/

Teachers of English to Speakers of Other Languages (TESOL): TESOL's mission is to ensure excellence in English language teaching to speakers of other languages. This international organization is one of the largest organizations for professionals in second language acquisition. The website contains a variety of information about the subject. http://www.tesol.org

Regional Educational Laboratories

Edvantia
States Served: Kentucky, Tennessee, Virginia, and West Virginia
National Leadership Area: Educational technology
http://www.edvantia.org/home.cfm?&section=home&area=home

Laboratory for Student Success
States Served: Delaware, Maryland, New Jersey, Pennsylvania, and
Washington, DC
National Leadership Area: Educational leadership
http://www.temple.edu/LSS/

Mid-continent Research for Education and Learning
States Served:
Colorado, Kansas, Missouri, Nebraska, North Dakota, South Dakota, and
Wyoming
National Leadership Area: Standards-based instructional practice
http://www.mcrel.org/

North Central Regional Educational Laboratory
States Served: Illinois, Indiana, Iowa, Michigan, Minnesota, Ohio, and Wisconsin
National Leadership Area: Educational technology
http://www.ncrel.org/

Northeast and Islands Regional Educational Laboratory at Brown University
States Served: Connecticut, Maine, Massachusetts, New Hampshire, New York, Rhode
Island, Vermont, Puerto Rico, and the Virgin Islands
National Leadership Area: Teaching diverse students
http://www.alliance.brown.edu/programs/lab/

Northwest Regional Educational Laboratory
States Served: Alaska, Idaho, Montana, Oregon, and Washington
National Leadership Area: Re-engineering schools
http://www.nwrel.org/

Pacific Resources for Education and Learning
States Served: American Samoa, Commonwealth of the Northern Mariana Islands, Feder-
ated States of Micronesia, Guam, Hawaii, the Republic of Palau, and the
Republic of the Marshall Islands
National Leadership Area: Area of curriculum and instruction related to reading and
language mastery
http://www.prel.org/

SERVE Center at the University of North Carolina and Greensboro
States Served: Alabama, Florida, Georgia, Mississippi, North Carolina, and
South Carolina
National Leadership Area: Expanded learning opportunities
http://www.serve.org/

Southwest Educational Development Laboratory
States Served: Arkansas, Louisiana, New Mexico, Oklahoma, and Texas
National Leadership Area: Family and community involvement
http://www.sedl.org/

WestEd
States Served: Arizona, California, Nevada, and Utah
National Leadership Area: Assessment of educational achievement
http://www.wested.org/

Glossary

Additive bilingualism: The learning of a majority language in an environment in which the addition of a second language and culture does not replace the first language and culture; rather, the first language and culture are promoted and developed (Lambert, 1982; NCELA, 2002).

Affective filter: Associated with Krashen's hypotheses of second language learning, the affective filter is a metaphor that describes a learner's attitudes that affect the relative success of second language acquisition. Negative feelings such as lack of motivation, lack of self-confidence, and learning anxiety act as filters that hinder and obstruct language learning (Baker & Prys Jones, 1998; NCELA, 2002).

Alternative assessment: Approaches for finding out what students know or can do other than through the use of multiple-choice testing (O'Malley & Valdez Pierce, 1996, p. 237).

Anecdotal records: Informal written notes on student learning products or processes, usually jotted down from direct observation (O'Malley & Valdez Pierce, 1996, p. 237).

Authentic assessment: Procedures for evaluating student achievement or performance using activities that represent classroom goals, curricula, and instruction, or real-life performance (O'Malley & Valdez Pierce, 1996, p. 237).

Benchmarks: Anchor papers used in defining exemplary performance on the levels of a scoring rubric. May also be a set of objectives, as in benchmark objectives, that define what is expected of a student in a particular area at a certain grade level (O'Malley & Valdez Pierce, 1996, p. 237).

BICS (Basic Interpersonal Communicative Skills): Also known as conversational fluency or social language (Cummins, 1984), everyday communication skills that are helped by contextual support (Baker & Prys Jones, 1998). Research indicates that students need approximately one to three years in order to be able to understand and talk in context-rich situations.

Bilingual education: Generally understood to be an instructional program for language minority students that makes use of the students' native language(s), bilingual education in practice takes many different forms. An important distinction is between those programs that use and promote two languages and those where bilingual children are present, but bilingualism is not fostered in the curriculum (Baker, 1993; NCELA, 2002).

Bilingualism: Simply defined, the ability to use two languages. However, individuals with varying bilingual characteristics may be classified as bilingual. Categories of bilingualism include ability and use of a language; proficiency across the language dimensions of listening, speaking, reading, and writing; differences in proficiency of both languages; and variation in proficiency over time (Baker, 1993; NCELA, 2002).

CALP (Cognitive Academic Language Proficiency): Also known as academic language proficiency (Cummins, 1984), the level of second language proficiency needed by students to perform the more abstract and cognitively demanding tasks of a classroom. Academic language is often abstract and has few contextual supports such as gestures and the viewing of objects (Baker & Prys Jones, 1998). Research indicates that students need approximately 4 to 10 years to use the second language in order to learn, read, and write cognitively complex academic material.

Cloze test: Reading test that consists of passages from which words are omitted at regular intervals; also provides an indication of overall language ability (Snow, 2000).

Cognates: Two words that have a common origin; most often, words in two languages that have a common etymology and thus are similar or identical in meaning (azure [English], *azul* [Spanish]).

Common underlying proficiency: Two or more languages contributing to the central, unified thinking system in an individual. The indications of linguistic interdependence in language learning are the understandings common across languages that make possible the transfer of such skills. Thus, ideas, concepts, attitudes, knowledge, and skills can transfer into either language (Baker & Prys Jones, 1998; Cummins, 1989).

Comprehensible input: A construct developed to describe understandable and meaningful language directed at second language learners under optimal conditions (Cloud et al., 2000, p. 203).

Content bias: Test content and procedures reflecting the dominant culture's standards of language function and shared knowledge and behavior (August & Hakuta, 1997, p. 115).

Context-embedded/context-reduced instruction: Context-embedded instruction provides a wide range of cues to meaning to support verbal input (facial expressions, gestures, visual clues). However, context-reduced instruction lacks such contextual support and provides few clues to meaning other than the words themselves (Cummins, 1984).

Conversational fluency: Also known as BICS or social language, the ability to carry on a conversation in familiar face-to-face situations (Cummins, 2002).

Culturally relevant curriculum and instruction: The selection of culturally relevant content, examples, modes of presentation, grouping structures, learning activities, reinforcers, motivational devices, and the like to promote understanding and learning (Cloud et al., 2000).

Developmental bilingual education (also known as maintenance or late-exit bilingual education): A program that uses two languages, the student's primary language and English, as a means of instruction. The instruction builds upon the student's primary language skills and develops and expands the English language skills of each student to enable him or her to achieve competency in both languages (U.S. General Accounting Office, 1994).

Discrete language skills: Aspect of language proficiency referring to the specific phonological, literacy, and grammatical skills that students acquire (Cummins, 2002).

Dual language program (also known as two-way immersion or two-way bilingual education): A bilingual program that allows students to develop language proficiency in two languages by receiving instruction in English and another language in a classroom that is usually made up of half native English speakers and half native speakers of the other language (Christian, 1994).

Early-exit bilingual education: See transitional bilingual education.

English as a second language (ESL): The field of English as a second language; courses, classes and programs designed for students learning English as an additional language (TESOL, 1997).

English language development: Instruction designed for English language learners to develop their listening, speaking, and writing skills in English (NCELA, 2002).

English language learners (ELLs): Students whose first language is not English and who are in the process of learning English. Unlike terminology such as "limited English proficient," this term highlights what the students are accomplishing, not their temporary deficits (Lacelle-Peterson & Rivera, 1994). Although these students are legally referred to as limited English proficient (LEP), the term English language learners (ELL), sometimes shortened to English learners (EL) has become the preferred term. The U.S. Department of Education is currently using the term English language learners.

False cognates: Words that are thought to be related (have a common origin) but are not (embarrassed, *embarazado* ["pregnant" in Spanish]).

FEP: Fluent English proficient.

Home language: Language(s) spoken in the home by significant others (e.g., family members, caregivers) who reside in the child's home; sometimes used as a synonym for first language, primary language, or native language (TESOL, 1997).

IDEA Language Proficiency Tests (IPT): A language test often used in initial assessment and placement of English language learners.

Inter-rater reliability: Technical measure of the degree of agreement between two raters rating the same assessment item (e.g., a student writing sample) using the same scale (Snow, 2000).

L1: First or native language.

L2: Second language.

Language Assessment Scales: A language test often used in initial assessment and placement of ELLs.

Language transfer: The effect of one language on the learning of another. There can be two types of transfer: negative transfer, sometimes called interference, and more often positive transfer, particularly in understandings and meanings of concepts (Baker & Prys Jones, 1998).

Late-exit bilingual education (also known as maintenance bilingual education or developmental bilingual education): See developmental bilingual education.

LEP: Limited English proficient.

Limited English Proficient (LEP): The term used by the federal government and most states to identify students who have insufficient English to succeed in English classrooms (Lessow-Hurley, 1991).

Linguistic and cultural biases: Factors that adversely affect the formal test performance of students from linguistic and cultural backgrounds, including timed testing, difficulty with English vocabulary, and the near impossibility of determining what bilingual students know in their two languages (August & Hakuta, 1997, p. 115).

Linguistically and culturally diverse (LCD): Term used to identify individuals from homes and communities where English is not the primary language of communication (García, 1991b).

Maculaitis Assessment: A language test often used in initial assessment and placement of English language learners.

Maintenance bilingual education (also known as developmental bilingual education or late-exit bilingual education): See developmental bilingual education.

Native language: First, primary, or home language (L1).

Native language instruction: Use of a child's home language (generally by a classroom teacher) to provide lessons in academic subjects or to teach reading and other language arts (Crawford, 1997; NCELA, 2002).

Native language support: Use of a child's home language (generally by a teacher aide) to translate unfamiliar terms or otherwise clarify lessons taught in English (Crawford, 1997; NCELA, 2002).

NEP: Non-English proficient.

Norming bias: Small numbers of particular minorities included in probability samples, increasing the likelihood that minority group samples are unrepresentative (August & Hakuta, 1997, p. 115).

Performance assessment: Assessment tasks that require students to construct a response, create a product, or demonstrate applications of knowledge (O'Malley & Valdez Pierce, 1996, p. 239).

Portfolio: A collection of student work showing student reflection and progress or achievement over time in one or more areas (O'Malley & Valdez Pierce, 1996, p. 239).

Preview-view-review method: An instructional approach in which content areas are previewed in the first language, presented in the second, and reviewed in the first (Lessow-Hurley, 1990).

Primary language: First, home, or native language (L1).

Professional learning community (PLC): The PLC conceptual framework can be grouped into three major themes that are evident in the policies, programs, and practices of the school or district. The themes are (1) a solid foundation consisting of collaboratively developed mission, vision, values, and goals; (2) collaborative teams that work interdependently to achieve common goals; and (3) a focus on results as evidenced by a commitment to continuous improvement (Eaker et al., 2002, p. 3).

Pullout ESL: Students are pulled out of their regular classrooms for specified periods of instruction to develop their English language skills.

Push-in ESL: Programs in which the ESL teacher goes into regular classrooms to work with English language learners.

Scaffolding: Adult support for learning and student performance through instruction, modeling, questioning, feedback, and so on. These supports are gradually withdrawn as students are able to demonstrate strategic behaviors in their own learning activities (Harris & Hodges, 1995).

Second language acquisition: The process of acquiring a second language. Some linguists distinguish between *acquisition* and *learning* of a second language, with acquisition used to describe the informal development of a second language, and learning used to describe the process of formal study of a second language. Other linguists maintain that there is no clear distinction between the two (NCELA, 2002).

Self-assessment: Appraisal by a student of his or her own work or learning processes (O'Malley & Valdez Pierce, 1996, p. 240).

Sheltered instruction (SI): An approach to teaching that extends the time students have for receiving English language support while they learn content subjects. SI classrooms, which may include a mix of native English speakers and English language learners or only ELLs, integrate language and content with sociocultural awareness. Teachers scaffold instruction to aid student comprehension of content topics and objectives by adjusting their speech and instructional tasks and by providing appropriate background information and experiences. The ultimate goal is accessibility for ELLs to grade-level content standards and concepts while they continue to improve their English language proficiency (Echevarria et al., 2000, p. 200).

Stanford English Language Proficiency Test: A language test often used in initial assessment and placement of English language learners.

Subtractive bilingualism: The learning of a majority language in an environment in which the second language and culture is intended to replace the first language and culture (Lambert, 1982).

Threshold hypothesis: Hypothesis that suggests that first language literacy transfers to a second language only when a person has reached a critical level of language competence in the first language in order to gain cognitive benefits from owning two languages (Baker & Prys Jones, 1998).

Transitional bilingual education (also known as early-exit bilingual education): An instructional program in which subjects are taught in two languages—English and the native language of the ELL students—and English is taught as a second language. English language skills, grade promotion, and graduation requirements are emphasized. The primary purpose of these programs is to facilitate ELL students' transition to an all-English instructional environment while they receive academic subject instruction in the native language to the extent necessary. Transitional bilingual education programs vary in the amount of native language instruction provided and the duration of the program (U.S. General Accounting Office, 1994).

Two-way immersion: See dual language program.

Universal aspects of literacy: Those characteristics of literacy that are similar for all languages and once learned in the first language can be transferred to learning a second language (Harris & Hodges, 1995).

References

Abedi, J. (2001). *Assessment and accommodations for English language learners: Issues and recommendations* (Policy Brief 4). Los Angeles: National Center for Research on Evaluation, Standards, and Student Testing.

Abedi, J. (2003). *Issues in content assessments and accommodations for English language learners.* Paper presented at the OELA Summit: Celebrate Our Rising Stars II Success in School: Everyone's Responsibility—Every Child's Right. Washington, DC.

Abedi, J., Courtney, M., & Leon, S. (2002). *Research-supported accommodations for English language learners in NAEP.* Los Angeles: University of California, Los Angeles, National Center for Research on Evaluation, Standards, and Student Testing.

Abedi, J., & Dietel, R. (2004). *Challenges in the No Child Left Behind Act for English language learners* (Policy Brief 7). Los Angeles: National Center for Research on Evaluation, Standards, and Student Testing.

Abedi, J., Lord, C., Kim, C., & Miyoshi, J. (2000). *The effects of accommodations on the assessment of LEP students in NAEP.* Los Angeles: University of California, Los Angeles, National Center for Research on Evaluation, Standards, and Student Testing.

Adger, C. T. (1996, October). *Language minority students in school reform: The role of collaboration* (Report No. EDO-FL-97-01). Washington, DC: ERIC Clearinghouse on Languages and Linguistics. (ERIC Document Reproduction Service No. ED400681)

American Educational Research Association. (2004, Winter). English language learners: Boosting academic achievement. *Research Points, 2*(1), 1–4.

American Educational Research Association, American Psychological Association, & National Council on Measurement in Education. (1985). *Standards of educational and psychological testing.* Washington, DC: American Psychological Association.

Anderson, R. C. (1994). Role of the reader's schema in comprehension, learning, and memory. In R. Ruddell, M. Ruddell, & H. Singer (Eds.), *Theoretical models and processes of reading* (4th ed., pp. 469–482). Newark, DE: International Reading Association.

Anderson, R. C. (1996). Research foundations to support wide reading. In V. Greaney (Ed.), *Promoting reading in developing countries* (pp. 55–77). Newark, DE: International Reading Association.

Anstrom, K. (1998, May). *What are the defining characteristics of effective instructional programs for language minority students?* (NCELA Pathways). Retrieved October 14, 2001, from http://www.ncela.gwu.edu/pathways/index.htm

Antunez, B. (2003). *Reading and English language learners.* Retrieved January 3, 2004, from http://www.readingrockets.org/article.php?ID=409

Arreaga-Mayer, C. (1998). Language sensitive peer mediated instruction for language minority students in the intermediate elementary grades. In R. Gersten & R. Jimenez (Eds.), *Promoting learning for culturally and linguistically diverse students: Classroom applications from contemporary research* (pp. 79–90). Belmont, CA: Wadsworth.

Ascher, C. (1990). *Assessing bilingual students for placement and instruction* (Report No. EDO-UD-90-5, Digest No. 65). New York: ERIC Clearinghouse on Urban Education. (ERIC Document Reproduction Service No. ED322273)

August, D. (2002). *English as a second language instruction: Best practices to support the development of literacy for English language learners.* Baltimore: Johns Hopkins University, Center for Research on the Education of Students Placed at Risk.

August, D. (2003). *Supporting the development of English literacy in English language learners: Key issues and promising practices* (Report No. 61). Baltimore: Johns Hopkins University, Center for Research on the Education of Students Placed at Risk.

August, D. (2004, October 6). *Developing literacy in English-language learners: Key issues and promising practices.* Presentation at the OELA Celebrate Our Rising Stars Third Annual Summit 2004, Washington, DC.

August, D. (2006). *Developing literacy in second language learners: Report of the National Literacy Panel on Language-Minority Children and Youth executive summary.* Retrieved March 6, 2006, from http://www.cal. org/natl-lit-panel/reports/Executive _Summary.pdf

August, D., & Hakuta, K. (Eds.). (1997). *Improving schooling for language-minority children: A research agenda.* Washington, DC: National Research Council, National Academy Press.

August, D., & Lara, J. (1996, February). *Systemic reform and limited English proficient students.* Washington, DC: Council of Chief State School Officers. Retrieved August 1, 2000, from http://www.ccsso.org/ pdfs/srandlep.pdf

August, D., & Pease-Álvarez, L. (1996). *Attributes of effective programs and classrooms serving English language learners.* Santa Cruz, CA: National Center for Research on Cultural Diversity and Second Language Learning. (ERIC Document Reproduction Service No. ED396581)

Baca, L., & Almanza, E. (1991). *Language minority students with disabilities.* Reston, VA: Council for Exceptional Children. (ERIC Document Reproduction Service No. ED339171)

Baker, C. (1993). *Foundations of bilingual education and bilingualism.* Clevedon, England: Multilingual Matters.

Baker, C., & Prys Jones, S. (1998). *Encyclopedia of bilingualism and bilingual education.* Philadelphia: Multilingual Matters.

Baptiste, H. P., Jr. (1999). The multicultural environment of schools: Implications to leaders. In L. W. Hughes (Ed.), *The principal as leader* (2nd ed., pp. 105–127). Upper Saddle River, NJ: Merrill.

Baruth, L. G., & Manning, M. L. (1992). *Multicultural education of children and adolescents.* Needham Heights, MA: Allyn and Bacon.

Batsis, T. M. (1987). *Translating the task: Administrators in language minority schools.* Washington, DC: ERIC Clearinghouse on School Administration. (ERIC Document Reproduction Service No. ED285266)

Battistich, V., Solomon, D., Watson, M., & Schaps, E. (1997). Caring school communities. *Educational Psychology, 32,* 137–151.

Beck, I. L., & McKeown, M. G. (2001). Text talk: Capturing the benefits of read-aloud experiences for young children. *The Reading Teacher, 55,* 10–20.

Beck, I. L., McKeown, M. G., & Kucan, L. (2002). *Bringing words to life: Robust vocabulary instruction.* New York: Guilford Press.

Bennici, F., & Strang, W. E. (1995). *Special issues analysis center, annual report, year 3: An analysis of language minority and limited English proficient students from NELS: 88* (Vol. V). Rockville, MD: Westat.

Berman, P., Aburto, S., Nelson, B., Minicucci, C., & Burkhart, G. (2000, September). *Going schoolwide: Comprehensive school reform inclusive of limited English proficient students.* Washington, DC: Institute for Policy Analysis and Research and the Center for Applied Linguistics, Center for the Study of Language and Education, The George Washington University.

Berman, P., Chambers, J., Gandara, P., McLaughlin, B., Minicucci, C., Nelson, B., Olsen, L., & Parrish, T. (1992). *Meeting the challenge of language diversity: An evaluation of programs for pupils with limited proficiency in English.* Berkeley, CA: BW Associates.

Berman, P., Minicucci, C., McLaughlin, B., Nelson, B., & Woodworth, K. (1995, August). *School reform and student diversity: Case studies of exemplary practices for LEP students.* Emeryville, CA: Institute for Policy Analysis and Research; Santa Cruz, CA: National Center for Research on Cultural Diversity and Second Language Learning. Retrieved June 13, 2001, from http://www.ncela.gwu.edu/miscpubs/schoolreform/index.htm

Bermúdez, A. B., & Márquez, J. A. (1996). An examination of a four-way collaborative to increase parental involvement in the schools. *The Journal of Educational Issues of Minority Students, 16,* 1–16.

Biemiller, A. (1999). *Language and reading success.* Cambridge, MA: Brookline Books.

Birch, B. M. (2002). *English L2 reading: Getting to the bottom.* Mahwah, NJ: Lawrence Erlbaum Associates.

Bishop, K. D., Foster, W., & Jubala, K. A. (1993). The social construction of disability in education: Organizational considerations. In C. A. Capper (Ed.), *Educational administration in a pluralistic society* (pp. 173–202). Albany: State University of New York Press.

Bliss, J., Firestone, W., & Richards, C. (Eds.). (1991). *Rethinking effective schools: Research and practice.* Englewood Cliffs, NJ: Prentice Hall.

Boethel, M. (2003). *Diversity: Family and community connections with schools.* Austin, TX: Southwest Educational Development Laboratory.

Bossert, T., Dwyer, D. C., Rowan, B., & Lee, G. V. (1982, Summer). The instructional management role of the principal. *Educational Administration Quarterly, 18*(3), 34–64.

Bradby, D., Owings, J., & Quinn, P. (1992, February). *Language characteristics and academic achievement: A look at Asian and Hispanic eighth graders in NELS:88* (Statistical analysis report, NCES 92-479). Washington, DC: U.S. Department of Education, Office of Educational Research and Improvement. Retrieved February 23, 2002, from http://nces.ed.gov/pubs92/92479.pdf

Brinton, D. M., Snow, M. A., & Wesche, M. B. (1993). Content-based second language instruction. In J. W. Oller, Jr. (Ed.), *Methods that work: Ideas for literacy and language teachers* (2nd ed., pp. 136–142). Boston: Heinle & Heinle.

Brown, H. D. (1992). Sociocultural factors in teaching language minority students. In P. A. Richard-Amato & M. A. Snow (Eds.), *The multicultural classroom: Readings for content area teachers* (pp. 73–92). White Plains, NY: Longman.

Brown, Z. A., Hammond, O. W., & Onikama, D. L. (1997, September). *Language use at home and school: A synthesis of research for Pacific educators.* Honolulu, HI: Pacific Resources for Education and Learning. Available: http://www.prel.org/products/ products/Language-use.pdf

Calderón, M. (1994). Mentoring, peer coaching, and support systems for first year minority/bilingual teachers. In R. A. DeVillar, C. J. Faltis, & J. P. Cummins (Eds.), *Cultural diversity in schools: From rhetoric to practice* (pp. 117–141). Albany: State University of New York Press.

Calderón, M., & Carreon, A. (1999). In search of a new border pedagogy: Sociocultural conflicts facing bilingual teachers and students along the U.S.-Mexico border. In C. J. Ovando & P. McLaren (Eds.), *The politics of multi-culturalism and bilingual education: Students and teachers caught in the cross fire* (pp. 167–187). Boston: McGraw Hill.

Calderón, M., Hertz-Lazarowitz, R., Ivory, G., & Slavin, R. E. (1997). *Effects of bilingual cooperative integrated reading and composition of students transitioning from Spanish to English reading* (CRESPAR Program 5, Report No. 10). Washington, DC: U.S. Department of Education, Office of Educational Research and Improvement. Retrieved February 23, 2002, from http://www.csos.jhu.edu/crespar/Reports/report 10entire.html

Calderón, M., Hertz-Lazarowitz, R., & Slavin, R. (1998). Effects of bilingual cooperative integrated reading and composition on students making the transition from Spanish to English. *The Elementary School Journal, 99,* 153–165.

California State Department of Education. (1994). *Building bilingual instruction: Putting the pieces together.* Sacramento, CA: Bilingual Education Office.

Capps, R., Fix, M., Murray, J., Ost, J., Passel, J.S., & Herwantoro, S. (2005). *The new demography of America's schools: Immigration and the No Child Left Behind Act.* Washington, DC: The Urban Institute.

Carlisle, J., Beeman, M., Davis, L., & Spharim, G. (1999) Relationship of metalinguistic capabilities and reading achievement for children who are becoming bilingual. *Applied Psycholinguistics, 20,* 459–478.

Carlo, M., August, D., McLaughlin, B., Snow, C. E., Dressler, C., Lippman, D. N., Lively, T. J., & White, C. E. (2004). Closing the gap: Addressing the vocabulary needs of English language learners in bilingual and mainstream classrooms. *Reading Research Quarterly, 39,* 188–215.

Carrasquillo, A. L., & London, C. (1993). *Parents and schools.* New York: Garland.

Carrasquillo, A. L., & Rodriguez, V. (1996). *Language minority students in the mainstream classroom.* Philadelphia: Multilingual Matters.

Carrow-Moffett, P. (1993). Change agent skills: Creating leadership for school renewal. *NASSP Bulletin, 77*(552), 57–62.

Carter, T., & Maestas, L. (1982). *Bilingual education that works: Effective schools for Spanish speaking children.* Sacramento, CA: California State Department of Education.

Carter, T. P., & Chatfield, M. L. (1986). Effective bilingual schools: Implications for policy and practice. *American Journal of Education, 95*(1), 200–234.

Cary, S. (2000). *Working with second language learners: Answers to teachers' top ten questions.* Portsmouth, NH: Heinemann.

Castañeda v. Pickard, 648 F. 2d 989 (5th Cir. 1981).

Cazabon, M., Nicoladis, E., & Lambert, W. E. (1998). *Becoming bilingual in the Amigos two-way immersion program* (Research Report No. 3). Santa Cruz, CA: Center for Research on Education, Diversity & Excellence.

Center on Education Policy. (2006). *From the capital to the classroom: Year 4 of the No Child Left Behind Act.* Washington, DC: Author. Available: http://www.cep-dc.org/ nclb/Year4/CEP-NCLB-Report-4.pdf

Chall, J. S., Jacobs, V., & Baldwin, L. (1990). *The reading crisis: Why poor children fall behind.* Cambridge, MA: Harvard University Press.

Chamot, A. U. (1992, August). Changing instruction for language minority students to achieve national goals. In *Third research symposium on limited English proficient student issues: Focus on middle and high school issues.* Washington, DC: U.S. Department of Education, OBEMLA.

Chamot, A. U., Dale, M., O'Malley, J. M., & Spanos, G. (1992). Learning and problem solving strategies of ESL students. *Bilingual Research Journal, 16*(3–4), 1–33.

Chamot, A. U., & O'Malley, J. M. (1987). The cognitive academic language learning approach: A bridge to the mainstream. *TESOL Quarterly, 21*(2), 227–249.

Chamot, A. U., & O'Malley, J. M. (1989). The cognitive academic language learning approach. In P. Rigg & V. G. Allen (Eds.), *When they don't all speak English: Integrating the ESL student into the regular classroom* (pp. 108–125). Urbana, IL: National Council of Teachers of English.

Chamot, A. U., & O'Malley, J. M. (1994). *The CALLA handbook: Implementing the cognitive academic language learning approach.* Reading, MA: Addison-Wesley.

Chavkin, N. F. (Ed.). (1993). *Families and schools in a pluralistic society.* Albany: State University of New York Press.

Cheung, O. M., Clements, B. S., & Mieu, Y. C. (1994). *The feasibility of collecting comparable national statistics about students with limited English proficiency: A final report of the LEP student counts study.* Washington, DC: Council of Chief State School Officers.

Christian, D. (1994). *Two-way bilingual education: Students learning through two languages* (Educational Practice Report No. 12). Washington, DC: Center for Applied Linguistics; Santa Cruz, CA: National Center for Research on Cultural Diversity and Second Language Learning. Retrieved December 17, 2001, from http://www.ncela.gwu.edu/miscpubs/ncrcdsll/epr12/index.htm

Cintron v. Brentwood Union Free School District, 455 F. Supp. 57, 6364 (E.D.N.Y. 1978).

Clair, N., & Adger, C. (1999, October). *Professional development for teachers in culturally diverse schools* (Report No. EDO-FL-99-08). Washington, DC: ERIC Clearinghouse on Language and Linguistics. (ERIC Document Reproduction Service No. ED435185)

Clements, B., Lara, J., & Cheung, O. (1992). *Limited English proficiency: Recommendations for improving the assessment and monitoring of students.* Washington, DC: Council of Chief State School Officers. (ERIC Document Reproduction Service No. ED347265)

Cloud, N., Genesee, F., & Hamayan, E. (2000). *Dual language instruction: A handbook for enriched education.* Boston: Heinle & Heinle.

Coady, M., Hamann, E. T., Harrington, M., Pacheco, M., Pho, S., & Yedlin, J. (2003). *Claiming opportunities: A handbook for improving education for English language learners through comprehensive school reform.* Providence, RI: The Education Alliance at Brown University Northeast and Islands Regional Educational Laboratory. Retrieved January 30, 2004, from http://www.alliance.brown.edu/pubs/claiming_opportunities/claimopp_1.pdf

Collier, V. P. (1989). How long? A synthesis of research on academic achievement in second language. *TESOL Quarterly, 23*(3), 509–531.

Collier, V. P. (1992). A synthesis of studies examining long-term language minority student data on academic achievement. *Bilingual Research Journal, 16*(1–2), 187–212.

Collier, V. P. (1995, Fall). *Acquiring a second language for school.* (Directions in Language and Education, No. 4). Washington, DC: National Clearinghouse for Bilingual Education. Retrieved September 10, 2001, from http://www.ncela.gwu.edu/ncbepubs/directions/04.htm

Collier, V. P., & Thomas, W. P. (1989). How quickly can immigrants become proficient in school English? *The Journal of Educational Issues of Language Minority Students, 5,* 26–38.

Commission on Chapter 1. (1992). *Making schools work for children in poverty.* Washington, DC: American Association for Higher Education.

Conley, D. T. (1996). *Are you ready to restructure? A guidebook for educators, parents, and community members.* Thousand Oaks, CA: Corwin Press.

Cooper, K., & Gonzalez, M. L. (1993). Communicating with parents when you don't speak the language. *Principal, 73,* 45–46.

Cooter, R. B., Jr., & Flynt, E. S. (1996). *Teaching reading in the content areas.* Englewood Cliffs, NJ: Prentice-Hall.

Corson, D. (1997). The learning and use of academic English words. *Language Learning, 47*(4), 671–718.

Cotton, K. (2003). *Principals and student achievement: What the research says.* Alexandria, VA: Association for Supervision and Curriculum Development.

Council of Chief State School Officers. (1996). *Interstate School Leaders Licensure Consortium (ISLLC) standards for school leaders.* Washington, DC: Author. Available: http://www.ccsso.org/content/pdfs/isllcstd.pdf

Crawford, J. (1997, March). *Best evidence: Research foundations of the Bilingual Education Act.* Washington, DC: National Clearinghouse for English Language Education. Retrieved February 23, 2002, from http://www.ncela.gwu.edu/ncbe pubs/reports/bestevidence/

Cummins, J. (1979). Cognitive/academic language proficiency, linguistic interdependence, the optimum age question and some other matters. *Working Papers on Bilingualism, 19,* 121 29.

Cummins, J. (1981a). Age on arrival and immigrant second language learning in Canada: A reassessment. *Applied Linguistics, 2*(2), 132 49.

Cummins, J. (1981b). The role of primary language development in promoting educational success for language minority students. In California State Department of Education, *Schooling and language minority students: A theoretical framework* (pp. 3–49). Los Angeles: Evaluation, Dissemination and Assessment Center, California State University.

Cummins, J. (1984). Wanted: A theoretical framework for relating language proficiency to academic achievement among bilingual students. In C. Rivera (Ed.), *Language proficiency and academic achievement* (pp. 79–90). Clevedon, England: Multilingual Matters.

Cummins, J. (1986). Empowering minority students: A framework for intervention. *Harvard Educational Review, 56*(1), 18–36.

Cummins, J. (1989). *Empowering minority students.* Sacramento, CA: California Association for Bilingual Education.

Cummins, J. (1991a). Interdependence of first- and second-language proficiency in bilingual children. In E. Bialystok (Ed.), *Language processing in bilingual children* (pp. 70–89). Cambridge, England: Cambridge University Press.

Cummins, J. (1991b). Language shift and language learning in the transition from home to school. *Journal of Education, 173*(2), 85–97.

Cummins, J. (1992). Language proficiency, bilingualism, and academic achievement. In P. A. Richard-Amato & M. A. Snow (Eds.), *The multicultural classroom: Readings for content area teachers* (pp. 16–26). New York: Longman.

Cummins, J. (1996). *Negotiating identities: Education for empowerment in a diverse society.* Los Angeles: California Association for Bilingual Education.

Cummins, J. (2000). *Language, power, and pedagogy: Bilingual children in the crossfire.* Clevedon, England: Multilingual Matters.

Cummins, J. (2001). *Negotiating identities: Education for empowerment in a diverse society* (2nd ed.). Los Angeles: California Association for Bilingual Education.

Cummins, J. (2002). Reading and the ESL student. *Orbit, 33*(1), 19–22.

Cunningham, A. E., & Stanovich, K. E. (1997). Early reading acquisition and its relation to reading experience and ability 10 years later. *Developmental Psychology, 33*(6), 934–945.

Cunningham, A. E., & Stanovich, K. E. (1998, Spring/Summer). What reading does for the mind. *American Educator, 22*(1 & 2), 8–15.

Curiel, H., Rosenthal, J. A., & Richek, H. G. (1986). Impacts of bilingual education on secondary school grades, attendance, retentions and drop-out. *Hispanic Journal of Behavioral Sciences, 8,* 357–367.

Darling-Hammond, L. (1997). *The right to learn: A blueprint for creating schools that work.* New York: Jossey-Bass.

Darling-Hammond, L., & McLaughlin, M. W. (1995). Policies that support professional development in an era of reform. *Phi Delta Kappan, 76*(8), 597–604.

De Avila, E. (1990, September). *Assessment of language minority students: Political, technical, practical and moral imperatives.* Paper presented at the Research Symposium on Limited English Proficient Students' Issues, Washington, DC. (ERIC Document Reproduction Service No. ED341266)

de la Luz Reyes, M. (1991). A process approach to literacy using dialogue journals and literature logs with second language learners. *Research in the Teaching of English, 25,* 291–313.

Delgado-Gaitan, C. (1990). *Literacy for empowerment: The role of parents in children's education.* New York: Falmer Press.

Delgado-Gaitan, C. (1991). Involving parents in the schools: A process of empowerment. *American Journal of Education, 100*(1), 20–46.

Dianda, M., & Flaherty, J. (1995). *Effects of Success for All on the reading achievement of first graders in California bilingual programs.* Los Alamitos, CA: The Southwest Regional Educational Laboratory.

Díaz, S., Moll, L., & Mehan, H. (1986). Sociocultural resources in instruction: A context specific approach. In C. E. Cortés & D. Holt (Eds.), *Beyond language: Social and cultural factors in schooling language minority students* (pp. 187–230). Los Angeles: Evaluation, Dissemination, and Assessment Center, California State University.

Doherty, R. W., Hilberg, R. S., Pinal, A., & Tharp, R. (2003, Winter). Five standards and student achievement. *NABE Journal of Research and Practice, 1,* 1–24.

Dole, J., Duffy, G., Roehler, L., & Pearson, P. D. (1991). Moving from the old to the new: Research in reading comprehension instruction. *Review of Educational Research, 61*(2), 239–264.

Doughty, C., & Williams, J. (Eds.). (1998). *Focus on form in classroom second language acquisition* (Cambridge Applied Linguistics Series). Cambridge, England: Cambridge University Press.

DuFour, R. (2001, Winter). In the right context. *Journal of Staff Development, 22*(1), 14–17.

DuFour, R. (2002). The learning-centered principal. *Educational Leadership, 59*(8), 12–15.

DuFour, R., & Eaker, R. (1998). *Professional learning communities at work: Best practices for enhancing student achievement.* Bloomington, IN: National Educational Service.

Duke, N., & Pearson, D. (2002), Effective practices for developing reading comprehension. In A. Farstrup & S. Samuels (Eds.), *What research has to say about reading instruction* (pp. 205–242). Newark, DE: International Reading Association.

Durán, R. P., & Szymanski, M. H. (1993, October). *Construction of learning and interaction of language minority children in cooperative learning* (CDS Report No. 45). Baltimore: Johns Hopkins University Center for Research on Effective Schooling for Disadvantaged Students.

Eaker, R., DuFour, R., & DuFour, R. (2002). *Getting started: Reculturing schools to become professional learning communities.* Bloomington, IN: National Educational Service.

Echevarria, J. (1998). Preparing text and classroom materials for English-language learners: Curriculum adaptations in secondary school settings. In R. Gersten & R. Jiménez (Eds.), *Promoting learning for culturally and linguistically diverse students: Classroom applications from contemporary research* (pp. 210–229). Pacific Grove, CA: Brooks/Cole Publishing.

Echevarria, J., & Graves, A. (1998). *Sheltered content instruction: Teaching English language learners with diverse abilities.* Boston: Allyn and Bacon.

Echevarria, J., Vogt, M., & Short, D. J. (2000). *Making content comprehensible for English language learners: The SIOP model.* Boston: Allyn and Bacon.

Echevarria, J., Vogt, M., & Short, D. J. (2004). *Making content comprehensible for English learners: The SIOP model.* (2nd ed.) Boston: Allyn and Bacon.

Edmonds, R. (1979). Effective schools for the urban poor. *Educational Leadership, 37*(1), 15–18, 20–24.

Elley, W. (1998). *Raising literacy levels in third world countries: A method that works.* Culver City, CA: Language Education Associates.

Elley, W. B. (1991). Acquiring literacy in a second language: The effect of book-based programs. *Language Learning, 41,* 375–411.

Elmore, R. (2003). *Knowing the right thing to do: School improvement and performance based accountability.* Washington, DC: NGA Center for Best Practices.

Epstein, J. (1990). School and family connections: Theory, research, and implications for integrating sociologies of education and family. In D. Unger & M. Sussman (Eds.), *Families in community settings: Interdisciplinary perspectives* (pp. 99–126). New York: Haworth Press.

Epstein, J. (1997, September/October). Six types of school-family-community involvement. *Harvard Education Letter.* Retrieved August 22, 2003, from http://www.edletter.org/past/issues/1997-so/sixtypes.shtml

Epstein, J., & Dauber, S. (1991). School programs and teacher practices of parental involvement in inner-city elementary and middle schools. *Elementary School Journal, 91*(3), 289–303.

Equal Educational Opportunities Act of 1974 (EEOA), 20 U.S.C. § 1703 (a)–(f) (1974).

Escamilla, K. (1993). Promoting biliteracy: Issues in promoting English literacy in students acquiring English. In J. Tinajero & F. Ada (Eds.), *The power of two languages: Literacy and biliteracy for Spanish speaking students* (pp. 220–233). New York: MacMillan/McGraw Hill.

Escamilla, K. (1994). Descubriendo la lectura: An early intervention literacy program in Spanish. *Literacy, Teaching and Learning, 1*(1), 57–70.

Escamilla, K., & Coady, M. (2001). Assessing the writing of Spanish-speaking students: Issues and suggestions. In S. R. Hurley & J. V. Tinajero (Eds.), *Literacy assessment of second language learners.* Needham Heights, MA: Allyn and Bacon.

ESCORT. (2001). *The help! kit: A resource guide for secondary teachers of migrant English language learners.* Oneonta, NY: ESCORT, State University of New York. Retrieved September 18, 2003, from http://www.escort. org/products/secondaryhelpkit.html

Espinosa, L. (1995). *Hispanic parent involvement in early childhood programs.* Champaign, IL: ERIC Clearinghouse on Elementary and Early Childhood Education.

Estrin, E. T., & Nelson-Barber, S. (1995). *Issues in cross-cultural assessment: American Indian and Alaska Native students* (Far West Laboratory Knowledge Brief No. 12). San Francisco: Far West Laboratory.

Feuerverger, G. (1994). A multicultural literacy intervention for minority language students. *Language and Education, 8*(3), 123–146.

Fielding, L. G., & Pearson, P. D. (1994). Reading comprehension: What works. *Educational Leadership, 51*(5), 62–68.

Fitzgerald, J. (1995a). English-as-a-second-language learners' cognitive reading processes: A review of research in the United States. *Review of Educational Research, 65*(2), 145–190.

Fitzgerald, J. (1995b). English-as-a-second-language reading instruction in the United States: A research review. *Journal of Reading Behavior, 27*(2), 115–152.

Fitzgerald, J. (1999). English-language learners' reading: New age issues. In P. R. Schmidt & P. B. Rosenthal (Eds.), *Reconceptualizing literacy in the new age of pluralism and multiculturalism* (pp. 19–20). Greenwich, CT: JAI Press.

Fleischman, H. L., & Hopstock, P. J. (1993). *Descriptive study of services to limited English proficient students. Volume 1: Summary of findings and conclusions.* Arlington, VA: Development Associates.

Freeman, D. E., & Freeman, Y. S. (2001). *Between worlds: Access to second language acquisition.* Portsmouth, NH: Heinemann.

Freeman, Y. S., & Freeman, D. (1998). *ESL/EFL teaching: Principles for success.* Portsmouth, NH: Heinemann.

Fullan, M. (2001). *The new meaning of educational change* (3rd ed.). New York: Teachers College Press.

Fullan, M. (with Stiegelbauer, S.). (1991). *The new meaning of educational change.* New York: Teachers College Press.

Fulton-Scott, M. J., & Calvin, A. D. (1983). Bilingual multicultural education vs. integrated and non-integrated ESL instruction. *NABE: The Journal for the National Association for Bilingual Education, 7*(3), 1–12.

Gandara, P. (1994). The impact of the education reform movement on limited English proficient students. In B. McLeod (Ed.), *Language and learning: Educating linguistically diverse students* (pp. 45–70). Albany: State University of New York Press.

García, E. (1987, Winter). *Effective schooling for language minority students* (New Focus, NCBE Occasional Papers in Bilingual Education, No. 1). Washington, DC: Office of Bilingual Education and Minority Languages Affairs, U.S. Department of Education. Retrieved September 16, 2001, from http://www.ncela.gwu.edu/ncbepubs/ classics/focus/01effective.htm

García, E. (1991a). *Characteristics of effective teachers for language minority students.* Santa Cruz: National Center for Research on Cultural Diversity and Second-Language Learning, University of California, Santa Cruz. (ERIC Document Reproduction Service No. ED338099)

García, E. (1991b). *The education of linguistically and culturally diverse students: Effective instructional practices* (Educational Practice Report No. 1). Washington, DC: Center for Applied Linguistics; Santa Cruz, CA: National Center for Research on Cultural Diversity and Second Language Learning.

García, E. (1994a). Addressing the challenges of diversity. In S. L. Kagan & B. Weissbourd (Eds.), *Putting families first* (pp. 243–275). San Francisco: Jossey-Bass.

García, E. (1994b). The education of linguistically and culturally diverse students: Effective instructional practices. In R. Rodriguez, N. J. Ramos, & J. A. Ruiz-Escalante (Eds.), *Compendium of readings in bilingual education: Issues and practices* (pp. 87–94). Austin, TX: Association of Bilingual Education.

García, E. (1994c). *Understanding and meeting the challenge of student diversity.* Boston: Houghton Mifflin.

García, E. (1997a). The education of Hispanics in early childhood: Of roots and wings. *Young Children, 52*(3), 5–14.

García, E. (1997b). Foreword. In O. B. Miramontes, A. Nadeau, & N. L. Commins, *Restructuring schools for linguistic diversity: Linking decision making to effective programs* (pp. ix–xi). New York: Teachers College Press.

García, E. (2001). *Student cultural diversity: Understanding and meeting the challenge* (3rd ed.). Boston: Houghton Mifflin.

Garcia, G. E. (2000). Bilingual children's reading. In M. Kamil, P. Mosenthal, P. D. Pearson, & R. Barr (Eds.), *Handbook of reading research* (Vol. 3, pp. 813–835). Mahwah, NJ: Lawrence Erlbaum.

Garcia, G. E., & Nagy, W. (1993). Latino students' concept of cognates. In D. J. Leu & C. K. Kinzer (Eds.), *Examining central issues in literary research, theory, and practice: Forty-second yearbook of the National Reading Conference* (pp. 367–373). Chicago, IL: National Reading Conference.

Garcia, G. E., & Pearson, P. D. (1990). *Modifying reading instruction to maximize its effectiveness for all students* (Tech. Report No. 489). Champaign, IL: University of Illinois, Center for the Study of Reading.

Garcia, G. E., & Pearson, P. D. (1994). Assessment and diversity. In L. Darling Hammond (Ed.), *Review of research in education* (Vol. 20, pp. 337–392). Washington, DC: American Educational Research Association.

Garcia, G. N. (2000). *Lessons from research: What is the length of time it takes limited English proficient students to acquire English and succeed in an all-English classroom?* (Issue Brief No. 5). Washington, DC: National Clearinghouse for Bilingual Education. Retrieved September 16, 2001, from http://www.ncbe.gwu.edu/ncbepubs/issue briefs/ib5.htm

Garcia-Vásquez, E., Vásquez, L. A., Lopez, I. C., & Ward, W. (1997). Language proficiency and academic success: Relationships between proficiency in two languages and achievement among Mexican-American students. *Bilingual Research Journal, 21,* 395–408.

Gardner, H. (1993). *Multiple intelligences: The theory in practice.* New York: Basic Books.

Genesee, F. (1993). *Cross-linguistic aspects of reading acquisition.* Atlanta, GA: American Association of Applied Linguistics.

Genesee, F. (Ed.). (1994). *Educating second language children: The whole child, the whole curriculum, the whole community.* Cambridge, England: Cambridge University Press.

Genesee, F. (Ed.). (1999). *Program alternatives for linguistically diverse students* (Educational Practice Report No. 1). Santa Cruz, CA: Center for Research on Education, Diversity, & Excellence. Retrieved April 26, 2001, from http://www.cal.org/crede/ pubs/edpractice/EPR1.pdf

Genesee, F., & Hamayan, E. (1994). Classroom-based assessment. In F. Genesee (Ed.), *Educating second language children: The whole child, the whole curriculum, the whole community* (pp. 212–239). Cambridge, England: Cambridge University Press.

Genesee, F., Lindholm-Leary, K., Saunders, W., & Christian, D. (2005). English language learners in U.S. schools: An overview of research findings. *Journal of Education of Students Placed at Risk, 10*(4), 363–385.

The George Washington University Center for Equity and Excellence in Education. (1996). *Promoting excellence: Ensuring academic success of limited English proficient students.* Arlington, VA: Author.

Gersten, R., & Baker, S. (2000, Summer). What we know about effective instructional practices for English-language learners. *Exceptional Children, 66*(4), 454–470.

Gersten, R., & Geva, E. (2003). Teaching reading to early language learners. *Educational Leadership, 60*(8), 44–49.

Gersten, R., & Jiménez, R. T. (1994). A delicate balance: Enhancing literature instruction for students of English as a second language. *The Reading Teacher, 47*(6), 438–449.

Gersten, R., & Woodward, J. (1992). The quest to translate research into classroom practice: Strategies for assisting classroom teachers' work with "at-risk" students and students with disabilities. In D. Carnine & E. Kameenui (Eds.), *Higher cognitive functioning for all students* (pp. 201–218). Austin, TX: Pro-Ed.

Geva, E. (2000). Issues in the assessment of reading disabilities in L2 children: Beliefs and research evidence. *Dyslexia, 6,* 13–28.

Gipps, C. (1994). *Beyond testing.* London: Falmer Press.

Goldenberg, C. (1992). *Instructional conversations and their classroom application* (Educational Practice Report No. 2). Washington, DC: Center for Applied Linguistics; Santa Cruz, CA: National Center for Research on Cultural Diversity and Second Language Learning. Retrieved February 22, 2002, from http://www.ncela.gwu.edu/miscpubs/ncrcdsll/epr2/

Goldenberg, C. (1996). The education of language-minority students: Where are we, and where do we need to go? *The Elementary School Journal, 96*(3), 353–361.

Goldenberg, C. (2001, January 25). Commentary: These steps can help us teach Johnny to read. *The Los Angeles Times,* p. B11.

Goldenberg, C. (2004a, March 5). *Effective practices to promote literacy development among language minority children and youth: Preliminary findings from the National Literacy Panel.* Presentation at the CORE Literacy Leadership Summit 2004, Oakland, CA.

Goldenberg, C. (2004b). *Successful school change: Creating settings to improve teaching and learning.* New York: Teachers College Press.

Goldenberg, C., & Gallimore, R. (1991a). Changing teaching takes more than a one-shot workshop. *Educational Leadership, 49*(3), 69–72.

Goldenberg, C., & Gallimore, R. (1991b). Local knowledge, research knowledge, and educational change: A case study of first-grade Spanish reading improvement. *Educational Researcher, 20*(8), 2–14.

Goldenberg, C., & Sullivan, J. (1994). *Making change happen in a language-minority school: A search for coherence* (Educational Practice Report No. 13). Santa Cruz, CA: National Center for Research on Cultural Diversity and Second Language Learning. Retrieved February 22, 2002, from http://www.ncela.gwu.edu/miscpubs/ncrcdsll/epr13/

Goldstein, B., Harris, K., & Klein, M. (1993). Assessment of oral storytelling abilities of Latin junior high school students with learning handicaps. *Journal of Learning Disabilities, 26*(2), 138–143.

Gómez, E. L. (1999). *Assessment portfolios and English language learners: Frequently asked questions and a case study of the Brooklyn International High School.* Providence, RI: The Education Alliance, LAB at Brown University.

Gomez v. Illinois State Bd. of Educ., 811 F. 2d 1030 (7th Cir. 1987).

Gonzáles, M. L. (1998). Successfully educating Latinos: The pivotal role of the principal. In M. L. Gonzáles, A. Huerta-Macías, & J. V. Tinajero (Eds.), *Educating Latino students: A guide to successful practice* (pp. 3–27). Basel, Switzerland: Technomic.

Gonzalez, L. (1992). Tapping their language: A bridge to success. *The Journal of Educational Issues of Language Minority Students, 10,* 27–39.

Gottlieb, M. (1995). Nurturing student learning through portfolios. *TESOL Journal, 5*(3), 18–23.

Gottlieb, M. (2000). Standards-based, large-scale assessment of ESOL students. In M. A. Snow (Ed.), *Implementing the ESL standards for pre-K–12 students through teacher education* (pp. 167–186). Alexandria, VA: Teachers of English to Speakers of Other Languages.

Gottlieb, M. (with the Language Proficiency Committee of the Illinois State Board of Education). (1999). *The language proficiency handbook: A practitioner's guide to instructional assessment.* Springfield, IL: Illinois State Board of Education.

Grabe, W. (1991). Current developments in second language reading. *TESOL Quarterly, 25*(3), 375–406.

Graves, M. F. (2005). *The vocabulary book: Learning & instruction.* Urbana, IL: Teachers College Press.

Griffith, J. (2002). A multilevel analysis of the relation of school learning and social environments to minority achievement in public elementary schools. *The Elementary School Journal, 102*(5), 349–367.

Guadarrama, I. (Ed.). (1993, Fall). Leadership for change in bilingual/ESL education. *Discovering our experiences: Studies in bilingual/ESL education.* Denton, TX: Mentor Teacher Training and Resource Center, Texas Women's University. (ERIC Document Reproduction Service No. ED373567)

Guarino, A. J., Echevarria, J., Short, D., Schick, J. E., Forbes, S., & Rueda, R. (2001). The sheltered instruction observation protocol. *Journal of Research in Education, 11*(1), 138–140.

Gusman, J. (2001). *Practical strategies for accelerating the literacy skills and content learning of your ESL students resource handbook.* Sacramento, CA: New Horizons in Education.

Guzman, F. M. (1990, June). Parenting skills workshops: Let's examine a success story. *IDRA Newsletter, 17*(6), 8.

Hafner, A. L. (2001, April). *Evaluating the impact of test accommodations on test scores of LEP students & non-LEP students.* Paper presented at the annual meeting of the American Educational Research Association, Seattle, WA.

Hamayan, E. V. (1993). Assessing the academic and cognitive growth of culturally and linguistically diverse students. In G. R. Tucker (Ed.), *Policy and practice in the education of culturally and linguistically diverse students* (pp. 9–12). Alexandria, VA: Teachers of English to Speakers of Other Languages.

Hargett, G. (1998). *Assessment in ESL and bilingual education: A hot topics paper.* Portland, OR: Northwest Regional Educational Lab. (ERIC Document Reproduction Service No. ED425645)

Harris, T. L., & Hodges, R. E. (Eds.). (1995). *The literacy dictionary: The vocabulary of reading and writing.* Newark, DE: International Reading Association.

Henderson, A., & Berla, N. (Eds.). (1994). *A new generation of evidence: The family is critical to student achievement.* Washington, DC: National Committee for Citizens in Education. (ERIC Document Reproduction Service No. ED375968)

Henderson, A., & Mapp, K. L. (2002). *A new wave of evidence: The impact of school, family, and community connections on student achievement.* Austin, TX: Southwest Educational Development Laboratory.

Henze, R. C., & Lucas, T. (1993). Shaping instruction to promote the success of language minority students: An analysis of four high school classes. *Peabody Journal of Education: Trends in Bilingual Education at the Secondary Level, 69*(1), 54–81.

Herman, J. L., Aschbacher, P. R., & Winters, L. (1992). *A practical guide to alternative assessment.* Alexandria, VA: Association for Supervision and Curriculum Development.

Hernandez, J. S. (1991). Assisted performance in reading comprehension strategies with non-English proficient students. *The Journal of Educational Issues of Language Minority Students, 8,* 91–112.

Heubert, J. P., & Hauser, R. M. (Eds.). (1999). *High stakes: Testing for tracking, promotion, and graduation.* Washington, DC: National Academy Press.

Hidalgo, N. M., Bright, J. S., Sui, F., Swap, S., & Epstein, J. (1995). Research on families, schools, and communities: A multicultural perspective. In J. A. Banks & C. A. Banks (Eds.), *Handbook of research on multicultural education* (pp. 498–524). New York: Macmillan.

Hiebert, E. H., Pearson, P. D., Taylor, B. M., Richardson, V., & Paris, S. G. (1998). *Every child a reader: Applying reading research to the classroom.* Ann Arbor, MI: Center for the Improvement of Early Reading Achievement, University of Michigan School of Education.

Hispanic Dropout Project. (1998, February). *No more excuses: The final report of the Hispanic Dropout Project.* Washington, DC: U.S. Department of Education, Office of the Under Secretary.

Hobbs, F., & Stoops, N. (2002). *Demographic trends in the 20th century. U.S. Census Bureau, Census 2000 special reports* (Series CENSR-4). Washington, DC: U.S. Government Printing Office.

Howard, J. (1990). *Getting smart: The social construction of intelligence.* Lexington, MA: The Efficacy Institute.

Huerta-Macaís, A. (1998). Learning for Latinos: The sociocultural perspective. In M. L. Gonzáles, A. Huerta-Macaís, & J. V. Tinajero, (Eds.), *Educating Latino students: A guide to successful practice* (pp. 29–45). Basel, Switzerland: Technomic Publishing.

Hurley, S. R., & Tinajero, J. V. (2001). *Literacy assessment of second language learners.* Needham Heights, MA: Allyn and Bacon.

Illinois Resource Center. (2004). *IRC e-kit.* Available: http://www.thecenter library.org/cwis/index.php

Inger, M. (1992). *Increasing the school involvement of Hispanic parents.* New York: Teachers College, Columbia University. ERIC Clearinghouse on Urban Education. (ERIC Document Reproduction Service No. ED350380)

Inger, M. (1993). Getting Hispanic parents involved. *Education Digest, 58,* 33–34.

Jiménez, R. (2000). Literacy and the identity development of Latina/o students. *American Educational Research Journal, 37,* 971–1000.

Jiménez, R. (2001). "It's a difference that changes us": An alternative view of the language and literacy needs of Latina/o students. *The Reading Teacher, 54*(8), 736–742.

Jiménez, R. T., Garcia, G. E., & Pearson, P. D. (1995). Three children, two languages, and strategic reading: Case studies in bilingual/monolingual reading. *American Educational Research Journal, 32,* 31–61.

Jiménez, R. T., Garcia, G. E., & Pearson, P. D. (1996). The reading strategies of bilingual Latina/o students who are successful English readers: Opportunities and obstacles. *Reading Research Quarterly, 31*(1), 90–112.

Joyce, B., & Calhoun, E. (1995). School renewal: An inquiry, not a formula. *Educational Leadership, 52*(7), 51–55.

Kagan, S. (1989). *Cooperative learning: Resources for teachers.* Riverside: University of California.

Kagan, S. (1995). *We can talk: Cooperative learning in the elementary ESL classrooms. Elementary Education Newsletter, 17*(2), 3–4.

Kane, M. B., & Khattri, N. (1995). Assessment reform. *Phi Delta Kappan, 77*(1), 30–32.

Katz, A. (2000). Changing paradigms for assessment. In M. A. Snow (Ed.), *Implementing the ESL standards for pre-K–12 students through teacher education* (pp. 137–166). Alexandria, VA: Teachers of English to Speakers of Other Languages.

Keyes v. School Dist. No. 1, 576 F. Supp. 1503, 1519 (D. Colo. 1983).

Kindler, A. (2002, October). *Survey of the states limited English proficient students & available educational programs and services 2000–2001 summary report* (Contract No. ED-00-CO-0113). Washington, DC: National Clearinghouse for English Language Acquisition and Language Instruction Educational Programs, The George Washington University. Retrieved October 28, 2005, from http://www.ncela.gwu.edu/ states/reports/ seareports/001/sea0001.pdf

Klesmer, H. (1994). Assessment and teacher perceptions of ESL student achievement. *English Quarterly, 26*(3), 8–11.

Kohl, G. O., Lengua, L. J., & McMahon, R. J. (2000). Parent involvement in school conceptualizing multiple dimensions and their relations with family and demographic risk factors. *Journal of School Psychology, 38*(6), 501–523.

Kopriva, R. (2000). *Ensuring accuracy in testing for English language learners.* Washington, DC: Council of Chief State School Officers.

Korinek, L., Walther-Thomas, C., Laycock, V. K. (1992). Educating special needs homeless children and youth. In J. H. Stronge (Ed.), *Educating homeless children and adolescents: Evaluating policy and practice* (pp. 133–152). Newbury Park, CA: Sage Publications.

Krashen, S. D. (1981). *Second language acquisition.* Oxford, England: Pergamon Press.

Krashen, S. D. (1985). *The input hypothesis.* New York: Pergamon Press.

Krashen, S. D. (1993). *The power of reading.* Englewood, CO: Libraries Unlimited.

Krashen, S. D. (2001, September/October/November). Are children ready for the mainstream after one year of structured English immersion? *TESOL Matters, 11*(1), 4.

Krashen, S. D., & Biber, D. (1988). *On course: Bilingual education's success in California.* Sacramento, CA: California Association for Bilingual Education.

Krashen, S. D., & Terrell, T. (1983). *The natural approach: Language acquisition in the classroom.* Oxford, England: Pergamon Press.

Krashen, S. D., Tse, L., & McQuillan, J. (1998). *Heritage language development.* Culver City, CA: Language Education Associates.

Kucer, S. B., & Silva, C. (1999). The English literacy development of bilingual students within a transition whole-language curriculum. *Bilingual Research Journal, 23,* 345–371.

Kwan, A. B., & Willows, D. M. (1998, December). *Impact of early phonics instruction on children learning English as a second language.* Paper presented at the National Reading Conference, Austin, TX.

LaCelle-Peterson, M. W., & Rivera, C. (1994). Is it real for all kids? A framework for equitable assessment policies for English language learners. *Harvard Educational Review, 64*(1), 55–75.

Ladson-Billings, G. (1995). Toward a theory of culturally relevant pedagogy. *American Educational Research Journal, 32*(3), 465–491.

Lambert, W. (1982). *Case for maintaining minority languages and cultures in America.* Oakland, CA: Luso-American Education Foundation.

Lambert, W. E., & Cazabon, M. (1994). *Students' view of the Amigos program* (Research Report No. 11). Santa Cruz, CA: National Center for Research on Cultural Diversity and Second Language Learning.

Lanauze, M., & Snow, C. E. (1989). The relation between first and second language writing skills: Evidence from Puerto Rican elementary school children in bilingual programs. *Linguistics and Education, 1*(4), 323–340.

Langer, J. A., Bartolome, L., Vasquez, O., and Luca, T. (1990). Meaning construction in school literacy tasks: A study of bilingual students. *American Educational Research Journal, 27,* 427–471.

Lapp, D., Fisher, D., Flood, J., & Cabello, A. (2001). An integrated approach to the teaching and assessment of language arts. In S. R. Hurley & J. V. Tinajero (Eds.), *Literacy assessment of second language learners* (pp. 1–26). Boston: Allyn and Bacon.

Lau v. Nichols, 414 U.S. 563, 94 S. Ct. 786 (1974).

Laufer, B. (2001). *Vocabulary acquisition in a second language: Do learners really acquire most vocabulary by reading?* Paper presented at the American Association of Applied Linguistics, St. Louis, MO.

Lee, V., & Patel, N. (1994). Making literacy programs work for immigrant families. *New Voices, 4,* 1–2.

Leighton, M. S., Hightower, A. M., & Wrigley, A. M. (1995). *Model strategies in bilingual education: Professional development.* Washington, DC: U.S. Department of Education.

Lein, L., Johnson, J. F., & Ragland, M. (1997). *Successful Texas schoolwide programs: Research study results.* Austin: The Charles A. Dana Center, The University of Texas at Austin. Retrieved May 16, 2001, from http://www.starcenter.org/products/pdf/ successfulreport.pdf

Leithwood, K. (1994). Leadership for school restructuring. *Educational Administration Quarterly, 30*(4), 498–518.

Lessow-Hurley, J. (1990). *The foundations of dual language instruction.* New York: Longman.

Lessow-Hurley, J. (1991). *A commonsense guide to bilingual education.* Alexandria, VA: Association for Supervision and Curriculum Development.

Lieberman, A. (1995). Practices that support teacher development. *Phi Delta Kappan, 76*(8), 591–596.

Lim, H., & Watson, D. (1993, February). Whole language content classes for second language learners. *The Reading Teacher, 46*(5), 384–393.

Lindholm, K. J. (1991). Theoretical assumptions and empirical evidence for academic achievement in two languages. *Hispanic Journal of Behavioral Sciences, 13,* 3–17.

Lindholm-Leary, K. J. (2001). *Dual language education.* Avon, England: Multilingual Matters.

Lindholm-Leary, K. J. (2005, April). *Synthesis of the scientific research on the academic achievement of ELL students.* Presentation at AERA, Montreal, Canada.

Lindholm-Leary, K. J., & Borsato, G. (2001). *Impact of two-way bilingual elementary programs on students' attitudes toward school and college.* Santa Cruz, CA: Center for Research on Education, Diversity and Excellence.

Linn, R. L. (1993). Educational assessment: Expanded expectations and challenges. *Educational Evaluation and Policy Analysis, 15,* 1.

Lipsky, D. K., & Gartner, A. (1997). *Inclusion and school reform: Transforming America's classrooms.* Baltimore: Paul H. Brookes.

Long, M., & Porter, P. (1985). Group work, interlanguage talk, and second language acquisition. *TESOL Quarterly, 19*(2), 207–228.

Lopez, G. R. (2001). *On whose terms? Understanding involvement through the eyes of migrant parents.* Paper presented at the Annual Meeting of the American Educational Research Association, Seattle, WA.

Louis, K. S., Kruse, S., & Raywid, M. A. (1996). Putting teachers at the center of reform. *NASSP Bulletin, 80*(580), 9–21.

Lucas, T. (1992). *Successful capacity building: An analysis of twenty case studies.* Oakland, CA: ARC Associates.

Lucas, T. (1993). *Applying elements of effective secondary schooling for language minority students: A tool for reflection and stimulus to change.* Washington, DC: National Clearinghouse for Bilingual Education. Retrieved September 16, 2001, from http:// www.ncbe.gwu.edu/ncbepubs/pigs/pig14.htm.

Lucas, T., Henze, R., & Donato, R. (1990). Promoting the success of Latino language-minority students: An exploratory study of six high schools. *Harvard Educational Review, 60*(3), 315–340.

Lucas, T., & Katz, A. (1994). Reframing the debate: The roles of native languages in English-only programs for language minority students. *TESOL Quarterly, 28*(3), 537–561.

Lyons, J. (1992). *Legal responsibilities of education agencies serving national origin language minority students.* Washington, DC: The Mid-Atlantic Equity Center, The American University.

Mace-Matluck, B. J., Alexander-Kasparik, R., & Queen, R. (1998). *Through the golden door: Educational approaches for immigrant adolescents with limited schooling.* McHenry, IL: Delta Systems and Center for Applied Linguistics.

McCollum, P. (1997). Two innovative El Paso schools bring together teachers and the community. *IDRA Newsletter, 24*(8), 3–6, 11. Retrieved June 19, 2002, from http:// www.idra.org/Newslttr/1997/Sep/Pam.htm

McKeon, D. (1994). When meeting "common" standards is uncommonly difficult. *Educational Leadership, 51*(8), 45–49.

McKeown, M. G., Beck, I. L., Omanson, R. C., & Pople, M. T. (1985). Some effects of the nature and frequency of vocabulary instruction on the knowledge and use of words. *Reading Research Quarterly, 20,* 522–535.

McLaughlin, B. (1992). *Myths and misconceptions about second language learning: What every teacher needs to unlearn* (Educational Practice Report No. 5). Santa Cruz, CA: National Center for Research on Cultural Diversity and Second Language Learning. Retrieved September 19, 2001, from http://www.ncbe.gwu.edu/miscpubs/ncrcdsll/epr5.htm

McLaughlin, B. (1995). *Fostering second language development in young children: Principles and practice* (Educational Practice Report 14). Santa Cruz, CA: National Center for Research on Cultural Diversity and Second Language Learning. Retrieved December 28, 2002, from http://www.ncbe.gwu.edu/miscpubs/ncrcdsll/epr14.htm

McLaughlin, B., August, D., Snow, C., Carlo, M., Dressler, C., White, C., Lively, T., & Lippman, D. (2000). *Vocabulary improvement in English language learners: An intervention study.* Paper presented at the Research Symposium on High Standards in Reading for Students from Diverse Language Groups: Research, Practice, and Policy. Washington, DC: Office of Bilingual Education and Minority Languages Affairs. Retrieved December 19, 2003, from http://www.ncela.gwu.edu/ncbepubs/symposia/ reading/vocabulary6.html

McLaughlin, M., & Oberman, I. (Eds.). (1996). *Teacher learning: New policies, new practices.* New York: Teachers College Press.

McLaughlin, M., & Vogt, M. E. (1996). *Portfolios in teacher education.* Newark, DE: International Reading Association.

McLeod, B. (1996, February). *School reform and student diversity: Exemplary schooling for language minority students* (NCBE Resource Collection Series No. 4). Washington, DC: U.S. Department of Education, Office of Research. Retrieved October 14, 2005, from http://www.ncela.gwu.edu/pubs/resource/schref.htm

McNamara, M. J., & Deane, D. (1995). Self-assessment activities: Toward autonomy in language learning. *TESOL Journal, 5*(1), 17–21.

McUsic, M. (1999). The law's role in the distribution of education: The promises and pitfalls of school-finance litigation. In J. Heubert (Ed.), *Law and school reform: Six strategies for promoting educational equity.* New Haven, CT: Yale University Press.

Medina, N., & Neill, D. M. (1990). *Fallout from the testing explosion: How 100 million standardized exams undermine equity and excellence in America's public schools* (3rd ed.). Cambridge, MA: Fair Test.

Melzi, G., Paratore, J. R., & Krol-Sinclair, B. (2000). Reading and writing in the daily lives of Latino mothers partic-ipating in an intergenerational literacy project. *National Reading Conference Yearbook, 49,* 178–193.

Menken, K., & Look, K. (2000, February). Meeting the needs of linguistically and culturally diverse students. *Schools in the Middle, 9*(6), 20–25.

Meyer, J. W. (1984). Organizations as ideological systems. In T. J. Sergiovanni & J. E. Corbally (Eds.), *Leadership and organizational culture: New perspectives on administrative theory and practice* (pp. 186–205). Urbana: University of Illinois Press.

Meyer, L. (2000). Barriers to meaningful instruction for English learners. *Theory Into Practice, 39*(4), 228–236.

Milk, R., Mercado, C., & Sapiens, A. (1992, Summer). *Re-thinking the education of teachers of language-minority chil-dren: Developing reflective teachers for changing schools* (NCBE FOCUS: Occasional Papers in Bilingual Educa-tion, No. 6). Washington, DC: National Clearinghouse for Bilingual Education. Retrieved June 12, 2002, from http://www.ncela.gwu.edu/ncbepubs/focus/focus6.htm

Minicucci, C., & Olsen, L. (1992, Spring). *Programs for secondary LEP students: A California study* (NCBE FOCUS: Oc-casional Papers in Bilingual Education, No. 5). Washington, DC: National Clearinghouse for Bilingual Edu-cation. Retrieved August 1, 2000, from http://www.ncela.gwu.edu/ncbepubs/focus/focus5.htm

Miramontes, O. B., Nadeau, A., & Commins, N. L. (1997). *Restructuring schools for linguistic diversity: Linking deci-sion making to effective programs.* New York: Teachers College Press.

Miron, L. F. (1997). *Resisting discrimination: Affirmative strategies for principals and teachers.* Thousand Oaks, CA: Corwin Press.

Moll, L. C. (1988). Some key issues in teaching Latino students. *Language Arts, 65*(5), 465–472.

Moll, L. C., Amanti, C., Neff, D., & Gonza´lez, N. (1992). Funds of knowledge for teaching: Using a qualitative ap-proach to connect homes and classrooms. *Theory Into Practice, 31*(2), 132–141.

Moll, L. C., & Diaz, S. (1987). Change as the goal of educational research. *Anthropology & Education Quarterly, 18*(4), 300–311.

Montecel, M. R., & Cortez, J. D. (2002). Successful bilingual education programs: Development and the dissemi-nation of criteria to identify promising and exemplary practices in bilingual education at the national level. *Bilingual Research Journal, 26,* 1–22.

Moss, M., & Puma, M. (1995). *Prospects: The congressionally mandated study of educational growth and opportunity. First year report on language minority and limited English proficient students.* Washington, DC: U.S. Department of Education, Planning and Evaluation Service.

Müller, E., & Markowitz, J. (2004, March). *Synthesis brief: English language learners with disabilities.* Alexandria, VA: NASDSE, Project Forum. Retrieved May 5, 2004, from http://www.nasdse.org/publications/ells.pdf

Muniz-Swicegood, M. (1994). The effects of metacognitive reading strategy training on the reading performance and student reading analysis strategies of third grade bilingual students. *Bilingual Research Journal, 18*(1–2), 83–97.

Murphy, C., & Lick, D. (2001). *Whole-faculty study groups: Creating student-based professional development.* Thousand Oaks, CA: Corwin Press.

Murphy, J., & Louis, K. S. (1994). *Reshaping the principalship: Insights from transformational reform efforts.* Thousand Oaks, CA: Corwin Press.

Nagy, W. E., Garcia, G. E., Durgunoglu, A., & Hancin-Bhatt, B. (1993). Spanish-English bilingual children's use and recognition of cognates in English reading. *Journal of Reading Behavior, 25*(3), 241–259.

Nagy, W. E., & Scott, J. A. (2000). Vocabulary processes. In M. Kamil, P. Mosenthal, P. D. Pearson, & R. Barr (Eds.), *Handbook of reading research* (Vol. 3, pp. 269–284). Mahwah, NJ : Lawrence Erlbaum.

National Association for Bilingual Education (NABE) & ILIAD Project. (2002). *Determining appropriate referrals of English language learners to special education: A self-assessment guide for principals.* Washington, DC: National As-sociation for Bilingual Education; Arlington, VA: Council for Exceptional Children.

National Association of Elementary School Principals (NAESP). (2001). *Leading learning communities: Standards for what principals should know and be able to do.* Alexandria, VA: Author. Retrieved October 29, 2001, from http://www.naesp.org//llc.pdf

National Center for Education Statistics. (1999, January). *Teacher quality: A report on the preparation and qualifications of public school teachers* (NCES 1999-080). Washington, DC: U.S. Department of Education, Office of Educa-tional Research and Improvement. Retrieved August 2, 2000, from http://nces.ed.gov/pubs99/1999080.pdf

U.S. Department of Education, National Center for Education Statistics. (2002). *Schools and staffing survey 1999–2000: Overview of the data for public, private, public charter, and Bureau of Indian Affairs elementary and sec-*

ondary schools (NCES 2002-313). Washington, DC: Author. Retrieved June 23, 2002, from http://nces.ed.gov/pubs2002/2002313.pdf

National Center for Education Statistics. (2002). *The condition of education 2002* (NCES 2002-025). Washington, DC: U.S. Department of Education. Retrieved June 12, 2003, from http://nces.ed.gov/pubsearch/pubsinfo.asp?pubid=2002025

National Center for Education Statistics. (2005). *The condition of education 2005* (NCES 2005-094). Washington, DC: U.S. Department of Education. Retrieved October 28, 2005, from http://nces.ed.gov/pubs2005/2005094.pdf

National Clearinghouse on English Language Acquisition. (2002). *NCELA FAQ No. 10: Glossary of terms related to the education of linguistically and culturally diverse students.* Retrieved May 23, 2005, from http://www.ncela.gwu.edu/expert/glossary.html

National Clearinghouse on English Language Acquisition. (2005). *The growing numbers of LEP students, 1993/94–2003/04.* Retrieved September 23, 2005, from http://www.ncela.gwu.edu/policy/states/reports/statedata/2003LEP/ GrowingLEP_0304.pdf

National Reading Panel. (2000). Teaching children to read: An evidence-based assessment of the scientific research literature on reading and its implications for reading instruction. Washington, DC: NICHD.

Navarrete, C., & Gustke, C. (1996). *A guide to performance assessment for linguistically diverse students.* Albuquerque, NM: Evaluation Assistance Center West, New Mexico Highlands University. Retrieved July 30, 2002, from http://www.ncela. gwu.edu/pubs/eacwest/performance/

Neuman, S., & Koskinen, P. (1992). Captioned television as comprehensible input: Effects of incidental word learning from context for language minority students. *Reading Research Quarterly, 27*(1), 94–106.

New Mexico State Department of Education. (2003). *Technical assistance manual for implementing bilingual education and Title III programs.* Santa Fe, NM: New Mexico State Department of Education, Bilingual Multicultural Education Unit. Retrieved January 7, 2004, from http://www.ped.state.nm.us/div/learn.serv/Bilingual/dl/TA%20Manual%2004-04-03/table.of.contents.hyperlink2.doc

New York State Education Department. (2001). *The teaching of language arts to limited English proficient/English language learners: A resource guide for all teachers.* Albany: The University of the State of New York, State Education Department, Office of Bilingual Education. Retrieved January 13, 2003, from http://www.emsc.nysed.gov/ciai/biling/resource/res.html

Newmann, F., & Wehlage, G. (1995). *Successful school restructuring: A report to the public and educators by the Center for Restructuring Schools.* Madison: University of Wisconsin.

Nicolau, S., & Ramos, C. L. (1990). *Together is better. Building strong relationships between schools and Hispanic parents.* Washington, DC: Hispanic Policy Development Project. (ERIC Document Reproduction Service No. ED325543)

Nieto, S. (1999). *The light in their eyes: Creating multicultural learning communities.* New York: Teachers College Press.

Nieto, S. (2002, December). Profoundly multicultural questions. *Educational Leadership, 60*(4), 6–10.

No Child Left Behind Act of 2001, Pub. L. No. 107-110, § 1111-1112, 115 Stat. 1425 (2002).

Noddings, N. (1995). A morally defensible mission for schools in the 21st century. *Phi Delta Kappan, 76*(5), 365–368.

Ochoa, A., & Mardirosian, V. (1996, Summer). Investing in the future of youth: Parent training. *The Journal of Educational Issues of Language Minority Students, 16.* Retrieved February 23, 2002, from http://www.ncela.gwu.edu/miscpubs/ jeilms/vol16/jeilms1607.htm

Ogbu, J. U., & Matute-Bianchi, M. E. (1986). Understanding sociocultural factors: Knowledge, identity, and school adjustment. In California State Department of Education, *Beyond language: Social and cultural factors in schooling language minority students* (pp. 73–142). Los Angeles: Evaluation, Dissemination, and Assessment Center, California State University.

Olsen, L. (Ed.). (1988). *Crossing the schoolhouse border: Immigrant students and the California public schools.* San Francisco: California Tomorrow.

Olsen, L., & Jaramillo, A. (1999). *Turning the tides of exclusion: A guide for educators and advocates for immigrant students.* Oakland, CA: California Tomorrow.

O'Malley, J. M., & Chamot, A. U. (1990). *Learning strategies in second language acquisition.* Cambridge, England: Cambridge University Press.

O'Malley, J. M., Chamot, A. U., Stewner-Manzanares, G., Russo, R., & Kupper, L. (1985). Learning strategy applications with students of English as a second language. *TESOL Quarterly, 19,* 557–584.

O'Malley, J. M., & Valdez Pierce, L. (1996). *Authentic assessment for English language learners: Practical approaches for teachers.* New York: Addison-Wesley.

Onosko, J. J. (1992). Exploring the thinking of thoughtful teachers. *Educational Leadership, 49*(7), 40–43.

Oosterhof, A. (1999). *Developing and using classroom assessments* (2nd ed.). Upper Saddle River, NJ: Prentice Hall.

Ortiz, A., & Wilkinson, C. (1990). Assessment and intervention model for the bilingual exceptional student. *Teacher Education and Special Education, 35*–42.

Osburne, A. G., & Mulling, S. S. (2001). Use of morphological analysis by Spanish L1 ESOL learners. *International Review of Applied Linguistics in Language Teaching, 39*(2), 153–159.

Palincsar, A. S., & Brown, A. L. (1984). Reciprocal teaching of comprehension-fostering and comprehension-monitoring activities. *Cognition and Instruction, 1*(2), 117–175.

Palincsar, A. S., & Klenk, L. (1992). Fostering literacy learning in supportive contexts. *Journal of Learning Disabilities, 25*(4), 211–225, 229.

Parker, L., & Shapiro, J. P. (1993). The context of educational administration and social class. In C. A. Capper (Ed.), *Educational administration in a pluralistic society* (pp. 36–65). Albany: State University of New York Press.

Patthey-Chavez, G., & Goldenberg, C. (1995). Changing instructional discourse for changing students: The instructional conversation. In R. Macias & R. G. Ramos (Eds.), *Changing schools for changing students: An anthology of research on language minorities, schools and society* (pp. 205–230). Santa Barbara: University of California Linguistic Minority Research Institute.

Pearson, B., & Berghoff, C. (1996). London Bridge is not falling down: It's supporting alternative assessment. *TESOL Journal, 5*(4), 28–31.

Pearson, P. D., & Fielding, L. (1991). Comprehension instruction. In R. Barr, M. L. Kamil, P. Mosenthal, & P. D. Pearson (Eds.), *Handbook of reading research* (Vol. 2, pp. 815–860). White Plains, NY: Longman.

Pease-Álvarez, L., García, E. E., & Espinoza, P. (1991). Effective instruction for language minority students: An early childhood case study. *Early Childhood Research Quarterly, 6*(3), 347–363.

Pellegrino, J., Chudowsky, N., & Glaser, R. (Eds.). (2001). *Knowing what students know: The science and design of educational assessment.* Washington, DC: National Academy Press.

Peregoy, S. F., & Boyle, O. F. (2000). *Reading, writing, & learning in ESL: A resource book for K–12 teachers* (4th ed.). Boston: Pearson Education.

Peregoy, S. F., & Boyle, O. F. (2005). English learners reading English: What we know, what we need to know. *Theory Into Practice, 39*(4), 237–247.

Pérez, B., & Torres-Guzmán, M. E. (1996). *Learning in two worlds: An integrated Spanish/English biliteracy approach* (2nd ed.). White Plains, NY: Longman.

Peyton, J. K., Jones, C., Vincent, A., & Greenblatt, L. (1994). Implementing writing workshops with ESOL students: Visions and realities. *TESOL Quarterly, 28*(3), 469–487.

Plyler v. Doe, 457 U.S. 202 (1982).

Postlethwaite, T. N., & Ross, K. N. (1992). *Effective schools in reading: Implications for educational planners. An exploratory study.* The Hague, Netherlands: The International Association for the Evaluation of Educational Achievement.

Pottinger, J. S. (1970, May 25). *Identification of discrimination and denial of services on the basis of national origin* [Memorandum from J. Stanley Pottinger, Director, OCR, to school districts with more than five percent national origin-minority group children]. Washington, DC: U.S. Department of Health, Education, and Welfare. Retrieved October 2, 2002, from http://www.ed.gov/about/offices/list/ocr/docs/lau1970.html

Power, B. (1999). *Parent power: Energizing home-school communication.* Portsmouth, NH: Heinemann.

Prawatt, R. S. (1992). From individual differences to learning communities: Our changing focus. *Educational Leadership, 49*(7), 9–13.

Pressley, M., & Woloshyn, V. (Eds.). (1995). *Cognitive strategy instruction that really improves children's academic performance.* Cambridge, MA: Brookline Books.

Procidano, M. E., & Fisher, C. B. (1992). *Contemporary families: A handbook for school professionals.* New York: Teachers College Press.

Purkey, S. C., & Smith, M. S. (1983). Effective schools: A review. *The Elementary School Journal, 83*(4), 427–452.

Quelmatz, E., Shields, P., & Knapp, M. (1995). *School-based reform: Lessons from a national study. A guide for school reform teams.* Menlo Park, CA: SRI International, U.S. Department of Education.

Ramirez, J. (1992). Executive summary of the final report: Longitudinal study of structured English immersion strategy, early-exit and late-exit transitional bilingual education programs for language-minority children. *Bilingual Research Journal, 16*(1–2), 1–62.

RAND Reading Study Group. (2002). *Reading for understanding: Toward an R & D program in reading comprehension.* Santa Monica, CA: RAND. Retrieved August 22, 2003, from http://www.rand.org/multi/achievement forall/reading/ readreport.html

Reese, L., Garnier, H., Gallimore, R., & Goldenberg, C. (2000). Longitudinal analysis of the antecedents of emergent Spanish literacy and middle-school English reading achievement of Spanish-speaking students. *American Educational Research Journal, 37*(3), 633–662.

Rennie, J. (1993). *ESL and bilingual program models.* Washington, DC: U.S. Department of Education. ERIC Clearinghouse on Languages and Linguistics. (ERIC Document Reproduction Service No. ED362072). Retrieved September 25, 2001, from http://www.ericfacility.net/databases/ERIC_Digests/ed362072.html

Ritter, P. L., Mont-Reynaud, R., & Dornbusch, S. M. (1993). Minority parents and their youth: Concern, encouragement and support for school achievement. In N. F. Chavkin (Ed.), *Families and schools in a pluralistic society* (pp. 107–119). Albany: State University of New York Press.

Rivera, C., & Stansfield, C. W. (1998). Leveling the playing field for English language learners: Increasing participation in state and local assessments through accommodations. In R. Brandt (Ed.), *Assessing student learning: New rules, new realities* (pp. 65–92). Arlington, VA: Educational Research Service.

Rollow, S. G., & Bryk, A. S. (1993). Democratic politics and school improvement: The potential of Chicago school reform. In C. Marshall (Ed.), *The new politics of race and gender. The 1992 yearbook of the Politics of Education Association* (pp. 97–106). Washington, DC: Falmer Press.

Rosebery, A. S., Warren, B., & Conant, F. R. (1992). Appropriate scientific discourse: Findings from language minority classrooms. *The Journal of the Learning Sciences, 1*(2), 61–94.

Rosenholtz, S. J. (1985). Effective schools: Interpreting the evidence. *American Journal of Education, 93*(3), 352–388.

Rosenshine, B., & Stevens, R. (1986). Teaching functions. In M. Wittrock (Ed.), *Handbook of research on teaching* (3rd ed., pp. 376–391). New York: MacMillan.

Rossi, R. J., & Stringfield, S. C. (1997). *Education reform and students at risk: Studies of education reform.* Washington, DC: Office of Educational Research and Improvement, U.S. Department of Education.

Rousseau, M. K., Tam, B. K. Y., & Ramnarain, R. (1993). Increasing reading proficiency of language-minority students with speech and language impairments. *Education and Treatments of Children, 16,* 254–271.

Rudd, T. J., & Gunstone, R.F. (1993). *Developing self-assessment skills in grade 3 science and technology: The importance of longitudinal studies of learning.* Paper presented at the annual meetings of the National Association for Research in Science Teaching and the American Educational Research Association, Atlanta, GA.

Ruddell, R. B., & Ruddell, M. R. (1995). *Teaching children to read and write: Becoming an influential teacher.* Boston: Allyn and Bacon.

Ruiz-de-Velasco, J., & Fix, M. (2000). *Overlooked & underserved: Immigrant students in U.S. secondary schools.* Washington, DC: The Urban Institute.

Samway, K. D., & McKeon, D. (1999). *Myths and realities: Best practices for language minority students.* Portsmouth, NH: Heinemann.

Saravia-Shore, M., & García, E. (1995). Diverse teaching strategies for diverse learners. In ASCD Improving Student Achievement Research Panel (Ed.), *Educating everybody's children: Diverse teaching strategies for diverse learners* (pp. 47–74). Alexandria, VA: Association for Supervision and Curriculum Development.

Saunders, W., O'Brien, G., Lennon, D., & McLean, J. (1996). Making the transition to English literacy successful: Effective strategies for studying literature with transition students. In R. Gersten & R. Jiménez (Eds.), *Effective strategies for teaching language minority students* (pp. 99–132). Belmont, CA: Wadsworth.

Saunders, W., O'Brien, G., Lennon, D., & McLean, J. (1999). *Successful transition into mainstream English: Effective strategies for studying literature* (Educational Practice Report No. 2). Santa Cruz, CA: Center for Research on Education, Diversity, and Excellence, University of California. Retrieved December 12, 2002, from http://repositories.cdlib.org/crede/edupractrpts/epr02/

Saunders, W. M., & Goldenberg, C. (1999). *The effects of instructional conversations and literature logs on the story comprehension and thematic understanding of English proficient and limited English proficient students* (Research Report No. 6). Santa Cruz, CA: Center for Research on Education, Diversity, and Excellence, University of California. Retrieved October 31, 2001, from http://repositories.cdlib.org/crede/ rsrchrpts/rr06

Saville-Troike, M. (1984). What really matters in second language learning for academic achievement? *TESOL Quarterly, 18*(2), 199–219.

Saville-Troike, M. (1991, Spring). *Teaching and testing for academic achievement: The role of language development* (NCBE FOCUS: Occasional Papers in Bilingual Education, No. 4). Washington, DC: National Clearinghouse for Bilingual Education. Retrieved February 23, 2002, from http://www.ncela.gwu.edu/ncbepubs/focus/focus4.htm

Scarcella, R. C. (1996). Secondary education and second language research: Instructing ESL students in the 1990's. *The CATESOL Journal, 9,* 129–152.

Scheurich, J. J. (1998). Highly successful and loving, public elementary schools populated mainly by low-SES children of color: Core beliefs and cultural characteristics. *Urban Education, 33*(4), 451–491.

Schinke-Llano, L.A. (1983). Foreigner talk in content classrooms. In H. W. Seliger & M. H. Long (Eds.), *Classroom-oriented research in second language acquisition* (pp. 146–165). Rowley, MA: Newbury House.

Schmoker, M. (1999) *Results: The key to continuous school improvement* (2nd ed.). Alexandria, VA: Association for Supervision and Curriculum Development.

Schunk, D. H., & Hanson, A. R. (1985). Peer models: Influence on children's self-efficacy and achievement. *Journal of Educational Psychology, 77*(3), 313–322.

Seaman, A. (2000, September/October). Evaluating an innovative elementary ESL program. *American Language Review, 4*(5). Retrieved March 2, 2003, from http://www. languagemagazine.com/internetedition/so2000/seaman.html

Section 504 at 34 C.F.R § 104.35, Section 504 of the Rehabilitation Act of 1973, 29 U.S.C. § 794 (Section 504).

Senge, P. (1990). *The fifth discipline: The art and practice of the learning organization.* New York: Doubleday Currency.

Senge, P., Ross, R., Smith, B., Roberts, C., & Kleiner, A. (1994). *The fifth discipline fieldbook: Strategies and tools for building a learning organization.* New York: Doubleday.

Senge, P., Kleiner, A., Roberts, C., Ross, R., Roth, G., & Smith, B. (1999). *The dance of change: The challenges to sustaining momentum in learning organizations.* New York: Doubleday/Currency.

Serna v. Portales Municipal Schools, 499 F. 2d 1147, 1153-54 (10th Cir. 1974).

Shachar, H. (1996). Developing new traditions in secondary schools: A working model for organizational and instructional change. *Teachers College Record, 97*(4), 549–568.

Shartrand, A., Weiss, H., Kreider, H., & Lopez, M. (1997). *New skills for new schools: Preparing teachers in family involvement.* Cambridge, MA: Harvard Family Research Project, Harvard Graduate School of Education.

Shore, K. (2001, March). Success for ESL students. *Instructor, 110*(6), 30–32, 106.

Short, D. (1999). Integrating language and content for effective sheltered instruction programs. In C. Faltis & P. Wolfe (Eds.), *So much to say: Adolescents, bilingualism, and ESL in the secondary school* (pp. 105–137). New York: Teachers College Press.

Sirotnik, K., & Oakes, J. (Eds.). (1986). *Critical perspectives on the organization and improvement of schooling.* Boston: Kluwer-Nijhoff.

Slavin, R. E. (1987). Ability grouping and student achievement in elementary schools: A best evidence synthesis. *Review of Educational Research, 57*(3), 293–336.

Slavin, R. E. (1995). *Cooperative learning: Theory, research and practice* (2nd ed.). Boston: Allyn and Bacon.

Slavin, R. E. (1999). *How Title I can become the engine of reform in America's schools.* Baltimore: Johns Hopkins University, Center for Research on the Education of Students Placed at Risk.

Slavin, R. E., & Cheung, A. (2003). *Effective programs for English language learners: A best-evidence synthesis.* Baltimore: John Hopkins University, CRESPAR.

Slavin, R. E., & Cheung, A. (2004, March). How do English language learners learn to read? *Educational Leadership, 61*(6), 52–57.

Slavin R. E., & Madden, N. (2001). Effects of bilingual and English-as-a-second-language adaptations of Success for All on the reading achievement of students acquiring English. In R. E. Slavin & M. Calderón (Eds.), *Effective programs for Latino students* (pp. 207–230). Mahwah, NJ: Lawrence Erlbaum Associates.

Slavin, R. E., & Yampolsky, R. (1992). *Success for All: Effects on students with limited English proficiency. A three-year evaluation* (Report No. CDS-R-29). Baltimore: Center for Research on Effective Schooling for Disadvantaged Students, Johns Hopkins University. (ERIC Document Reproduction Service No. ED346199)

Sleeter, C. E., & Grant, C. A. (1994). *Making choices for multicultural education: Five approaches to race, class, and gender* (2nd ed.). New York: Merrill.

Smolen, L., Newman, C., Wathen, T., & Lee, D. (1995). Developing student self-assessment strategies. *TESOL Journal, 5*(1), 22–27.

Snow, C. E. (1990). Rationales for native language instruction. In A. M. Padilla, H. H. Fairchild, & D. M. Valadez (Eds.), *Bilingual education: Issues and strategies* (pp. 60–74). Alexandria, VA: Association for Supervision and Curriculum Development.

Snow, C. E., Burns, M. S., & Griffin, P. (Eds.). (1998). *Preventing reading difficulties in young children.* Washington, DC: National Academy Press.

Snow, M. A. (Ed.). (2000). *Implementing the ESL standards for pre-K–12 students through teacher education.* Alexandria, VA: TESOL.

Sosa, A. (1990). *Making education work for Mexican Americans: Promising community practices.* Charleston, WV: ERIC Clearinghouse on Rural Education and Small Schools. (ERIC Document Reproduction Service No. ED319580)

Sosa, A. (1997, Spring & Summer). Involving Hispanic parents in educational activities through collaborative relationships. *Bilingual Research Journal, 21*(2 & 3), 1–8.

Soto, L., Smrekar, J., Nekcovei, D. (1999, Spring). *Preserving home languages and cultures in the classroom: Challenges and opportunities* (Directions in Language and Education, No. 13). Washington, DC: National Clearinghouse for Bilingual Education. (ERIC Document Reproduction Service No. ED436085). Retrieved February 23, 2002, from http://www.ncbe.gwu.edu/ncbepubs/directions/13.htm

Spangenberg-Urbschat, K., & Pritchard, R. (Eds.). (1994). *Kids come in all languages: Reading instruction for ESL students.* Newark, DE: International Reading Association.

Sparks, D. (2003, October). *Significant change begins with leaders: Results.* Oxford, OH: National Staff Development Council. Retrieved January 23, 2004, from http://www.nsdc.org/library/publications/res10-03spar.cfm

Stahl, S. A., & Fairbanks, M. M. (1986). The effects of vocabulary instruction: A model-based meta-analysis. *Review of Educational Research, 56,* 72–110.

Stedman, L. C. (1987). It's time we changed the effective schools formula. *Phi Delta Kappan, 69*(3), 215–224.

Sternberg, R. J. (1986). Cognition and instruction: Why the marriage sometimes ends in divorce. In R. F. Dillon & R. J. Sternberg (Eds.), *Cognition and instruction* (pp. 375–382). Orlando, FL: Academic Press.

Stigler, J. W., & Hiebert, J. (1999). *The teaching gap: Best ideas from the world's teachers for improving education in the classroom.* New York: Free Press.

Suro, R. (1998). *Strangers among us: How Latino immigration is transforming America.* New York: Alfred A. Knopf.

TESOL. (1997). *ESL standards for pre-K–12 students.* Alexandria, VA: Author.

Texas Education Agency. (2000). *The Texas successful schools study: Quality education for limited English proficient students.* Austin, TX: Texas Education Agency. Retrieved May 16, 2001, from http://www.ncela.gwu.edu/miscpubs/tea/tsss.pdf

Tharp, R. G., Estrada, P., Dalton, S., & Yamauchi, L. (2000). *Teaching transformed: Achieving excellence, fairness, inclusion, and harmony.* Boulder, CO: Westview Press.

Tharp, R. G., & Gallimore, R. (1991). *The instructional conversation: Teaching and learning in social activity* (Research Report No. 2). Santa Cruz, CA: National Center for Research on Cultural Diversity and Second Language Learning. Retrieved October 31, 2001, from http://www.ncela.gwu.edu/miscpubs/ncrcdsll/rr2.htm

Thomas, W. P., & Collier, V. P. (1997, December). *School effectiveness for language minority students.* Washington, DC: National Clearinghouse for Bilingual Education, The George Washington University Center for the Study of Language and Education. Retrieved May 16, 2001, from http://www.ncela.gwu.edu/ncbepubs/resource/effectiveness/thomas-collier97.pdf

Thomas, W. P., & Collier, V. P. (2002). *A national study of school effectiveness for language minority students' long-term academic achievement.* Santa Cruz, CA: Center for Research on Education, Diversity and Excellence, University of California, Santa Cruz. Retrieved March 12, 2003, from http://www.crede.ucsc.edu/research/llaa/1.1_final.html

Thurlow, M. L. (2001, April). *The effects of a simplified-English dictionary accommodation for LEP students who are not literate in their first language.* Paper presented at the annual meeting of the American Educational Research Association, Seattle, WA.

Tierney, R., & Pearson, P. D. (1994). Learning to learn from text: A framework for improving classroom practice. In R. Ruddell & H. Singer (Eds.), *Theoretical models and processes of reading* (4th ed.). Newark, DE: International Reading Association.

Tikunoff, W. J. (1983). *An emerging description of successful bilingual instruction: Executive summary of part I of the SBIF study.* San Francisco: Far West Laboratory for Educational Research and Development. (ERIC Document Reproduction Service No. ED297561)

Tikunoff, W. J. (1985). *Applying significant bilingual instructional features in the classroom.* Rosslyn, VA: National Clearinghouse for Bilingual Education. (ERIC Document Reproduction Service No. ED338106)

Tikunoff, W. J. (1987). Providing instructional leadership: The key to effectiveness. In S. H. Fradd & W. J. Tikunoff (Eds.), *Bilingual education and bilingual special education: A guide for administrators* (pp. 231–246). Boston: College Hill Press.

Tikunoff, W. J., Ward, B. A., van Broekhuizen, L. D., Romero, M., Vega-Casteneda, L., Lucas, T., & Katz, A. (1991). *A descriptive study of significant features of exemplary special alternative instructional programs (SAIPs): Final report* (Contract No. T288001001). Los Alamitos, CA: Southwest Regional Laboratory.

Tinajero, J. V., Calderon, M., & Hertz-Lazarowitz, R. (1993). Cooperative learning strategies: Bilingual classroom applications. In J. V. Tinajero & A. F. Ada, (Eds.), *The power of two languages: Literacy and biliteracy for Spanish speaking students* (pp. 241–253). New York: MacMillan/McGraw Hill.

Tinajero, J. V., & Hurley, S. R. (2001). Assessing progress in second-language acquisition. In S. R. Hurley & J. V. Tinajero (Eds.), *Literacy assessment of second language learners* (pp. 27–42). Boston: Allyn and Bacon.

Title VI of the Civil Rights Act of 1964, 42 U.S.C. § 2000d (Title VI).

Tomeson, M., & Aarnoutse, C. (1998). Effects of an instructional program for deriving word meanings. *Educational Studies, 24,* 107–128.

Tse, L. (1996, Summer/Fall). Language brokering in linguistic minority communities: The case of Chinese- and Vietnamese-American students. *The Bilingual Research Journal, 20*(3 & 4), 485–498.

U.S. Census Bureau. (2002). *American fact finder.* Available: http://factfinder.census.gov/servlet/BasicFactos Servlet?lang=en.

U.S. Census Bureau. (2004, March). *Children and the households they live in: 2000.* Available: http://www.census.gov/prod/2004pubs/censr-14.pdf

U.S. Department of Education, Office for Civil Rights. (2000, August). *The provision of an equal education opportunity to limited–English proficient students.* Washington, DC: Author. Retrieved October 2, 2002, from http://www.ed.gov/about/offices/list/ocr/eeolep/index.html

U.S. General Accounting Office. (1994). *Limited English proficiency: A growing and costly educational challenge facing many school districts* (Publication No. GAO/HEHS-94-38). Washington, DC: United States General Accounting Office. Retrieved September 3, 2003, from http://archive.gao.gov/t2pbat4/150611.pdf

U.S. General Accounting Office. (2001, February). *Report to Congressional requesters: Meeting the needs of students with limited English proficiency* (Publication No. GAO-01-226). Washington, DC: United States General Accounting Office. Retrieved March 1, 2001, from http://www.gao.gov/new.items/d01226.pdf

Valdés, G. (1996). *Con respeto: Bridging the distance between culturally diverse families and schools: An ethnographic portrait.* New York: Teachers College Press.

Valdés, G., & Figueroa, R. A. (1994). *Bilingual and testing: A special case of bias.* Norwood, NJ: Ablex Publishing.

Valdez Pierce, L. (2001). Assessment of reading comprehension strategies for intermediate bilingual learners. In S. R. Hurley & J. V. Tinajero (Eds.), *Literacy assessment of second language learners* (pp. 64–83). Boston: Allyn and Bacon.

Valdez Pierce, L., & O'Malley, J. M. (1992). *Performance and portfolio assessment for language minority students* (NCBE Program Information Guide Series, No. 9). Washington, DC: National Clearinghouse for Bilingual Education. (ERIC Document Reproduction Service No. ED346747). Available: http://www.ncela.gwu.edu/pubs/pigs/pig9.htm

Valverde, L. A., & Armendáriz, G. J. (1999). Important administrative tasks resulting from understanding bilingual program designs. *Bilingual Research Journal, 23*(1), 1–10.

Van Wagenen, M. A., Williams, R. L., & McLaughlin, T. F. (1994). Use of assisted reading to improve reading rate, word accuracy, and comprehension with ESL Spanish-speaking students. *Perceptual and Motor Skills, 79,* 227–230.

Villareal, A. (2001, January). Challenges and strategies for principals of low-performing schools. *IDRA Newsletter, 28.* Retrieved February 23, 2002, from http://www.idra.org/Newslttr/2001/Jan/Lalo.htm

Violand-Sánchez, E., Sutton, C. P., & Ware, H. W. (1991, Summer). *Fostering home-school cooperation: Involving language minority families as partners in education.* Washington, DC: National Clearinghouse on Bilingual Education.

von Vacano, M. J. (1994, May). Using the home language in the education of language minority children. *NABE News, 17*(6), 27–29.

Vygotsky, L. S. (1978). *Mind and society: The development of higher psychological processes.* Cambridge, MA: Harvard University Press.

Wagner, T. (1994). *How schools change: Lessons from three communities.* Boston: Beacon.

Walqui, A. (2000). *Contextual factors in second language acquisition.* Washington, DC: Center for Applied Linguistics.

Waters, J. T., Marzano, R. J., & McNulty, B. A. (2003). *Balanced leadership: What 30 years of research tells us about the effect of leadership on student achievement.* Aurora, CO: Mid-continent Research for Education and Learning.

White, T. G., Graves, M. F., & Slater, W. H. (1990). Growth of reading vocabulary in diverse elementary schools: Decoding and word meaning. *Journal of Educational Psychology, 82,* 281–290.

Wiggins, G. (1992). Creating tests worth taking. *Educational Leadership, 49*(8), 26–33.

Williams, M. L. (1991, September 27). *Policy update on schools' obligations toward national origin minority students with limited-English proficiency (LEP students).* [Memorandum from Michael L. Williams, Assistant Secretary for Civil Rights, to OCR senior staff]. Washington, DC: U.S. Department of Education, Office for Civil Rights. Retrieved October 2, 2002, from http://www.ed.gov/about/offices/list/ ocr/docs/lau1991.html

Wong Fillmore, L. (1985). When does teacher talk work as input? In S. Gass & C. Madden (Eds.), *Input in second language acquisition* (pp. 17–50). New York: Newbury House.

Wong Fillmore, L. (1991a). Second language learning in children: A model of language learning in social context. In E. Bialystok (Ed.), *Language processing in bilingual children* (pp. 49–69). Cambridge, England: Cambridge University Press.

Wong Fillmore, L. (1991b). When learning a second language means losing the first. *Early Childhood Research Quarterly, 6*(3), 323–347.

Wong Fillmore, L., Ammon, P., McLaughlin, B., & Ammon, M. S. (1985). *Learning English through bilingual instruction* [Final report submitted to the National Institute of Education]. Berkeley: University of California. (ERIC Document Reproduction Service No. ED259579)

Wong Fillmore, L., & Meyer, L. M. (1992). The curriculum and linguistic minorities. In P. W. Jackson (Ed.), *The handbook of research on curriculum* (pp. 626–658). New York: Macmillan.

Wong Fillmore, L., & Snow, C. E. (2000). *What teachers need to know about language* (Contract No. ED-99-CO-0008). Washington, DC: U.S. Department of Education's Office of Educational Research and Improvement, Center for Applied Linguistics.

York-Barr, J., Sommers, W., Ghere, G. S., Montie, J. (2001). *Reflective practice to improve schools.* Thousand Oaks, CA: Corwin Press.

Zehler, A., Hopstock, P., Fleischman, H., & Greniuk, C. (1994). *An examination of assessment of limited English proficient students.* Arlington, VA: Special Issues Analysis Center.

Zehler, A., Fleischman, H., Hopstock, P., Stephenson, T., Pendzick, M., & Sapru, S. (2003). *Descriptive study of services to LEP students and LEP students with disabilities. Volume I: Research report.* Arlington, VA: Development Associates.

Zelasko, N., & Antunez, B. (2000). *If your child learns in two languages: A parent's guide to improving educational opportunities for children learning English as a second language.* Washington, DC: National Clearinghouse for Bilingual Education. Retrieved May 29, 2002, from http://www.ncela.gwu.edu/pubs/parent/

Zimmerman, B. J., & Martinez-Pons, M. (1990). Student differences in self-regulated learning: Relating grade, sex, and giftedness to self-efficacy and strategy use. *Journal of Educational Psychology, 82*(1), 51–59.